D1384181

THE OPENNESS OF BEING

THE GIFFORD LECTURES IN THE
UNIVERSITY OF EDINBURGH
1970–1971

THE OPENNESS OF BEING

Natural Theology Today

E. L. MASCALL

*Professor of Historical Theology in the University of
London, Emeritus Student of Christ Church, Oxford,
Priest of the Oratory of the Good Shepherd*

When an animal has nothing to do, it goes to
sleep.
When a man has nothing to do, he may ask
questions.
Bernard Lonergan.

Videtur quod Deus non sit. . . . Sed contra . . .
St Thomas Aquinas.

PHILADELPHIA

THE WESTMINSTER PRESS

© E. L. MASCALL, 1971

ISBN 0–664–20944–0

LIBRARY OF CONGRESS CATALOG CARD NO. 72–75839

PUBLISHED BY THE WESTMINSTER PRESS ®
PHILADELPHIA, PENNSYLVANIA

PRINTED IN GREAT BRITAIN

Library of Congress Cataloging in Publication Data

Mascall, Eric Lionel, 1905–
  The openness of being

  (The Gifford lectures, 1970–71)
  Bibliography: p.
  1. Natural theology. 2. Theism. I. Title.
II. Series.
BL182.M35   210   72–75839
ISBN 0–664–20944–0

TO THE RIGHT REVEREND FATHER IN GOD
GRAHAM DOUGLAS
LORD BISHOP OF WILLESDEN
WITH AFFECTION AND ESTEEM

FOREWORD

WHEN THE SENATUS ACADEMICUS of the University of Edinburgh did me the honour of appointing me as Gifford Lecturer in Natural Theology for the session 1970–71 I felt specially grateful for the stimulus which this gave me to return for a brief period to the branch of theology in which I had produced my first serious academic work twenty-seven years before. Since my book *He Who Is* and its sequel *Existence and Analogy* appeared in 1943 and 1949 respectively I had become more and more absorbed in questions of dogmatic theology, though the philosophical aspects of Christian theism had never ceased to interest me, as was indicated by the publication of my small work *Words and Images* in 1957. Now, however, I have been given the welcome opportunity of making a fresh survey of the field of natural theology and the present volume embodies its results. Even within the ample time provided for a Gifford Lecturer some selection was inevitable; I therefore decided to devote a large proportion of it to the discussion of certain recent work, such as that of the transcendental Thomists, which is not as widely known as it deserves to be in English-speaking philosophical and theological circles. My chief desire, however, has been to vindicate, against the generally positivist attitude of Anglo-Saxon philosophy in recent years, a fundamentally and unashamedly metaphysical approach to theism. In pursuing this aim some reference to my earlier work was inevitable, but I have tried to keep it to a minimum; for there is little merit in mere repetition. The ten main chapters of this book contain, apart from some passages in chapter three which were omitted through limitations of time, the lectures as actually delivered, and in preparing them for publication I have retained the conversational form. Certain material which, either on grounds of length or because it fell outside the limits proper to natural theology, was not delivered orally I have included as Appendices. Some repetitions have been allowed to remain. In the text and footnotes I have mentioned the dates of books referred to only when it seemed relevant to the argument to do so; the dates of all will, however, be found in the Bibliography.

Most of chapter eight appeared as a review-article and a review in the *Downside Review*, most of appendix one as a review in *The Thomist*, most of appendix three as an article in the *Church Quarterly Review* and appendix four as an article in the *American Church Quarterly*; for consent to reproduce these I am grateful to the editors and publishers of the journals concerned.

Finally, I must express my gratitude to the University of Edinburgh for electing me to the Lectureship, to the many friends in Edinburgh who made my visits so fruitful and delightful, to the Council of King's College, London, for granting me the necessary leave of absence, and to Miss Patricia V. Connor for the care and patience with which she typed my manuscript.

King's College, London   E. L. M.
June, 1971

ACKNOWLEDGMENTS

The author and publishers would like to thank the following publishers for their courtesy in permitting the publication of extracts from copyright works: Messrs Routledge & Kegan Paul for *God and the Soul* (P. Geach); A. R. Mowbray and Co. for *The Theology of Grace and the Oecumenical Movement* (C. Moeller *and* G. Philips); Search Press for *The Foundations of Belief* (L. Dewart). Acknowledgment is also made to: Macmillan Services Ltd. for *The Many-Faced Argument: Recent Studies on the Ontological Argument for the Existence of God* (J. Hick *and* A. C. McGill); The S.C.M. Press Ltd. for *Theism and Empiricism* (A. B. Gibson); Geoffrey Bles Ltd. for *The Degrees of Knowledge: Distinguish to Unite* (J. Maritain); Messrs Sheed & Ward Ltd. for *The Future of Belief: Theism in a World Come of Age* (L. Dewart); Longman Group Ltd. for *Insight: A Study of Human Understanding* (B. J. F. Lonergan); A. & C. Black Ltd. for *Metaphysics* (E. Coreth); Penguin Books Ltd. for *A Rumour of Angels: Modern Society and the Rediscovery of the Supernatural* (P. L. Berger); and Editions Téqui for *Le Réalisme Méthodique* (E. Gilson).

CONTENTS

Catholicism involve basic questions about the relation between God and man. Two important discussions will be considered.

(1) The Chevetogne conference of 1953 between
Catholics, Orthodox and Calvinists, characterised
by notions of 'created grace', 'deification' and 'extrinsic grace' respectively.

Orthodox 'deification' and the doctrine of divine
energies. The importance of St Gregory Palamas.
Palamism and Thomism not as opposed as commonly
believed. Ecumenical significance of Palamism.

The development of the notion of 'created grace'.
Grace as a *habitus*. Bonaventure: *Habere est haberi*.
Luther and nominalism. Justification and sanctifi-
cation.

The trinitarian character of grace. Philosophical
systematisation. The possibility of synthesis: outstanding problems.

(2) Karl Rahner. The *potentia oboedientialis* of
nature for grace: re-examination of the scholastic
doctrine. Grace and the beatific vision. Uncreated
and created grace. A digression on J. Maritain.

Importance of the *openness* of created being for a
satisfactory doctrine of grace.

CHAPTER ONE

INTRODUCTION

Theology is the happy result of a daring trust in the coherence of faith and reason.

—M.-D. Chenu, *Faith and Theology*, p. 30.

'THERE IS NOT and never has been in the world such a monster as a professor of purely natural religion.' When Dom John Chapman wrote those words in 1911 he was not, as might appear, intending to draw attention, in a wider context, to that void in the academic realm which, as far as Scotland was concerned, led Adam, Lord Gifford, to found the lectureship which I have the honour at this moment to occupy. He was asserting, from the standpoint of Roman Catholic theology, that in concrete fact no religious man is left to find his way to God by his own unaided natural powers, unassisted by that personal and gratuitous intervention of God himself which is technically known as grace. 'It is obviously not possible *in practice*', he wrote, 'to disentangle the Supernatural from the Natural. The two are warp and woof from which our whole experience is woven. But it *is* possible to do so *in theory*, and SCHOLASTIC PHILOSOPHY deals ONLY with the Natural, and therefore not with life in all its complexity as we know it, but with the world as it would be without revelation and without grace (of all kinds), which are disturbing factors.' And again: 'The crucial instance of this abstract nature of pure philosophy is in *Natural Theology*, which is a *part* of philosophy: its subject matter is what man can know of God *without revelation and without grace*; whereas it is (really) OF FAITH that it is within the power of every man to have divine faith (of some kind) and that no one is ever without "sufficient grace".... A human being falls lower or rises higher, but is never a simply *natural* man.'[1]

[1] *Spiritual Letters of Dom John Chapman*, pp. 192 ff.

Not all Christians would, of course, make the distinction between the natural and the supernatural in religion as Chapman made it. Some would deny that, even in theory, there could be purely natural religion, for they would maintain that, just because God is present in all his creatures as their creator and sustainer, it is impossible for a man to seek God in his creatures without becoming the recipient of personal address on the part of God; God will not wait passively for man to discover him. They will thus, as Austin Farrer pointed out in his Bampton Lectures,[1] wish to make a distinction not between natural and revealed religion, or between 'reason' and 'revelation' *tout court*, but between *Natural* Reason and *Supernatural* Revelation, throwing the emphasis upon the adjectives rather than upon the nouns. 'We have not to distinguish', wrote Farrer, 'between God's action and ours, but between two phases of God's action—his supernatural action, and his action by way of nature. It is difficult', he continued, 'to see how anything resembling Christianity can survive the denial of this distinction. For Christianity is faith in Christ, and Christ is God acting not by way of nature, but supernaturally. If you reduce Christ to a part of God's natural action, is he Christ any longer?'[2] Dr James Richmond has remarked that the Augustinian tradition makes a distinction between general and special revelation where the Thomist tradition makes the different, but related, distinction between rational and revealed theology.[3]

Some Christian thinkers, however, will deny that, outside the revelation which God has given in Jesus Christ, any knowledge of God is to be found at all, or at any rate any knowledge of God that is not so distorted by human finitude and sin as to be worse than no knowledge at all; they will in fact deny that such a discipline as natural theology has any right to exist. Thus, one of the most distinguished of modern theologians, when invited to become Gifford Lecturer, had serious qualms of conscience about accepting the invitation, qualms which were alleviated only by the very reasonable assurance that if he made it plain in his lectures why he held that there was not, or ought not to be, such a disreputable subject as natural theology he would

---

[1] *The Glass of Vision* (1948), p. 3.
[2] ibid.
[3] *Theology and Metaphysics* (1970), p. 3.

certainly be lecturing about it.[1] John Baillie, in his projected Gifford Lectures of 1961, devoted a complete lecture to the difficulty felt by many modern thinkers in maintaining the traditional demarcation between natural and revealed theology and expressed his own support of the distinction between general and special revelation.[2] Many of the earlier courses of Gifford Lectures open with somewhat anxious protestations by the lecturer that his chosen topic, in spite of appearances, does in fact fall within the terms of Lord Gifford's trust, and contain from time to time regretful suggestions that the lecturer could interestingly develop certain points in more detail if his conscience and the Trustees allowed it. It is a matter for satisfaction, since many modern thinkers find the old barrier between natural and revealed religion difficult or impossible to maintain, that more recently this kind of apologia has become much less prominent. Indeed a careful reading of the very wide conditions laid down in Lord Gifford's Deed of Foundation makes it quite plain that, as long as he does not appeal to revelation to support or take the place of argument, the Lecturer has very great latitude indeed. He can argue either for the existence of God or against it; he can discuss religion as a historical and cultural phenomenon without expressing any judgment on either its value or its truth. Indeed, from one example it would appear that he can discourse about modern science without any reference to religion at all, even in the widest sense of that very elastic term.[3]

My own position, if I may be permitted to come clean at the start, is very much that of Dom John Chapman. Speaking as a Christian theologian, I do not believe that any religious awareness is a purely natural or purely rational thing, from which specific intervention by God can be excluded a priori. Therefore I do not think that religious experiences can be sharply classified into definite types within which individual differences are minimal or irrelevant, in the way in which, for example, a geologist may feel satisfied when he has lumped together one

[1] Karl Barth, *The Knowledge of God and the Service of God* (1938), Gifford Lectures at Aberdeen, 1937–8.
[2] *The Sense of the Presence of God*, ch. ix. Baillie's death prevented the actual delivery of the lectures.
[3] W. Heisenberg, *Physics and Philosophy* (1959), Gifford Lectures at St Andrews, 1955–6.

lot of specimens as bauxite, another lot as pyrites and so on. Nevertheless, because I believe that God has created man as a rational animal and has endowed him with natural powers, of which reason itself is one of the most significant, I hold that in religious experience there is a common element which is highly important and which with proper precautions can be brought under rational examination. Furthermore, because I believe that all natural objects have the common characteristic of being created and sustained by God, I hold that rational investigation of them may disclose rational grounds for believing in his existence. All that I have just said is, of course, said in order to justify a Christian theologian having an interest in natural theology. His natural theologising itself must be purely rational activity making no appeal to revelation. It may well be that in all religious awareness there are, closely intertwined, both a natural and a supernatural element or, if you like, aspects of both general and special revelation. It may none the less be the case that the two elements or aspects can be distinguished and separately discussed. The point may be illustrated by a simple parallel from electrodynamics. All electric circuits contain both resistance and inductance; both factors exist in every circuit, though in particular cases one or the other may be vanishingly small. The circuit with zero resistance or with zero inductance is a pure abstraction. Nevertheless, it may be useful to discuss these fictitious cases, both because some actual circuits may approximate very closely to them and also because the cases in which both factors are significantly involved may be easier to understand if the two factors have previously been discussed separately. Similarly, it is, I would hold, useful to discuss what knowledge of God, if any, can in principle be acquired by purely rational investigation, even if we hold that the knowledge that matters most cannot be acquired in this way. We must also recognise that the activity and the objects of revelation itself can be investigated by rational means.

I would suggest at this point that a great deal of unnecessary confusion may be avoided if we carefully distinguish between two contrasts which are closely related and, for that very reason, often unreflectively assumed to be identical. The first is the contrast between natural and revealed knowledge of God as distinct elements in religious experience; the second is the contrast between natural reason and supernatural revelation as distinct sources of material for theological investigation and as distinct criteria for theological judgment.

Austin Farrer, writing in 1943, pointed out that even the most convinced believer in revelation cannot afford to repudiate or ignore reason altogether.

> Illumination [he wrote], whether direct or by reflection from historical revelation, may be a *sine qua non* of conviction; but without the presentation of some intelligible object, it cannot be the total and sufficient cause. A man may be under the influence of the illumination and yet require to hear reason for the object to be made intelligible and the illumination to take effect in convincing him; and since it is never possible for anyone to know certainly that no illumination direct or reflected is falling upon himself or any other man, we can proceed cheerfully with our rational theology, for we need never despair of its convincing anyone.

And again:

> Unless I had some mental machinery for thinking the bare notion of God, could I recognise his revelatory action as that of God? That machinery might never have worked before. Let us suppose it works now for the first time, when the revelation occurs. Still it does work now, and it is possible to study it and see how it works and what is the notion it produces. As we shall learn, to study this notion of God, of a supreme and original being, is to study what the mind can only see in and through the general nature of finite and dependent being. And this is to study rational theology.[1]

Thus it appears that, even if it is held that all knowledge of God is revealed in the strictest sense, it will still be true that we have to exercise our reason in order to understand it and make sense of it. Mr H. P. Owen, in his brilliant work *The Christian Knowledge of God*, indeed goes further. 'Revelation', he writes, 'is not a special way in which we know; it is a special way in which God makes himself known.'[2] I am not sure that I would go as far as this, for I should want to say that, in giving the revelation, God may also give us the supernatural discernment ('faith' in

[1] *Finite and Infinite*, pp. 1f.
[2] op. cit., p. 122.

the scholastic sense) to recognise and understand it. But I should want to add—and this would bring me closer to Mr Owen—that this enlightenment will neither annul nor supersede the use of reason and man's other natural powers; it will, on the contrary, embrace them and fortify them, making them not less but more able to do their own jobs correctly.

In deciding on a subject for these lectures, it seemed to me that the time was ripe for a new survey of the basic structure of natural theology. Much has been written on and around the subject during the last quarter of a century from a great variety of angles. I have, however, found myself faced with certain difficulties. I have myself written at some length on the subject during that period, and I should still wish, apart from comparatively minor points of emphasis, to defend the position which I set forth in my books *He Who Is* (1943), *Existence and Analogy* (1949) and *Words and Images* (1957). There does not seem to me to be much virtue in repetition for the sake of repetition. A more serious obstacle arises from the extraordinarily divided condition of the philosophical world today. The lack of comprehension on the political plane between the Western democracies and the Marxist states is as nothing compared with the almost total lack of mutual interest between philosophers in the English-speaking world and those on the continent of Europe.[1] (A partial exception should be made for the United States of America, where some measure of interchange is visible.) It is not so much that the Anglo-Saxon linguistic analysts and the continental existentialists and phenomenologists disagree with each other's arguments and conclusions as that each side apparently finds it impossible to recognise that what the other side is doing is philosophy at all or is even intellectually respectable. Only in those departments of theological faculties which are concerned with the philosophy of religion is a slightly wider range of interest to be found. On the other hand, together with this formidable obstacle there goes a corresponding advantage. Just because the work of continental philosophers is unknown or neglected here discussion of it may at least have the attrac-

[1] Cf. the remarks on the 'cultural solipsism' of Oxford philosophy by C. M. Taylor in reference to the philosophical conference held at Royaumont in 1959 (cit. I. Mezoros, *British Analytical Philosophy*, ed. B. Williams and A. Montefiore, p. 312).

tion of novelty. And I shall devote a good deal of space to one continental school, namely that of the so-called transcendental Thomists, and this not because I agree with all their conclusions or even with their basic philosophical assumptions but because they are highly influential in some very vigorous and intelligent Christian circles and because there is a great deal that we can learn from both their achievements and their failures.

Considerations of space as well as of competence impose upon me further limitations. I shall almost entirely restrict myself to considering those approaches to theism which can rather narrowly lay claim to the title, not widely respected today, of metaphysical; these are exemplified by the ontological and the various forms of cosmological argument for theism. With some reluctance I have decided to make only passing reference to the approach to theism from the data of the moral consciousness. This has received eloquent and, in my view, convincing expression in Mr H. P. Owen's small but very impressive book *The Moral Argument for Christian Theism*. This, published in 1965, seems to me to be as important as, if not indeed more important than, A. E. Taylor's massive work *The Faith of a Moralist*, which consists of the Gifford Lectures delivered in St Andrews from 1926 to 1928.[1] With equal reluctance, and indeed perhaps with more reluctance in view of the fact that its approach is much closer to that which I am myself adopting, I shall say only a few words, and those in this first lecture, about Dom Illtyd Trethowan's recent book *Absolute Value;* it is the first volume of a two-volume work and an adequate discussion can hardly be attempted until the work is complete. In its general form Trethowan's argument is similar to that which he has expounded in earlier works and which is shared in its main features by such writers as Dom Mark Pontifex, Dr H. D. Lewis, Mr H. P. Owen, Austin Farrer and myself.[2] It is cosmological, in the sense that it takes its starting point in the existence of finite beings and of the universe of which they are parts, but it sees the purpose of

[1] Cf. also the late G. F. Woods's impressive book *A Defence of Theological Ethics* (1966).

[2] Illtyd Trethowan, *Certainty* (1948), *An Essay in Christian Philosophy* (1954), *The Basis of Belief* (1961); Mark Pontifex, *The Existence of God* (1947); H. D. Lewis, *Our Experience of God* (1959); H. P. Owen, *The Christian Knowledge of God* (1969); A. M. Farrer, *Finite and Infinite* (1943), *Faith and Speculation* (1967); E. L. Mascall, *He Who Is* (1943), *Existence and Analogy* (1949).

theistic argumentation not as the construction of syllogisms but
as the evocation of a recognition of God as present in finite
beings as the ground of their existence. 'If I had to talk about
the concept of "being"', writes Trethowan, 'I should suggest
that it is properly a double one, that it refers both to the
finite and to the infinite in that it refers to the finite in its
relation to the infinite.'[1] Trethowan's special feature, and it is
much more prominent in his latest work, is the emphasis which
he places on the moral consciousness and its recognition of
value. Indeed, when he asserts that 'the awareness of obligation
is an awareness of God'[2] and goes on to support this assertion,
he would seem to be introducing a moral rather than a cosmological argument. Nevertheless he is clear that he is not appealing to any abstract notion of morality but to moral value as a
datum apprehended by us in the concrete finite world. 'I am
not', he writes, 'proposing an argument from conscience according to which an inference is made from the existence of a law to
the existence of a lawgiver. What I am proposing is an interpretation of our moral experience.'[3] And in relation to St Thomas's
famous 'Five Ways' he writes:

> They draw our attention to features of our experience which
> provoke or bring into focus an awareness of God. If in fact the
> values of our world not only derive from absolute Value but are
> in this peculiar sense 'like' it, it is in contemplating them that
> we may be most naturally led to realise that such is the case.
> But they are no more than the natural occasions in which the
> awareness of God may arise or rather become more explicit.[4]

Thus, Trethowan's argument might be described as cosmological with a moral slant rather than as a typical example of
the moral argument. He is, in fact, a thinker of unusual and
sometimes startling originality, as is shown by his refusal to
admit any intelligibility in the notion that there could be any
possible worlds other than the world that actually exists. He is
insistent that we can, with the right precautions, reach absolute
certainty and there are places where he appears to be basing his
conviction of God more upon the capacity of the mind to achieve

---

1 *Absolute Value*, p. 90.
2 ibid., p. 84.
3 ibid., p. 87.
4 ibid., p. 123.

this than upon the objects which it perceives. Thus he writes:

> What I have been trying to show or rather to suggest (for
> these things can be seen only if people are prepared to look for
> them) is that our knowledge will not be recognised as the meta-
> physical experience which I believe it to be unless we realise
> that it is, in so far as metaphysical, a knowledge of God. We do
> not reach definitive conclusions about the nature and workings
> of the mind until we discover its source and its ground. I am not
> saying that we must first be certain of God *before* we can become
> certain of anything else. I am saying that *in* becoming certain of
> anything else, in recognising truth as such, we are in touch—in
> cognitive contact—with God, and that if we were not we should
> not be thus certain. So in the end it is a question of all or nothing.
> Either metaphysics *is* meaningless or it must be a theistic meta-
> physics.[1]

The lack of mutual interest and understanding in the philosophical world, to which I have referred, may be usefully
emphasised by quoting a passage from the preface which Dr
Louis Dupré has contributed to the English edition of M. Henry
Duméry's book *Faith and Reflection*.

> Henry Duméry, of the University of Paris, [he writes] is probably
> the best known philosopher of religion in France today. Born in
> 1920, he remained relatively obscure until 1957 when he pub-
> lished five books in one year. His work touched off a storm of
> controversy, particularly among Catholic theologians, which has
> never subsided. Only one of his books, *The Problem of God*, has
> been translated into English and, except for a few specialists,
> his name is virtually unknown in America. This obscurity seems
> to be due to the silence which separates Anglo-Saxon from
> Continental philosophers. Most of the time one group acts
> simply as if the other did not exist or was not worth talking to.
> Yet both pay dearly for this neglect, for the absence of any signi-
> ficant dialogue between the two Western traditions is one of the
> major reasons that philosophical discussion more and more
> spins around itself far from the real world. To the ordinary
> intellectual, philosophy seems to be the business of a group of
> inbred academic coteries which have removed their interests
> to a distance sufficient from those of ordinary mortals to be
> safe from any outside criticism. What ought to be the most

[1] ibid., p. 170.

stimulating of all disciplines has turned into an esoteric game totally irrelevant to what really matters in life.[1]

Duméry's main theme is original and stimulating, though many readers will no doubt judge it as paradoxical and perverse. From one angle it might be described as an attempt to drive out the atheism from Jean-Paul Sartre's existentialism, and to do this by taking every step with him except the last. Duméry agrees with Sartre that if there were a pre-existing realm of truth and value, to which man was morally bound to conform, man's intellectual and moral autonomy would be denied and his freedom destroyed. Man, he holds, must be the creator of his own values. But he denies, against Sartre, that this necessitates the denial of God; on the contrary, it is only as the gift of a transcendent God that man's power to create values can be explained. The immediate influence upon Duméry's thought is that of Husserl and phenomenology, but he finds an earlier justification for it in the neo-Platonism of the great third-century philosopher Plotinus, for whom the ultimate and absolute One is beyond both intelligibility and being.[2] 'In the creation of meaning and value *the self expresses its essential relation to the One.*'[3] And like all existentialism Duméry's system detaches man metaphysically from the rest of the finite world.

> Definitely eliminated in Duméry's thought is a revelation of God through nature. Nature may help man find his way to God, but it can never teach him anything *about* God. Nature has no voice of its own—all revelation is essentially human, for man alone can give meaning and expression. So, if God is to speak at all, he must do it through man. Man alone is the image of God.[4]

Thus, for Duméry, it is only through man that divine revelation can come and it is man who gives the religious object its religious meaning; this takes place in the act of faith, which involves a personal commitment. The question whether the object *as religious* has any reality outside the human mind clearly be-

---

[1] *Faith and Reflection*, p. ix.
[2] Duméry himself writes: 'We have drawn a certain inspiration from Plotinus' doctrine, but that is not to say that it served as a point of departure. . . . For us, Plotinus was an indirect encounter' (*The Problem of God*, p. 75n.).
[3] Dupré, loc. cit., p. xxvi.
[4] ibid., p. xxix.

comes acute. Duméry strongly denies that religion is a purely subjective experience and he sees the criterion of authenticity as given in Jesus Christ and developed and transmitted by the historic Christian community. Much more discussion than there is room for at this moment would be needed to locate Duméry's argument in the contemporary theological and philosophical scene and to make possible a judgment about its truth or falsehood. It is none the less astonishing that thought of such originality and provocativeness should be so little known in the Anglo-Saxon world.

I must now give some indication of the line which I propose to follow in these lectures. In defiance of the contemporary climate I shall be uncompromisingly metaphysical. I shall be primarily concerned with that type of argumentation for theism that is exemplified in the ontological and the cosmological argument. One of the surprising happenings in recent religious thinking has been the sudden revival of interest in the ontological argument, especially in the form which it takes in the *Proslogion* of St Anselm of Canterbury. This is largely due to the influence of the energetic American philosopher Dr Charles Hartshorne, though, as I shall emphasise later on, the ontological argument undergoes in his hands a transformation that would certainly have astonished St Anselm. Behind this, somewhat surprisingly, lies the revival of interest in the writings of A. N. Whitehead, which has given birth to a so-called 'process-theology' that has driven the short-lived 'death-of-God' theology almost entirely off the American theological scene. Before investigating this ontological revival, however, it will be necessary to pay some attention to the linguistic aspect of theology, and to this I shall devote the second lecture. The nature and function of language does, of course, hold a central, and indeed an all-embracing, status in present-day Anglo-Saxon philosophy as exemplified by the various types of linguistic analysts. Their approach has, however, been almost entirely positivistic and behavioristic, and even under the influence of the cryptic aphorisms of the later Wittgenstein they have shown little interest in the function of language as an instrument of cogitation and communication on the part of intelligent inhabitants of the material world. It is surprising that they have had so little contact with their colleagues in the realm of philology and linguistics, and one is tempted to wonder whether it may not be the latter group of specialists, rather than the professional philosophers, who will in the near future have most help to give towards the solution of problems in the area where linguistics impinges upon philosophy. It is no doubt too early to expect a final judgment on the much publicised work of Dr Noam Chomsky, but, if his theory of a universal human grammar underlying the grammars of the various human languages establishes itself, the linguistic approach to philosophy may have the result of rehabilitating rather than of excluding a metaphysical outlook on the universe. In any case there are certain questions about language that are of importance to natural theology and which need attention at an early stage in the discussion.

After these preliminaries I propose, in the third lecture, to give as detailed an examination as time permits of the recent work on the ontological argument. Here, as I have said already, the most important figure is that of Dr Charles Hartshorne. He is himself a fervent supporter of the argument, especially in the Anselmian form, though, as we shall see, he gives a highly idiosyncratic interpretation or reformulation of it. What is surprising is to find how much attention has been recently given to the argument by persons who, unlike Dr Hartshorne, do not accept the argument's validity. There is, in fact, a widespread feeling that, even if the argument is defective, a great deal of importance is to be learnt by a detailed understanding of its deficiencies and perhaps even more by an examination of the reasons why many people have thought not only that it is valid but also that it uncovers the ultimate secrets of the nature of reality. Here I shall also briefly refer to the school of 'reflexive philosophy', whose best-known members are Maurice Blondel, Louis Lavelle and Aimé Forest.

I shall pass on from this to consider the approach to theism which is commonly given the name 'cosmological', since it takes as its datum the actual concrete existence of the *cosmos* or world. In one form or another this has of course become the central, and one might say the typical, argument in the Catholic philosophical tradition. However, at least since the time of Immanuel Kant, it has been rejected by the main body of empiricist philosophers, often on the ground, which I believe to be false, that it involves a covert appeal to the ontological argument.[1] I have discussed it at some length in the books which I mentioned earlier in this lecture.[2] Before I make any further remarks on the cosmological approach as such I shall devote two lectures to one particular type of it, which has produced a large number of works, many of which are available in English translations but which have received little attention in these islands. These are the works of the writers who describe themselves as Transcendental Thomists. They are distinguished from the Neo-Thomists such as Jacques Maritain and Étienne Gilson by the fact that, instead of rejecting the Kantian critique of knowledge, which is generally understood as having demoted God from the status of a constituent principle of reality to that of a regulative principle of human thought, they accept the necessity of beginning with a critique of human knowledge but reject the destructive consequences for theology which have generally been held to follow from it. The founder of this school was the French Jesuit Joseph Maréchal, who wrote an immense work on the foundations of metaphysics between the two World Wars, but, apart from respectful and laudatory utterances from those who managed to read it, it provoked little really fresh thinking until it inspired a group of German-speaking writers of whom the most important are Karl Rahner, J. B. Lotz and Emerich Coreth. Rahner's great work *Geist im Welt* was written in 1939.

While the theological and philosophical inspiration of this group was provided by Maréchal, its literary idiom was derived from Martin Heidegger, the famous existentialist thinker under whom many of its members, including Rahner, studied. My own judgment, which I make under correction, is that Heidegger's influence on Rahner was less on his philosophical outlook than on his literary idiom and style, which some readers find fascinating and others infuriating. Standing aside from these is the Canadian Jesuit Bernard Lonergan, whose chief works, while voluminous and unsparingly exacting on the reader, are free from the influence of Heidegger and are basically lucid and rigid. In the opinion of many, he is the greatest Christian thinker alive today, more profound and more penetrating even than

[1] Cf., on this point, A. E. Taylor, *Encycl. of Religion and Ethics*, XII, p. 278, s.v. 'Theism'.
[2] Cf. p. 6 *supra*.

Rahner; he has had the experience, rare among philosophers and theologians, of having a full-scale congress assembled in his lifetime and devoted to the sole purpose of understanding and developing his thought. I would hazard the guess that, if transcendental Thomism is to make itself heard in the Anglo-Saxon philosophical milieu, it will be *via* Lonergan rather than *via* Rahner and Coreth, in spite of the fact that his literary output, unlike Rahner's, consists entirely of top-level professional work with no direct popular appeal. If anybody was ever a philosopher's philosopher and a theologians' theologian, it is Bernard Lonergan.

In the sixth and seventh lectures I shall develop my own argument and discuss the basic requirements of cosmological theism. In particular, calling upon a little-known but entertaining work of M. Gilson, I shall argue for a fundamentally realist epistemology and I shall maintain that all forms of idealism, placing the object of knowledge entirely within the mind, are inherently incapable of getting outside it. They lock themselves up inside their own mentality and then find that they have thrown away the key. The fashionable linguistic philosophy which is so familiar to us today is little more than a desperate attempt to escape from the mental prison of idealism, and it results in the equally unhappy fate of incarceration in the verbal prison of sentential analysis. (May I add in passing that linguistic analysis is a perfectly legitimate activity, so long as it does not substitute itself for metaphysics.) I shall restate, as convincingly as I can, the only doctrine of perception which, in my view, does not saw off the branch on which it is sitting. I shall then try to show that the contingent world of our experience manifests the presence, at its metaphysical root, of that absolute being which Christian theology calls God. That the knowledge about God which we can thus acquire is minimal in the extreme I shall not only admit but shall emphasise. This does not matter; once the point can be located in which finite being manifests the presence in it of the infinite, the knife-blade can be inserted and the cavity widened later on. I shall further maintain that the purpose, in this context, of argumentation in the strict sense is to induce and defend this 'contuition' of God in finite beings, and not to ignore it or usurp its place. In this connection I shall question the utility of the phenomenological method, as very possibly excluding from its purview the very factor in our experience for which it ought to be looking and upon which the recognition of God depends. Holding as I do that all finite beings, and not only some of them, are sustained by God's creative activity, I maintain that any of them, if we only know how to grasp it, can be seen as embodying that character of contingency which manifests God as its sustainer. In contradiction to the Christian existentialists, for whom it is only in my experience of my own subjectivity, as one who finds himself hurled into an uncongenial world, that I can come to recognise God, and in contrast to Austin Farrer, for whom my own soul is, not the *only* place, but certainly the *easiest* place in which I can recognise the creative activity of God, I shall point to extra-mental being, and in particular extra-mental material being, as providing the clearest example of sheer contingency. Just because it is the object and not also the subject of my awareness, I can, when I contemplate it, recognise its radical contingency uncontaminated by other factors which intrude themselves when I reflect upon my own self. I would therefore claim that my approach is metaphysical in the strictest sense of the word; it does not depend on the special characteristics or properties of any particular being or type of being, but upon the universal element of contingency which is common to all the objects of our perception. In taking this line quite intransigently I do not, however, wish to rule out other approaches; though I do wish to add that, without an implicit or explicit appeal to the element of contingency I do not see how they can establish their case. What the consideration of contingency may claim to have shown is the existence of transcendent self-existent being as the creative ground of the universe; and I shall go on to argue that such a creative ground must have the attributes of thought, will and power, and can therefore, in however analogical a sense, be rightly described as personal.

In the eighth lecture I shall interrupt the course of my argument to take account of a position which has achieved some measure of acceptance in certain religious circles, both Catholic and Protestant, but which, if it is accepted, seems to me to deal the death-blow not only to the kind of approach which I have adopted but to any rational form of theism. This is the view that truth itself, and not only our apprehension of it, is a historically conditioned value which changes from age to age and from place to place. The most distinguished recent exponent of it is Dr Leslie Dewart, and I shall give a detailed examination of the two books in which he has stated it. I hope to show that if it is adopted it destroys itself no less than the positions which it overtly denies.

Resuming my own argument in the ninth lecture I shall develop the notion of the openness of finite being. I shall argue that, just because of its radically dependent and non-self-sufficient character, finite being is open to fresh influxes of creative power which will elevate and transform it, but not destroy it. This, as I see it, provides the natural basis for both grace, as the Catholic tradition conceives it, and the Incarnation. To follow up the consequences of this in detail would take one beyond the limits proper to Gifford Lectures, but it is proper to indicate that natural theology itself shows finite being to have a receptive capacity, a *potentia oboedientialis*, for a supernaturalisation that it cannot achieve by its own natural powers. Finite being is essentially dependent, and because dependent incomplete, and because incomplete open to indefinite transformation. Of what kind and degree that transformation may be it is not for natural theology to say.

In the tenth and final lecture I shall discuss the relation of God and the world to time. I shall have nothing very original to say about this, but I shall take the opportunity to comment on the central importance which temporality has for some contemporary thinkers and in particular on the noteworthy resuscitation of the metaphysics of A. N. Whitehead by the promoters of 'process-theology'. And there, leaving many loose threads untied and remembering that Gifford Lectures, like other things finite, are necessarily incomplete, I shall end.

The volume of writing on natural theology that has appeared in recent years is quite enormous. If some of it will receive little or no mention this will imply no slight on its quality but will merely indicate my own limits of space and of competence. I shall, for the most part, concentrate on material which, while it is of real importance and interest, may be less familiar to my audience than some that has been more widely discussed. I shall make no attempt to tell again in detail the story that begins with logical positivism and ends for the time being with the

death of God. It is with real regret that I shall have to pass by
in silence the profound and judicious, but inadequately appreciated, books of my friend and colleague the late George F.
Woods, *Theological Explanation* (1958) and *A Defence of Theological Ethics* (1966). I can only mention the names of two quite
recent works that I have found of great value, Professor A.
Boyce Gibson's *Theism and Empiricism* (1970)[1] and Dr James
Richmond's *Theology and Metaphysics* (1970). And, while I
believe that the line which I shall follow provides a valid
approach to theism, I fully recognise that there are others which
are equally valid and are very possibly much more interesting.

[1] I have discussed this book at length in Appendix I *infra*.

CHAPTER TWO

THEOLOGY AND LANGUAGE

I am not yet so lost in lexicography, as to forget that words are the daughters of earth, and that things are the sons of heaven.
—Samuel Johnson, *Dictionary*, Preface.

NEITHER A GIFFORD LECTURER nor anyone else could give a course of lectures without making use of language, and if his subject is theology his language will be largely theological. That there are peculiar problems concerning theological language was discovered by English-speaking philosphers in the nineteen-thirties, though it had been a commonplace among theologians for centuries. And, although few philosophers today would adhere to the sweeping dismissal by the logical positivists of all metaphysical, ethical and theological statements as neither true nor false but strictly meaningless, most of them would still be unwilling, at any rate in English-speaking circles, to accept theological statements as assertions of matters of fact. It will, I think, therefore be useful, at this early stage in this course, to devote some time to the question of theological language.

The first point which I wish to stress is that, although there are special problems concerning theological language, there are serious and difficult problems concerning language as such. There has indeed been no lack of discussion about language and languages among analytic philosophers in recent years, from the time of Carnap and the Vienna Circle onwards. And behind this, round about the beginning of the century, there was the work of the mathematical logicians, with their disquieting discovery of the famous paradoxes; their heirs today are such persons as Dr Kurt Gödel, with his theorem stating that, in any logical system elaborate enough to be of practical use, it is possible to formulate statements whose truth or falsehood cannot be determined within the system. These philosophers, however, brilliant as they are, have been occupied almost entirely with the internal logical structure of languages (often highly artificial languages at that) or with the behaviour of words and sentences, and have paid remarkably little attention to the fact that human beings, unlike other living creatures, make use of language in order to clarify, order and communicate their thoughts. Their pursuit has in fact been rather like that type of sociological study which limits itself to the observable behaviour of human beings and ignores the whole realm of their mental life, their curiosity, their anxieties, their aspirations, loves and hates. It has interested itself chiefly with the behaviour of words and, even in the phase when its methodology was expressed by the maxim 'Don't ask for the meaning, look for the use', the word 'use' referred simply to the *way* in which words were used rather than to the intention of the user. Such a predominantly descriptive concern with language has, of course, its place and, properly used, it can deliver us from a great deal of confusion; but it condemns itself by its very method to leave out the most significant fact about languages, namely their function in the life of intelligent, self-conscious beings, the fact to which Sir Julian Huxley has drawn attention when he describes the evolution of language as 'the invention of words as symbols for things, in place of sounds as signs for feelings.'[1]

Right at the start of any discussion about language we must take account of the awkward fact that we have to make use of language whenever we wish to discuss it. Thus any doctrine about language which denies its basic competence as an instrument of intelligent enquiry and communication simply saws off the branch on which it is sitting. The late George F. Woods warned the doctrinal critic 'to have in mind the perpetual problem of the adequacy of language as an instrument for use in examining the adequacy of language'.[2] This warning, salutary as it is for the doctrinal critic, is even more important for the linguistic critic, who, even when treating of the language which he studies in a purely behavioristic way, must claim

[1] *Evolution in Action*, Penguin ed., p. 36, Cf. Naom Chomsky: 'These studies [*sc.* of animal communication] simply bring out even more clearly the extent to which human language appears to be a unique phenomenon, without 'significant analogue in the animal world' (*Language and Mind* (1968), p. 59).
[2] 'Doctrinal Criticism', in F. G. Healey, ed., *Prospect for Theology*, p. 83.

B

more than a behavioristic status for his own assertions. It will not do for him to say that his own assertions are expressed in a metalanguage which is not itself subject to the judgments that it makes about the first-order language which is the object of its own study; for, even if it cannot be judged by itself, there is a meta-metalanguage in which it can be judged. We can easily get involved in an infinite regress of a familiar type, but I do not think the difficulty can be resolved by saying that, although there is no archetypal language in which all languages including itself can be judged, any particular language can be judged in the language which is immediately above it in the sequence. For unless, somewhere inside or outside the sequence, language ceases to be simply a dance performed by marks on paper or vibrations in the air and becomes the instrument of intelligent thought it fails to state anything at all and so loses the very end for which it exists. I do not want to involve myself in the intricacies of the higher logic, but simply to urge that, legitimate and illuminating as the logical study of language is, it must not be allowed to exclude the recognition that language is essentially an instrument and a medium of human thought and communication. I do not think that even the later Wittgenstein and his successors have clearly seen that the nature and function of language are not exhausted by a discussion of either its internal logical structure or the speech-behaviour of people who use it. Time and again, when reading discussions about the nature and function of language, one finds oneself wondering whether the writer has ever seriously applied his own theories about language to the language which he himself uses in formulating and defending them.

Now, just because language is an instrument and a medium of thought and communication—that is to say, just because it is something that we use in order to clear our minds and to talk to other people—language can never be adequately understood except with reference to the social and linguistic context in which it is used. Even the most specialised discussion of mathematical topology, atomic nuclear structure or the coding of genetic characters in a living cell assumes the existence of a group of intelligent persons having a common conceptual framework and a common interest; the man who constructs a purely private language in which to talk only to himself must be a very rare person outside mental hospitals. I do not mean to suggest that, without, for example, achieving a perfect identification with the life and mentality of ancient Babylonia, I cannot in any degree understand the Code of Hammurabi, but I do mean that I am likely to misinterpret statements emanating from a culture other than my own unless I can achieve some degree of imaginative identification with it. It is, to give one example, his power to evoke the climate of thought and life in fourth-century North Africa in the mind of the modern reader that gives Mr Peter Brown's study of St Augustine a value that is absent from many equally learned but less inspiring works on the same subject. To achieve the desired end will, of course, need a good deal of sheer factual information; to understand the Decree of the Council of Chalcedon I must find out as much as I can about the fifth-century context and usage of such terms as *prosopon*, *hypostasis* and *physis*. Nevertheless, more than a purely lexicographical mass of information is necessary; we need to understand the way that the minds of fourth- and fifth-century Christians were working, and the way that their problems were puzzling them, if we are really to understand why they used the kind of language that they did. No arrangement of computers, however intricate, bombinating *in vacuo* can perform this task of understanding, though they may perhaps assist it; it involves the living thought of living intelligent beings. Nor is this task necessary only in studying the documents of the past; it is just as necessary in trying to understand our own contemporaries to the extent that they live in a different cultural and mental setting from our own. To take one instance, the difficulty which most Europeans and Americans have in taking seriously many of the utterances of the Russian and Chinese governments may arise largely from this cause. More is needed to remove the sense of frustration which accompanies this than the study of Russian and Chinese grammar-books and dictionaries; the trouble is that, as we sometimes significantly say, we do not 'know how their minds work'.

If what I have been saying is true, there is a real sense in which meaning is fundamentally mental and is logically prior to language. To adapt a famous phrase of Pope John XXIII, meaning is one thing and its verbal formulation is quite another. And, for reasons which I shall shortly indicate, no linguistic statement can do justice to the complexity of the situation to which it refers. This does not mean that all statements are equally and indifferently inadequate, so that it does not really matter what we say about anything. They are indeed all inadequate but some are less inadequate than others. And their degree of inadequacy will at least partly depend on the degree to which those who utter them share a genuine mental and linguistic community. It is said that there was once a group of American linguistic scholars who were convinced that the structure of Indo-European languages was so different from that of the real world as to make them useless for accurate philosophical purposes. Some of the Amerindian (Red-Indian) languages were alleged, in contrast, to be almost ideal. It might seem strange, in view of this, that the scholars in question, instead, as might have seemed reasonable, of writing books in Amerindian languages about Indo-European languages, wrote books about Amerindian languages in English. No doubt the reason for this was that they were writing for English-speaking people and not for Red Indians; it therefore seemed preferable to write somewhat misleading books for their fellow-scholars than logically perfect books for a non-existent public. I do not know whether this story is true, but I have seen an article by an English philosopher in which it was alleged that the English language was, in virtue of its sentential structure, unsuitable for theological purposes, and that theology could be conducted much better, if not absolutely ideally, in Classical Chinese. The writer fell indeed into a simple logical fallacy on the second page of her argument, but this might no doubt be taken as confirming her thesis of the unsuitability of English for theological purposes; though in fact the fallacy occurred when the English had been re-stated in the symbolism of *Principia Mathematica* and would have been unlikely to occur if the writer had been content with the ordinary language of the palace and the bus-queue. The significant fact, however, is that her article was written in the disreputable English language and not in the respectable Chinese. This was, no doubt, because she was writing in the context of an English-speaking linguistic community; she was trying to convert the English rather than to confirm the Chinese. And this does, I think, emphasise the fact that language cannot in practice be dissociated from its social context.

In the theological realm we have, I think, come to recognise that more is involved in understanding the classical statements of the Christian Church than the kind of knowledge that can be acquired from grammar-books and dictionaries. I will illustrate this by a passage from the Gifford Lectures of the late Leonard Hodgson, which is instructive both positively and negatively. He wrote as follows:

> I have described the history of human thought as God seeking to make himself known to man through minds inevitably conditioned by the forms of thought and linguistic usage of their age and culture. This conditioning has to be taken into account in our study of the books of the Bible just as much as in that of the conciliar creeds, the patristic writings, and the works of scholastic and Reformation divines. We have to learn all we can about their authors' ways of thinking and linguistic self-expression in order to discover in what way their insight into truth was coloured by this outlook and to what extent there was miscolouring which needs to be discounted. We ourselves have to think and speak as twentieth-century Western Europeans, in terms of the thought and language of our time and place. As we study the writings of the past the question we have always to be asking is; what must the truth have been and be if men who thought and spoke as they did saw it and spoke of it like that?[1]

Hodgson clearly attached great importance to the last sentence of this passage, since, with slight variations, he repeated it three times in another place;[2] and I agree that he was making a valuable point. I am, however, doubtful whether he appreciated its full implications. For, if we try to answer the question 'What must the truth have been and be if men who thought and spoke as they did saw it and spoke of it like that?', in what terms are we to answer it? It would, of course, be possible to try to answer it in terms of thirteenth-century Western scholasticism or of eighth-century Hinayana Buddhism, and this might indeed be a useful academic exercise, though we who were performing it would be for the most part twentieth-century Europeans and not thirteenth-century scholastics or eighth-century Buddhists and we should be in danger of producing only a rather self-conscious pastiche. This is, in any case, not what Hodgson had

[1] *For Faith and Freedom*, II, pp. 4f.
[2] ibid., I, pp. 87, 88.

in mind. As he himself recognised, we can only answer his question in terms of the thought and language of our own particular time and place, as twentieth-century Western Europeans.[1] And what guarantee have we that those terms are more adequate than those of some earlier Christian period? If the suggestion is that the ways of thinking and speaking of all times and places are equally adequate, though those of our time and place are more suitable for us, this would surely need to be shown; *prima facie* it does not seem likely that the language of, say, an aboriginal tribe in Australia today will be as adequate a vehicle for Christian theology as the Greek of St Gregory Palamas. Or is the suggestion that, although they are not absolutely adequate and final, our twentieth-century thought and language are so much more developed than those of other times and places that, for all practical purposes, we can take them as if they were? Again this would need proving and it would be surprising if it were true, since our modern Western European words and concepts were not devised with the needs of Christian or any other theology in mind. Whatever may be the limitations of the traditional theological forms of thought and expression and however difficult it may be to make them intelligible and inspiring to our contemporaries, they were not simply adopted by the Church as given and fixed categories but were transformed and moulded by the Church for the purposes for which it needed them. This should be recognised even by writers like Dr Leslie Dewart, who holds that in the interplay between Christianity and Hellenism Christianity came off second best. Or did Hodgson perhaps mean that truth itself, and not merely its linguistic and conceptual expression, is relative and fluid, as Dewart has alleged in his books *The Future of Belief* and *The Foundations of Belief*? One of the variants of Hodgson's question might seem to suggest this: 'If the truth about God's revelation in Christ be such that those men saw it and wrote of it like that, *what must it be for us?*'[2] I find it difficult to believe, in view of his writings as a whole, that Hodgson was quite such a relativist as that. It seems to me more likely that, in his anxiety to express

[1] I suspect that Hodgson would have included citizens of North America under the description 'Europeans', as the South African government did until it discovered them making use with the Bantu of the facilities labelled 'Non-Europeans'.

[2] ibid., p. 88 (italicisation mine).

the unchanging truth in terms that would appear intelligible and relevant to his contemporaries, he tended over-hastily to give our twentieth-century modes of thought and expression a specially privileged status. Another way in which to make my point is by remarking that, if Hodgson's question is legitimate, it must also be legitimate to ask 'What must the truth have been and be if men who think and speak as we do think and speak of it like *this*?' And this is patently unanswerable by us, except in a sheer tautology, since we have only our own thought and speech by which to answer it. The real lesson to be learnt from Hodgson's question is, I suggest, that, while we have only our own human languages in which to assert truths, the truths themselves are something other than our assertions of them and are not in themselves linguistic at all.[1] That is to say, a statement is true to the extent that, in the social and linguistic context in which it is uttered, it accurately describes some feature of the real or the logical world, and it can perform this function even if it can never reproduce with complete adequacy the feature's total complexity. Language has inevitably a certain looseness of fit at both the objective and the subjective poles. In extreme cases this may render it practically useless; the statement 'A plane leaves at 3.15' will be minimally informative if it is divorced from all reference to the day, the place of departure and the destination; there are far too many situations to which it could apply. And the word 'gut' will fail to identify its object unless we know whether it is used in the context of German or of English discourse. This inevitably imprecise character of language should act as a warning, but it does not deprive language of its function as a means of thought and expression; I can state with perfect accuracy that a battle was fought at Waterloo in A.D. 1815, even if I am unable to specify the identity of the opposing forces, the details and the outcome of the conflict and the day of the week on which it was fought.

We may add at this point that it is because of the contextual character of language that there is danger in making use of the

---

[1] Mr J. A. Baker (*The Foolishness of God* (1970), pp. 364f) has criticised Hodgson's methodological question on the ground that 'truth does not come to men clothed in words, it comes to them as words; and when as far as possible we know what the words meant to them, then as far as possible we know what the truth was to them.' I am not quite clear whether this criticism is the same as mine or not.

compendia of documents from past ages which the more erudite and diligent scholars compile for the benefit of their less learned or lazier colleagues; such works, for example, as Denzinger's *Enchiridion*, Mr J. Stevenson's *New Eusebius* and *Creeds, Councils and Controversies*, Dr C. K. Barrett's *New Testament Background* and Mr H. Bettenson's *Documents of the Christian Church*. In spite of the helpful notes with which they are furnished, these indispensable and time-saving works can easily mislead the unwary user. For, especially in the case of the briefer items, they are inevitably read out of their context; both the emphasis and sometimes the very meaning of a verbal formula may thus be completely misunderstood. Thus, to give one example, the doctrine of a *limbus infantium* appears in a very different light if it is recognised that it was directed not against people who held that babies dying unbaptised might share in the joys of heaven but against those who held that they were inevitably condemned to the flames of hell. Furthermore—and this is an even more dangerous limitation—the user is entirely at the mercy of the principle, or lack of principle, of the compiler in selecting his material; however conscientious the latter may be, his own views as to what is important will influence his choice. Thus it has been said, not without truth, that what in practice decides the influence of a papal or conciliar decree in the Roman Catholic communion is not, in the last resort, the authority with which it was promulgated but the value which it appeared to have in the eyes of Denzinger and his successors and which determined its inclusion in or exclusion from the indispensable *Enchiridion*. The selection of material and its arrangement in such a compendium inevitably provides it with a new and artificial context different from that in which it originated; both the overall picture and the nuance of an individual item may thus be seriously distorted.

We must look a little more closely at the question of the relation between a statement and the objective situation which it describes. It has sometimes been supposed that if a sentence is true it must picture precisely and in detail the situation to which it refers and that a language can be adequate only if sentences can be formed in it which picture precisely and in detail the whole universe or some part of it. Because no existing language measures up to this requirement philosophers have sometimes tried to construct, or at least to lay down principles for constructing, ideal languages which would satisfy it. Such an ambition was characteristic of the sense-datum epistemology of Russell and Broad in the period between the wars and, in a different way, of the work of such members of the Vienna Circle as Carnap and Neurath, though it could never be more than an ambition. Wittgenstein held a similar view when he wrote his celebrated *Tractatus Logico-Philosophicus*, though he abandoned it later.[1] He thought that, because a language consists of discrete elements, the world must consist of discrete 'atomic facts', to which the language's elementary statements would be in biunique, or one-to-one, correspondence; only if this were the case would it seem possible for language to 'picture' the world. It is, however, pretty clear that the world and language are not related in this way. So far from consisting of atomic facts which can be put in one-to-one correspondence with atomic linguistic statements, the world (at least as it appears to us) is a continuous, multidimensional, dynamic entity, while language is discrete, unidimensional and static. And even if we interpret current physical theory as showing that the universe consists of discrete 'fundamental particles', probably finite in number, so that its ostensible continuity is only an appearance, it will still be of such vast complexity that it cannot possibly be pictured biuniquely by any set of statements that we could ever manage to formulate.

What I am in fact arguing is that it is a mistake to suppose that the function of language is, even ideally, to picture reality by being in biunique correspondence with it, except in certain limited and highly specialised cases. Its function is rather to be an instrument by which intelligent beings are able both to clarify their own thinking and to communicate their thoughts to one another. Many of these thoughts, of course, have as their content the world in which the thinker lives and the people whom he meets in it; he is not concerned merely with his own subjectivity. Language is therefore essentially an activity of human beings living in a real world and in community, and it can be understood only as such. Any attempt to reduce it either to a set of labels attached to facts or to a set of noises emitted more or less systematically by human bodies in response to

[1] Cf. J. O. Urmson, *Philosophical Analysis: its Development between the Two World Wars* (1956).

stimuli ignores its basic nature as an invention and instrument of intelligent persons. What is necessary for the fruitful use of language is the sharing of some degree of social and cultural life on the part of those who try to communicate by means of it. This calls for a genuine effort of understanding and not merely a grammatical, syntactical and logical expertise; it is, as I have said, largely through the lack of such understanding and of the effort to attain it that many political discussions in the contemporary world end in deadlock and frustration. It is significant that this situation is often described by saying that the several parties 'simply do not speak the same language'; this means more than that they are uninstructed in one another's grammar, syntax and vocabulary. It is parallel to the phrase previously quoted, that 'we do not know how one another's minds work'. And it is because it does make this much-to-be-desired effort at mutual understanding that so much value can be seen in such a work as the Marxist scholar Roger Garaudy's *From Anathema to Dialogue*, with the appended essays by the Catholic priests Karl Rahner and Johannes Metz.

We must in fact avoid two opposite extremes. One is that of assuming that the ideal to which language should strive is simply that of picturing facts by statements logically isomorphous with them; this was the view of the earlier Wittgenstein. For it, an ideal language would be one in which every object and relation had been given a label and all the thinking could be done by a computer. The other extreme is that of minimising the function of language as expressing and communicating truth, or of redefining truth so that it no longer consists of the conformity of thought with reality but of an ever-changing vocalisation of man's subjective experience as a changing inhabitant of a changing world. This is the view defended by Dr Dewart with his repeated denunciations of 'Hellenism'. There are, needless to say, elements of truth in both the extreme positions. There are occasions and areas of reality to which the proto-Wittgensteinian ideal is proper, such as that of mathematics and much of the positive sciences. There are also legitimate uses of language—some of which are indeed of great importance—in which it expresses emotions, announces decisions of action, recommends policies and so forth. But all these uses are subsidiary to, and emergent from, man's basic character as a being who is capable of acquiring knowledge and so of apprehending truth. Mr J. R. Lucas has argued, quite convincingly in my opinion, that the essential functions of intelligent mentality cannot, even in principle, be simulated by any machine, however elaborate.[1] And, next to his possession of intelligence itself, language is man's most important endowment both for extending his own knowledge and for communicating it to others. He is, of course, neither infallible nor impeccable; he may unwittingly make mistakes and he may deliberately tell lies. If it is alleged, as it has been by some, that language has taken the form that it has simply because of its survival-value for man in the evolutionary process and not because of its capacity to express truth about reality, the first part of the assertion may be accepted but the implied denial in the second part is to be rejected. For unless man's thinking and the language which he used to clarify and express it had in fact developed in conformity with reality, their survival-value for him would indeed have been small. We need only ask ourselves what chance man would have had of survival if his thought and speech had borne no relation to the facts of the world around him. On the other hand, his speech would presumably have been extremely rudimentary, if not non-existent, had he lived in complete isolation and not in company with others of his kind. Down to the present day it is by living as members of a speaking community that children learn to speak. And all this may be briefly summed up in the simple statement that man makes use of language because he is an intelligent and social being.

This has been a far from exhaustive discussion of the nature of language and the problems that it raises, but it must suffice for the present. All that I have tried to do has been to defend the common-sense position that, in spite of these problems, language can, if due care is taken, be a reliable, though limited, medium of thought and communication. And I repeat that anyone who denies this position will have to use language in order to argue against it. I must devote the remainder of this lecture to considering the type of language with which we shall be specially concerned, namely theological language.

[1] 'Minds, Machines and Gödel' in *Minds and Machines*, ed. by A. R. Anderson; and replies to objectors, 'Satan Stultified', *The Monist*, LII (1968), pp. 145ff; *The Freedom of the Will* (1970), pp. 124ff.

Much of the language which theology employs does not differ in any relevant respect from that of ordinary discourse and it raises no special problems. Some of it, however, purports to describe, or at least to refer to, realities beyond those that are immediately perceived by the senses; in this it has a feature in common with metaphysics, in the traditional sense of that term. It goes, however, even beyond metaphysics in that the reality with which it claims to be specially concerned—what it denotes by the word 'God'—transcends not merely the realm of the immediately sensible, but the realm of all finite objects. The grounds on which it has been alleged that statements containing the word 'God' are meaningless, and that therefore there can be no being, God, to which they apply, are well known to philosophers and theologians at the present day; they range from the crude complaint of the logical positivists, that theological statements fail to conform to what is in fact an arbitrary definition of meaningfulness, to Professor Flew's oft-repeated assertion that such statements must be meaningless since the people who affirm them refuse to admit that they could be shown to be false by any conceivable circumstances whatever. I shall not attempt to recapitulate the vast mass of writing on this matter. It is difficult to separate discussion of the meaningfulness of theological assertions from discussion of the arguments put forward in support of their truth; I shall have more to say about this later on. I will, however, mention in passing two very useful works on the subject, Dr Frederick Ferré's *Language, Logic and God* and Dr John Macquarrie's *God-Talk*, though I must add that the most penetrating discussion which I know is contained in a brief, and unfortunately not easily accessible, article by Fr W. Norris Clarke, S.J., entitled 'Analytic Philosophy and Language about God', in the volume *Christian Philosophy and Religious Renewal*.[1] The position which I myself wish to maintain is the very simple one that, since meaningfulness means the capacity to be understood, the only way in which to discover whether a statement or a concept is meaningful is to see whether people can understand it. The apparently tautologous character of this definition of meaningfulness is in fact its strong point; for any attempt to define it in terms of a more fundamental concept must perforce assume that that concept is itself meaningful. The

[1] Edited by George F. McLean, O.M.I. (Washington, D.C., 1967), pp.39ff.

famous attempt of Professor A. J. Ayer to define meaningfulness by his verification principle[1] died the death of a simple suicide by a thousand qualifications, for, in spite of all its death-writhings, it never managed to conform to its own standard of meaningfulness.[2]

[1] *Language, Truth and Logic*, 2nd ed., 1946.

[2] Dr Alvin Plantinga remarks, at the end of a careful investigation:

> The fact is that no one has succeeded in stating a version of the verifiability criterion that is even remotely plausible; and by now the project is beginning to look unhopeful. . . .
>
> If the notion of verifiability cannot so much as be explained, if we cannot so much as say what it is for a statement to be empirically verifiable, then we scarcely need worry about whether religious statements are or are not verifiable. How could we possibly tell? As a piece of natural theology, verificationism is entirely unsuccessful. And this makes the dizzy gyrations of those theologians who accept it more puzzling than ever; perhaps they would do well to *study* it before rushing to embrace it. [*God and Other Minds* (1967), pp. 167, 168 and footnote].

More recently still, Dr Raeburne S. Heimbeck, in his minutely detailed work *Theology and Meaning: A Critique of Metatheological Scepticism* (1969), has argued for the meaningfulness of the language of classical theism and has shown the weakness of the verificationism of both A. G. N. Flew and R. B. Braithwaite. His conclusion is

> that having checking procedures (verification and falsification procedures) is a sufficient but not a necessary condition of cognitive significance, and that having semantic entailments and incompatibles . . . is both a necessary and a sufficient criterion of cognitive significance [p. 37].

He quotes Karl Popper, against Flew, that falsifiability is not a criterion of meaning, while disagreeing with Popper's view that falsifiability is the criterion for demarcating scientific theories from non-scientific (p. 88n). He charges Flew with

> three important mistakes: the assumption that the meaning of a sentence is equivalent to the empirical expectations of the statement it makes, the identification of the 'counts against' and the 'is incompatible with' relations, and the suggestion that G-statements expressing the love of God and the existence of God are in principle unfalsifiable [p. 123].
>
> The root error in both [Flew and Braithwaite] was seen to be the conflation of evidence with criteria, of the grounds for believing a statement to be true or false (the checking conditions) with the conditions which would actually make a statement true or false (the truth-conditions) [p. 163].

Heimbeck also remarks, in line with Plantinga as quoted above:

> I would hold that [Schuman M.] Ogden has conceded prematurely to Flew's metatheological condemnation of classical theism. There seems to be a tendency on the part of representatives of the newer theologies to regard metatheological scepticism as an ally in the struggle against classical theism. The metatheological sceptic from his side may

In defining meaningfulness, however, in terms of capacity to be understood, I am, of course locating it in the setting of a linguistic community. Apart from this context language is just marks on paper or vibrations in the air. God-talk, can of course, like any other talk, be mere psittacism; people can talk in their sleep and gramophones can talk in an empty room. Nevertheless, talk can be the medium of intelligent communication within a community, and only within a community can it be intelligible. For a linguistic empiricist to declare, with all the fervour of a Welsh evangelist, that he cannot give any intelligible meaning to the sentence 'God exists' may indicate nothing more than that he has never made a serious effort to enter into the linguistic community of those who affirm it. Religious people can, of course, talk nonsense without recognising it, when they are weary or off their guard, but then so too can linguistic analysts; nobody has yet made sense of the famous sentence 'Pirits karulise elatically', because there is (so far as is known) no linguistic community within which the words that compose it have been used in intelligent conversation. Nevertheless, I would maintain that, when religious people, including theologians, speaking carefully and responsibly, make statements containing the word 'God', they do understand what they are saying. This is, as they would themselves be the first to admit, very surprising and mysterious; and to outsiders who have some arbitrary and extrinsic criterion of meaningfulnessness it may be downright stupefying.

not be as sanguine about such an alliance. Flew, for one, finds Ogden's Whitehead-Hartshorne-Bultmann reconstruction as unintelligible as classical theism [p. 42n.].

It would be premature at this stage to assess the significance for theism of the advocates of 'transformational generative grammar', of whom the best known in Britain is Dr Noam Chomsky. These scholars dispute the assumption of the logical empiricists and the 'ordinary-language analysts' that natural languages are unsystematic. Though their primary concern is linguistic and not metaphysical, their work may have implications for metaphysics and theology. Dr Earl R. MacCormac has written as follows:

If the transformational grammar allows for the possibility of certain meaningful religious statements, then the question of the validity of those statements will be decided outside of that theory. Deciding upon whether it is cognitively meaningful or not to claim that a spiritual being exists will depend upon a religious epistemology. Advocates of such theological claims will have to defend them by constructing an adequate theory of religious knowledge. ['A New Programme for Religious Language: the Transformational Generative Grammar', in *Religious Studies*, VI (1970), p. 55.]

Like other statements these may need a good deal of clarification. What, however, one should never do is to deny facts on the grounds of preconceived theories; and I maintain that, as a fact of experience, theological statements are meaningful, in the context in which theological talk occurs. Whether they are in addition true is, of course, another question. It will occupy our attention a great deal later on.

It is indeed remarkable that we should be able to make meaningful statements about a being who is alleged by the very people who make the statements to be altogether transcendent to the finite world and radically different from it; for all the words and concepts that we use in this discourse are, or are constructed from, words and concepts that are normally used in talking about finite beings of everyday experience. Christian philosophers have in fact elaborated a great mass of theory to deal with this surprising situation; it is known as the Doctrine of Analogy. I have devoted a book to the subject and I shall not attempt to recapitulate it here.[1] It may just be worth while mentioning, for those who are interested in the technicalities of the subject, that a suggestion which I make in that book, to the effect that a satisfactory doctrine of analogy cannot be built up on analogy of proportionality alone but requires in addition analogy of attribution, seems to have been confirmed by more recent Thomist scholars, who find in Aquinas himself the notion of analogy of causal participation.[2] I have in any case come to see more clearly that one is already loading the question if one puts it in the form 'How can terms which in their normal and natural application refer to finite beings refer analogically to God?' The primary datum, though many modern empirical philosophers may not be ready to admit this, is that the terms apply *both* to finite beings *and* to God, and the question is how this dual application can be explained. From an ultimate standpoint a theologian will indeed assert that their primary application is to God and only their secondary application is to finite beings, but this will come at the end of the story, not at the beginning. To anticipate future argument, I will merely say here that the explanation of this dual application of terms to

---

[1] *Existence and Analogy*, 1949. For more recent developments cf. the second edition of my *He Who Is*, 1966, Introductory Essay.

[2] Cf. *He Who Is*, 2nd ed., pp. xiiiff. Also W. Norris Clarke, art. cit., pp. 7of.

God and to finite being is that God and finite beings are in a definite causal relation. If God and his creation were as totally unrelated as some opponents of natural theology affirm, no terms could apply to both, however analogically. I am not, of course, asserting that the dual application of terms can be made the basis of a proof of God's existence; with all due respect to supporters of the ontological argument, I do not think that one can make that kind of transition from language to reality. What I do think, on the other hand, is that only the notion of a God who is related to the world—and who is related to it in a very particular way—can make the fact of this dual applicability of terms intelligible.

A final point of importance is this. Believers not only believe that God exists; they also believe a number of things about him. In consequence, as Fr Norris Clarke has pointed out, the word 'God' is used with a good deal of latitude, so that it may be legitimately asked whether 'God' is a proper name or a description and, if the latter, what description it is.[1] The word 'God' is not alone in this respect. Suppose I speak about 'the Queen' and somebody says to me 'What do you mean by "the Queen"?' In order to make it plain that I am referring to the Queen of England and not to the Queen of Holland or Greece, I may reply 'the lady whose head appears on our fourpenny stamps' or 'the legitimate successor of King George VI'. If I adopt the former definition, then the statement 'The Queen's head appears on the fourpenny stamps' is an analytic proposition and 'The Queen is the legitimate successor of King George VI' is a synthetic one; and conversely if I adopt the latter. If I adopt some other definition, both statements will be synthetic.

This particular instance may appear to be trivial, but the matter is far from trivial when statements are made about God. Since, as I have said, believers believe a number of things about God, it is not always clear how many of these things are explicitly or implicitly included in the definition which they assume of the word 'God'. In consequence, when they use the word 'God' they may not all be meaning precisely the same things by it. For one man the word 'God' may simply signify the ultimate ground of the universe, and the question whether that ground is personal or impersonal may seem to him of little importance;

[1] art. cit., pp. 51ff.

for another the question may be so important that he would refuse to apply the word 'God' to the ground of the universe unless he was convinced of its personal character. Thus to these two men the question 'Is there a God?' may have very different meanings, and if this is not recognised confusion and frustration may arise. As a matter of common honesty it is essential not to take a minimal definition of the word 'God' in arguing for God's existence and subsequently to slip over quietly into a notion of God that is stored with all the fullness of Christian belief and devotion. Consider the following dialogue:

Titus: 'God' means the ultimate ground of the universe.
Balbus: Agreed.
Titus: The universe must have an ultimate ground.
Balbus: Agreed.
Titus: Therefore God must exist.
Balbus: Agreed. But what is God like?
Titus: Well, he must be loving, wise and all-powerful.
Balbus: How do you know that?
Titus: Well, I wouldn't call him 'God' unless he was.
Balbus: Shouldn't you have thought of that before?

This kind of intellectual cheating is by no means fictitious, and it is all the more insidious for being usually unintentional and unconscious. Some critics have detected it in Dr J. A. T. Robinson's persuasive book *Honest to God*.[1] There is, of course, no harm in using the word 'God' with different definitions in different contexts. When the Christian theologian uses it he will often mean by it the Holy Trinity of Father, Son and Holy Spirit, who are one divine unity of love. It is clear to me that St Anselm used a different definition of 'God' in the *Proslogion* from that which St Thomas Aquinas assumed in the *Summa Theologiae*; this does not mean that St Anselm and St Thomas believed different things *about* God. Two things are, however, essential. The first is to be quite clear about the meaning we are giving the word in any particular discussion; the second is to refrain from slipping from one meaning to another in the course of the same argument. If we fail in this we shall constantly confuse the two questions that need to be kept distinct: 'Is there a God? and 'What is God like?'

[1] Cf. my *Secularisation of Christianity*, p. 121; D. E. Jenkins, *The Honest to God Debate*, p. 198.

CHAPTER THREE

GOD AND LOGIC

'But why drives on that ship so fast,
Without or wave or wind?'
'The air is cut away before,
And closes from behind.'
—S. T. Coleridge, *The Ancient Mariner.*

THE POINT WHICH we reached at the end of the last lecture was this: that in conducting any argument for theism it is imperative to be clear and consistent about the definition which we are employing of the word 'God'. Otherwise we shall be constantly confusing the two questions 'Is there a God?' and 'What is God like?'; and we shall in all probability fall into the fallacy of implicitly assuming a minimal definition of God in arguing for his existence and a much more ample definition in discussing his nature. There can be no harm in adopting different definitions of 'God' in different arguments for God's existence, provided we are quite clear what we are doing and carefully check each against the others. Thus, in one argument we might define God as a being having the attribute X and, having proved the existence of such a being, go on to argue that in addition it possessed the attributes Y and Z. In another argument we might define God as a being possessing the attributes X and Y and, having proved the existence of such a being (a more difficult task than the former but perhaps a possible one), go on to prove that it possessed in addition the attribute Z. We should then have two arguments proving the existence of a being possessing the attributes X, Y and Z, though a further argument might be necessary to prove that there is only one such being. Alternatively, we might have two arguments, one of which proved the existence of God defined as a being possessing the attribute P and the other proving the existence of God de-

fined as a being possessing the attribute Q, and we might further argue that any being possessing one of these attributes also
possessed the other and that there was only one being that
possessed either. Again, we might even have an argument that
proved the existence of God defined as a being possessing the
attribute L and find that, in the very act of proving its existence,
we had also proved that it possessed the attribute M. I shall not
attempt to catalogue all the possible variants; they would
appear to be in principle unlimited. But I shall do my best to
heed my own warning; and in discussing any argument for the
existence of God I shall try to make it plain what is the definition
of God that is presupposed to the argument. And I shall devote
the rest of this lecture to a consideration of the ontological argument, which, after having fallen into apparently irreparable
discredit, has recently made a remarkable recovery.

The ontological argument, or, in view of their diversity, it
would perhaps be better to say, ontological arguments, attempt
to prove the existence of God simply from the definition of the
word 'God' or from the concept which that word connotes.
Thus an argument such as that in Descartes' Third Meditation,
which is based on the fact that the concept of God is found in
the thinker's own mind, is not strictly speaking an ontological
argument; on the other hand the argument in his Fifth Meditation, based on the content of the concept itself, is an ontological
argument in the strictest sense. As a matter of history, arguments of this type spring from two chief sources: the *Proslogion*
of St Anselm of Canterbury in the eleventh century and the
Third of the *Meditations* of René Descartes in the seventeenth. It
is the Anselmian argument that has received most attention in
recent years as an important contribution to philosophical
theology, while that of Descartes still holds its position in academic syllabuses for its historical interest but does not appear to
be taken very seriously in itself.

The definition of 'God' from which Anselm begins is that of
'something than which nothing greater can be thought', *aliquid
quo majus nihil cogitari potest*;[1] that from which Descartes begins
is that of a supremely perfect being.[2] These definitions are not

---

[1] *Proslogion*, II.

[2] *Meditations*, III. It is disputed whether Descartes had first-hand knowledge of Anselm's argument; cf. M. Charlesworth, *St Anselm's Proslogion*, p. 6
and n. 2.

identical, though it might not be difficult to argue that they are equivalent, that is to say that anything which corresponded to either also corresponded to the other. It is Anselm's with which we shall be chiefly concerned. There are two statements of the argument in the *Proslogion*, or, as some recent writers would insist, statements of two similar but importantly different arguments, in chapters II and III of that work respectively. Both claim to prove that God exists, but the former merely asserts that the non-existence of God is false, while the latter asserts that it is not only false but impossible.

Proslogion II, having defined God as something than which nothing greater can be thought, draws a distinction between a purely mental existence of any object—its existence 'in the understanding'—and its existence in concrete reality; it then asserts that an object which exists both in the mind and in reality is 'greater' than an object, otherwise precisely similar, which exists only in the mind. It is then argued that 'that than which nothing greater can be thought' must exist in reality as well as in the mind, since if it existed only in the mind we could think of a being otherwise precisely similar which did exist in reality as well. We should thus have been led into a contradiction, having thought of something greater than something than which nothing greater can be thought. Thus the hypothesis that God exists only in the mind must be false, and it follows that God exists in reality. The argument is thus a *reductio ad absurdum*, proving a proposition—'God exists in reality and not only in the mind'—by showing that the supposition of its falsehood leads to a contradiction. The argument in *Proslogion* III derives a similar contradiction from a logically weaker hypothesis, namely the hypothesis that God can be *conceived* as not existing; and the conclusion is correspondingly stronger. It is that the non-existence of God is not merely false but is inconceivable. Philosophers have in general seen little difference between the two arguments and have tended to take *Proslogion* III as a restatement or, at most, a clarification or amplification of *Proslogion* II. We shall, however, see later on that for some modern philosophers the difference is quite fundamental.

Among recent literature on the subject I would single out two symposia as specially useful. *The Ontological Argument from St Anselm to Contemporary Philosophers*, edited by Alvin Plantinga, covers both Anselm and Descartes, before going on to G. E. Moore, William P. Alston, J. N. Findlay, Charles Hartshorne and Norman Malcolm. It includes Anselm's controversy with his contemporary Gaunilo and the criticism made by the later scholastic St Thomas Aquinas. To Descartes' own exposition it adds his controversy with Caterus, Gassendi and others and the relevant later writings of Spinoza, Leibniz, Kant and Schopenhauer. The other book, *The Many-faced Argument: Recent Studies on the Ontological Argument for the Existence of God*, edited by John Hick and Arthur C. McGill, pays little attention to Descartes, but it contains several critical and interpretative studies of Anselm, including those by Karl Barth and Anselm Stolz, and a very useful survey by McGill, before going on to contemporary or quite recent material. When it is added that in October 1968 a special section of the journal *Religious Studies* was devoted to five essays on the ontological argument and that other issues have contained articles on it as well, it should be evident that interest in it is anything but dead.

As with other philosophical and theological topics, much of the discussion has been concerned with the nature and purpose of the argument as its author St Anselm conceived it. This may at first sight be surprising, in view of the brevity and clarity of the argument itself, but its brevity may in fact provide the explanation; Anselm, so far from telling us exactly what was in his mind, leaves us to find this out for ourselves. It is therefore understandable that we do not all come to the same conclusion. Dr McGill, in his survey, distinguishes several schools of interpretation. The first, including both admirers and critics, sees Anselm as the supreme rationalist among Christian thinkers; he claims to prove everything by reason, even the deepest and most mysterious truths of the faith.[1] Others see Anselm as, before all else, the Christian believer, who insists on the primacy of faith, whose desire to understand God arises from his love and hunger for God, and who, even in his most intensive arguments, always argues from the data of revealed faith for the satisfaction of loving faith. The most striking, and indeed paradoxical,

[1] Dr Frederick Sontag writes: 'Anselm introduces a subtle distinction into his discovery that God's perfection requires an ultimately ineffable nature by asserting that, although our terms refer to a being beyond comprehension, the meanings of the terms used in describing God are in themselves fully comprehensible' (*Divine Perfection*, p. 40).

presentation of this point of view is to be found in Karl Barth's work *Fides quaerens Intellectum*, published in German in 1931 and later translated into English. For Barth, what Anselm intended to do was to show by reason that reason could tell us nothing about God except that he is altogether out of the reach of reason. Others, such as André Hayen, while less extreme than Barth, see Anselm as a theologian rather than a philosopher; Hayen asserts that his argument with the 'fool' who 'says in his heart "There is no God"' is inspired by an apostolic love for all men which includes even the fool in its scope. Others, again, like Anselm Stolz, contend that the *Proslogion* is a work of mystical theology, that its presentation in the form of a prayer is not a literary device but is of its very essence and that it 'represents an effort of the soul to raise itself to a kind of vision of God, by means of a dialectical investigation of the rationality of Christian dogmas'.[1] Where experts disagree so widely it is temerarious for the layman to express an opinion, but I venture to suggest that the various views are not, with the possible exception of Barth's, incompatible. Anselm did not, as I see the matter, make the kind of distinction between faith and reason which we find, for example, in St Thomas, and which in some later theologians becomes not a distinction but an impenetrable barrier. He believed in God by faith, and the definition which he gives of God is, for him, only a clarification, in terms appropriate to discussion, of the truth about God as supreme and transcendent which is central to the religion of both the Old and the New Testament. But he believed by faith that God is supremely rational, and it therefore seemed obvious to him that, if one could only find out how to do it, it must be possible to prove the existence, and indeed the necessary and inevitable existence, of this supremely rational being. He believed that God had shown him how to do this, and he could never thank God sufficiently for it. I think, therefore, that one key at least to the *Proslogion* is to be found in the fact that it could never occur to Anselm that there was anything irrational or anti-rational about faith and revelation. Whether his arguments are rationally valid or not is, of course, another question.

Almost, if not quite, all of the many criticisms which have been made of Anselm's arguments accuse him of making an

[1] McGill, op. cit., p. 65.

illicit transition from the conceptual or ideal to the actual realm. Even if I cannot think of God except as existing, the objection runs, this does not show that he actually exists. This holds equally against *Proslogion* II and *Proslogion* III; it holds also against the modified form of the argument in the *Reply to Gaunilo*, in which Anselm argues, first that his definition of God implies that God is an eternal existent, and then that an eternal existent cannot be a merely possible one. One way—it might be called the 'classical' way—of stating the objection is by saying that 'exists' is not a predicate; more precisely we might say that it is certainly not a predicate like other predicates.[1]

Grammatical predicates can indeed have a number of logical, epistemological and metaphysical kinds of function. If the horses in the field are brown, each one of them is brown; but if the horses in the field are numerous, it does not follow that each of them is numerous. More relevantly to our present concern, while most predicates refer to qualities of things and thus to components or aspects of their essence, 'exists' refers to the concrete actuality of things and not, except indirectly, to their essences at all. Many modern writers, as for example Étienne Gilson and Bernard Lonergan, have emphasised in this connection the radical difference between the apprehension of a concept and the affirmation of a judgment, and have pointed out that, while qualities are conceived as constituents of the essence of a being, its existence is affirmed in a judgment; and, we must add, not the judgment that its essence includes certain qualities but the more basic judgment that it *is*. Thus it is really misleading to speak of 'existence' at all; for the very shape of the word, parallel in its formation to 'essence', might suggest that it is a kind of quality or a complex of qualities. It is noteworthy that St Thomas Aquinas in his most characteristic works does not use the word *existentia* at all; he avoids its abstract flavour by using instead the verbal noun *esse*. It may be added that in a recent article in *Religious Studies*[2] Mr M. J. A. O'Connor has claimed—as it seems to me, with justice—that Anselm's three arguments involve further fallacies of a logical character hitherto

[1] David M. Lochhead, in a vigorous criticism of M. J. Charlesworth's *St Anselm's Proslogion* (Religious Studies, II (1966), pp. 121ff), has defended Anselm from the accusation of taking 'exists' to be a predicate. Cf. A. Plantinga's discussion, pp. 55ff *infra*.

[2] *Religious Studies*, IV (1968), pp. 133ff.

undetected. He points to the peculiarly psychological character of Anselm's definition of God—'something than which nothing greater can *be thought*'—and remarks that a more natural definition would be 'something than which nothing greater can *be*'. The difference is, he maintains, not trivial, for it leads Anselm to compare God's existence in the mind with God's existence in reality, as if the mind and reality were two locations in which God could exist; whereas in fact what exists in the mind is not God but the thought of God.[1] 'In point of fact', writes O'Connor 'Anselm deceives us into thinking he is treating G.C.B. [the greatest conceivable being] as a concept, when he is actually treating it as a given entity at different levels of ontology—mental and actual. From the supposed agreement of the unbeliever that G.C.B. exists at the one level he argues that it must also exist at the other.'[2] And O'Connor shows how, for example, this inadvertence on Anselm's part leads him to suppose that he has proved that 'G.C.B. cannot be imagined as existing and yet not actually exist' when all he has in fact proved is that 'G.C.B. cannot be imagined as existing and yet be *known* not to exist'—a very different proposition.

Anselm, we have just said, speaks of God, and not just the thought of God, as existing in the mind; as if the mind was itself a place in which God actually exists.[3] It must now be recognised that, according to one school of interpreters, a sympathetic school at that, this is precisely what Anselm did mean. (We must note, of course, that by 'existence in the mind' here we mean not that existence of God in all things by 'essence, presence and power', as St Thomas puts it, which arises from the fact that he is their creator and sustainer,[4] but an actual identification of the *idea of God* in the mind with God's own entitative being.) In McGill's words, 'At the beginning of the argument, ... Anselm is not looking at or thinking about some mental notion and wondering whether this is a true notion which represents a real object. *Through* this idea he is looking at and thinking

---

[1] I have slightly paraphrased O'Connor's argument, but I hope not misleadingly.

[2] art. cit., p. 136.

[3] Wallace I. Matson, in *The Existence of God* (1965), condemns Anselm's argument on the ground that 'exists in the understanding' cannot validly mean more than 'is understood' (op. cit., pp. 49ff).

[4] *S. Th.*, I, viii, 3.

about reality, specifically about the unique perfection of God's nature.' 'According to the realists, then, since Anselm begins with a direct cognition of God's reality, it is better not to call this an "idea" at all, but an awareness. Some say that he views it in this way because of his Platonic doctrine of ideas. . . . Other historians explain this realism as the product of a decisive religious experience. . . . According to the realists, therefore, those who deny the conclusion cannot be accused of a logical blunder. They simply fail to recognise the awareness which is being analysed.'[1]

A very different interpretation of Anselm which McGill lists asserts the purely psychological character of the idea of God in the mind and sees the saint as arguing to God as the cause of this psychological datum with its peculiar character of compulsiveness; in this, as he remarks, it would appear to have much in common with Descartes' argument in his *Third Meditation*. A variant of this interpretation is found in Étienne Gilson, who sees Anselm as appealing to God's reality as causing not the idea as such, but the logical necessity which the mind discovers in analysing it; this, however, means for Gilson that the argument contains only the initial datum for a proof. Still another interpretation finds importance in the distinction, in Anselm, between the words 'conceive' (*cogitare*) and 'understand' (*intelligere*). 'Cogitare . . . might be called the cognition of objective possibility, just as *intelligere* is the cognition of objective actuality.' The fool in the argument *understands* the definition of God, because he has it in his mind, but when he tries to *conceive* God as non-existent he finds this impossible. Conceiving operates within a noetic limit, imposed by reality itself. 'The logic simply demonstrates that this initial limit whereby the mind is not able to conceive of anything greater than God, involves other limits, such as its not being able to affirm (*Proslogion* II) or even to conceive of (*Proslogion* III) God's non-existence.'[2]

In contrast with such interpretations as these Karl Barth maintains that for Anselm the definition of God from which he begins is itself a datum of revelation, so that all the argument shows—but for Barth it is a great deal—is that revelation does not allow us to conceive of a non-existent God. I find Barth's

[1] *The Many-faced Argument*, pp. 71ff.
[2] McGill, op. cit., pp. 86f.

argument tortuous and unconvincing, but, as I have discussed it at some length elsewhere,[1] I shall not repeat myself here. It is also dealt with exhaustively by Henri Bouillard in his book *The Knowledge of God*. I think, however, that Barth is right in seeing Anselm's definition as emerging from the Christian revelation. I agree with Gilson that 'the inconceivability of the non-existence of God could have no meaning at all save in a Christian outlook where God is identified with being, and where, consequently, it becomes contradictory to suppose that we think of him and think of him as non-existent.'[2] And I agree further with Gilson that, significant as it is, Anselm's attempt to pass from the realm of concepts to the realm of actuality is a failure, though a heroic one. One further school of interpreters to whom McGill refers see the argument of the *Proslogion* as a sequel to Anselm's earlier work the *Monologium*, in which he seeks to prove the existence of God from the existence of things in this world; they do in fact admit the inadequacy of the *Proslogion* as providing arguments for God's existence, though it is difficult to suppose that Anselm would agree with them.

McGill's discussion of the purpose and character of Anselm's arguments is a magnificent example of erudition and of analytical ability; as he somewhat disconcertingly shows, almost any of the interpretations proposed comes into conflict with statements made by Anselm himself. Perhaps all these interpretations are over-subtle and the truth is simply, as I have suggested, that Anselm saw no conflict between reason and revelation and that it seemed to him to be the most natural thing in the world to look for a rational proof of the existence of God, as he looked for rational proofs of the Trinity and the Incarnation. That his thought, like that of other Christians down to the thirteenth century, moved naturally in a Platonic realm of ideas and essences is not surprising. Like some other achievements of the saints (not, I hasten to add, like all), it calls for our admiration rather than our imitation. I am, however, startled by the grounds on which, at the end of his brilliant survey, McGill expresses his hopes of the future vindication of Anselm. I have in an earlier lecture said something about the importance of language as a means of communication between human per-

---

[1] *He Who Is*, 2nd ed., Appendix.
[2] *The Spirit of Medieval Philosophy*, p. 59.

sons and as an instrument for the clarification of human thought. McGill, however, attributes to words an inherent character as bearers of meaning which is apparently quite independent of their utilisation as tools by human beings. After referring to the dominant view of language as derivative and expressive, he writes as follows:

> Today, for the first time in centuries, a serious challenge is being raised against this subjectivistic theory of language. Words, according to Martin Heidegger, are not primarily the tools by which men express what is already in their heads. Rather they are the *instruments of reality itself*, the medium through which being discloses itself, using man's voice as its spokesman. Language is not about reality, it is reality in the state of unveiledness and in every statement it is the subject matter—not the subjectivity of the author—which addresses man's thought.
>
> This view has begun to liberate readers from the axiom that language expresses merely *human* ideas. We may expect, therefore, that eventually it will lead to a new approach to *Proslogion* II. When that occurs, interpreters will give full weight to Anselm's *intelligere quod auditur*, and will be able to understand why he thinks that nothing else is needed except uttering the words 'that than which a greater cannot be conceived'.[1]

I am not surprised that Mr Thomas McPherson mildly remarks, in a review of *The Many-faced Argument*, that 'this kind of approach seems to create more problems than it solves'. 'The trouble with this', he writes, 'surely is that men utter falsehoods as well as truths, are obscure as well as lucid. It is no doubt true, if one chooses to put it that way, that reality expresses itself through man's voice. But so does unreality and confusion, and it is not always easy to tell the difference simply on the basis of the words we hear.'[2] Such logolatry as this might well seem too great a price to pay for one's deliverance from the ghost-world of linguistic empiricism.

I have postponed to this point one group of thinkers to whom McGill makes brief reference, first because the symposium contains an essay by Aimé Forest which is devoted entirely to them, secondly because it seems to me to be of considerable importance, and thirdly because little attention has been paid to it in

---

[1] op. cit., p. 110.
[2] *Religious Studies*, V (1969), p. 124.

professional English-speaking philosophical circles. This is the school of so-called 'reflexive philosophy', in which the leading figures are Maurice Blondel, Jacques Paliard, Louis Lavelle and Ferdinand Alquié, not to mention Aimé Forest himself. In McGill's words:

> This view is based on a fundamental distinction between what may be called 'projective' and 'reflexive' thought. In every moment of consciousness the mind reaches outward away from itself toward some object; it thus acts intentionally and projectively. At the same time, however, while grasping for things, the mind is also aware of its own operations, of its own intellectual, moral and emotional processes. In other words, alongside the knowledge which each man has of the world, he also possesses a *reflexive knowledge* of himself as an inner spiritual activity, as an *élan*, or dynamism, of consciousness and will.[1]

It is emphasised that this reflexive knowledge is not to be confused with introspection, in which the mind becomes the deliberate object of its own attention; indeed it seems to me that the choice of the word 'reflexive' is unfortunate and could be misleading. 'In the latter [introspection] the mind turns away from the world and looks at its own mental processes as if they were objects. Reflexive knowledge, on the other hand, is what the mind learns about itself *while in the process of thinking about objects*. It accompanies, and does not replace projective thought.'[2] It is thus, in the language of Karl Rahner and the other protagonists of transcendental Thomism, essentially *unthematic* and unformulated, though it can become formulated by subsequent thought. It is, so to speak, my knowledge of myself *at the near end* of my consciousness of the world around me and of my willing and acting within it. And it is something which the neo-behaviourists such as Professor Ryle find it even more difficult to bring within their self-imposed limits than they find the facts of introspection. It is what the scholastics are referring to when they insist that we know ourselves not apart from, but in, the acts through which we know other beings.

Now it is the contention of the school of reflexive philosophy that in our awareness of ourselves we can also become aware of God as our creative ground and as the supreme reality; and it is

[1] op. cit., p. 89.
[2] ibid., p. 92.

held that it is the function of the ontological argument to enable us to recognise this. In Ravaisson's words, quoted by Forest: 'From the interior and central point of view of reflection, the soul does not discern only itself, but also, at its foundation, the absolute from which it emanates.'[1] For Blondel, with his basic metaphysical principle of 'action', the ontological argument complements and does not supersede the various forms of cosmological argument. In the meeting of the truth of being with the dynamism of the consciousness which not merely perceives but affirms it, action enables us to perceive not only what we are but what is at the root of our being. We do not perceive God himself, but we do perceive God in ourselves. Whereas Blondel's starting-point is our *action*, Jacques Paliard's is our *self-consciousness*, while for Louis Lavelle it is by reflection on our action that we form the idea of God, as enveloping our existence because he is the cause of it; it is an idea that is reflexive, not representative. For Ferdinand Alquié, too, the weight of the ontological argument is carried by reflection and not by representation: 'the ontological argument consists in naming the presence which becomes manifest when the mind is aware of returning to itself.'[2] Central to Alquié's thought, we are told, is the distinction between 'ideas' and 'presences'. 'The characteristic of an idea is that we can delimit it; it is in us in such a way that in principle nothing can prevent us from saying that we are its author. A presence, on the contrary, is not objective, if by this term we understand the character of that which lends itself to being determined. The ontological argument is the discovery of the absolute; it is necessary to affirm its existence because of the discovery that a presence cannot be reduced to the objectivity of ideas. By reflecting upon an interior presence, the spirit sees its limits and at the same time recognises what sustains its vitality.'[3] It is emphatically asserted that this position is, in spite of appearances, utterly opposed to philosophical idealism. And Forest sums it up in the sentence: 'Alquié's thought is the movement from Kant to St Anselm, from critical philosophy to spiritual philosophy.'[4]

[1] F. Ravaisson, *Rapport sur la philosophie contemporaine en France*, p. 271, cit. Forest, op. cit., p. 277.
[2] Forest, op. cit., p. 293.
[3] ibid., p. 294.
[4] ibid., p. 295.

Even from such a brief summary as I have been able to give here we might be led to wonder whether this very impressive and deeply devout movement of thought is really very closely related to St Anselm's. Forest indeed admits this. 'One will hesitate', he writes, 'to acknowledge an accord between reflexive philosophy and St Anselm's teachings. We cannot say that these extremely original endeavours hold to the letter of the argument in the *Proslogion*.'[1] His conclusion is that 'the reflexive proof is authorised by St Anselm, rather than in agreement with him'— a somewhat enigmatic remark! His final remarks are, however, moving, and thought-provoking:

> We may recall that at the end of his life Husserl was assessing the difficulties and possible failure of his religious philosophy. He said that his mistake had been to want to seek God without God. That is the temptation of idealism. More than any other experience, the Anselmian kind of self reflection is able to deliver us from it.[2]

We shall later on be considering a group of thinkers who have much in common with the reflexive school, when we discuss the cosmological approach to theism; this is the school of 'transcendental Thomism', of which Karl Rahner, Emil Coreth and Bernard Lonergan are leading exponents.

I shall now make some remarks about a very different attempt to rehabilitate the ontological argument which has been made by Norman Malcolm and Charles Hartshorne. Their most important papers are included in Hick and McGill's volume, but mention should also be made of several full-scale treatises in which Hartshorne expounds and defends his argument at length, *The Logic of Perfection*, *Anselm's Discovery* and *A Natural Theology for our Time*. The special feature of this approach is that it very sharply distinguishes between the arguments in chapters II and III of the *Proslogion* and takes the latter as expressing Anselm's real intention, as well as being in fact valid. The difference between the two chapters, it will be remembered, is that the former claims to prove simply that God exists, whereas the latter claims to prove that he exists necessarily. To put the contrast in negative terms, the former claims to prove that God's

[1] ibid., p. 299.
[2] ibid., p. 300.

non-existence is false, the latter that it is impossible. Most critics have taken *Proslogion* III as merely dotting the i's and crossing the t's of *Proslogion* II; after proving that God exists, they tell us, Anselm goes on to point out that, unlike other existents, he exists necessarily. Malcolm and Hartshorne, however, are in principle prepared to admit the criticism which accuses *Proslogion* II of wrongly treating 'exists' as a predicate and thus of making an illicit transition from the ideal to the real realm; though it would perhaps be fairer to say that they would admit the criticism if they thought that *Proslogion* II stood on its own feet without assistance from *Proslogion* III. The heart of their defence is that, whether or not 'exists' is a predicate and ascribes an attribute to God, 'necessarily exists' certainly is and does. Saying that God exists may not say what kind of being he is, but saying that he necessarily exists certainly does. Thus, *existence* may not be an attribute, but *necessary existence* is; and it is this latter that *Proslogion* III shows God to possess. For Hartshorne the argument is a rigid one in modal logic, that is to say the logic which considers propositions as not merely true or false, but also as necessary, contingent or impossible; in one place he sets it out in symbolic form in ten successive steps.[1] His basic conviction is that to deny the existence of a being that has been proved to have necessary existence as an attribute is to utter a self-contradictory statement. I cannot see, however, that it makes any difference whether the attribute in question is existence *tout court* or necessary existence; in either case the most that can be validly argued is that if God exists he exists necessarily, but it does not follow that he exists. Hartshorne may be quite correct in arguing that necessary existence is included in God's essence, that is, in the kind of being that he is if he exists; but the existence by which an existing being exists in reality is not an essence or a constituent or aspect of an essence; it is an *act*. If God exists, we can, with St Thomas, identify his essence with his act of existing and say that it is his essence to exist; but until we know that he exists all that we can say is that *if* he exists this identification can be made. Hick makes the point by accusing Hartshorne of confusing two quite distinct notions, that of logical necessity and that

---

[1] *Logic of Perfection*, pp. 49ff; reprinted in *The Many-faced Argument*, pp. 334ff.

of ontological or factual necessity. He writes as follows:

> We have distinguished the following two concepts: (1) the logically necessary truth of a proposition, arising from the meaning of the terms employed in it; and (2) the factual necessity of a Being who exists eternally and *a se*. The two concepts are quite distinct; logical necessity is not a case of ontological necessity, nor vice versa. The necessary existence of an object, *x*, is defined as the existence of *x* without beginning or end and without dependence upon anything other than itself. The logically necessary truth of a proposition, *p*, on the other hand, reflects the circumstances that *p* is formed so as to be true by definition. . . . From the concept of God as ontologically necessary we can derive the analytic truth that if God exists, he exists eternally and *a se*, but we cannot deduce that it is a logically necessary truth that God exists, i.e., that the concept of an eternal Being who exists *a se* is instantiated in extramental reality. And yet this is precisely what Malcolm and Hartshorne try to do. They observe (rightly) that while 'existence' is not a real predicate (i.e., cannot figure as an element in the concept of a kind of being), 'necessary existence' in the ontological sense *is* a real predicate and can be a constituent element in the concept of deity. However, having established that ontological necessity (i.e., eternal existence *a se*) is a real predicate, they proceed as though what they had established is the quite different conclusion that logically necessary existence is a real predicate.[1]

And Hick is furthermore able to show the precise point in Hartshorne's statement at which the illicit shift of meaning is made; the plausibility of Hartshorne's argument depends on the fact that he has used the same symbol, 'N', to denote both kinds of necessity.

Substantially the same criticism as Hick's has been made by Dr David A. Pailin in an article published in *Religious Studies*.[2] It is interesting to note that he defends the notion of 'necessary existence' against those modern philosophers who have asserted that the only proper application of the attribute 'necessary' is to propositions and that it is a misuse of the term to speak of a 'necessary *being*'. My own comment on the question is that there

[1] op. cit., pp. 347f.
[2] 'Some Comments on Hartshorne's Presentation of the Ontological Argument', *Religious Studies*, IV (1968), pp. 103ff.

is no harm in making both applications of the adjective as long as we do not fall into Hartshorne's fallacy of failing to distinguish between them. If the proposition 'X exists' is a necessary proposition, it does not seem unreasonable to describe X as a 'necessary being'. I think that, as a matter of fact, most of the philosophers who object to the term 'necessary being' do so because they believe that no proposition asserting existence could be necessarily true; in this it seems to me that they are themselves failing to recognise the distinction drawn by Hick between logical and ontological necessity. There may, however, be something to be said for abandoning the term 'necessary being'. Fr Norris Clarke has pointed out that it is far from universal in Christian usage. 'St Thomas', he reminds us, 'never uses it as an attribute proper to God. This came in only through the Augustinian tradition stemming from Anselm. . . . St Thomas in no way deduces the existence of God from his essence, but rather defines his essence completely in terms of his existence: God is *ipsum Esse Subsistens*, pure subsistent act of existence.' And again: 'For St Thomas, "contingent" and "necessary" have quite different meanings from their now traditional use in modern philosophy, including modern scholasticism. For him, "contingent" meant simply any composite of matter and form, any generable and corruptible. . . . "Necessary" means just the opposite: any pure form that is not subject to substantial change. Both angels and God are such.'[1]

My conclusion is that, for all his ingenuity, Hartshorne has not been successful in his attempt to rehabilitate the ontological argument. There are indeed indications that Hartshorne's own thought on the question is not altogether finalised. Pailin quotes

[1] 'Analytic Philosophy and Language about God', in *Christian Philosophy and Religious Renewal*, ed. George F. McLean, p. 55 and n. 13. Dr Anthony Kenny makes the same point:

> To say that God is a necessary being is not necessarily to say that 'God exists' is a necessary proposition: when Aquinas uses this description of God in the *Summa Theologiae* he means simply that God is imperishable. Moreover, it has not been shown that the necessity of necessarily true propositions derives from human convention; there is much evidence, in the recent history of philosophical logic, in the contrary direction. The notion of *necessary being*, therefore, has not been shown to be incoherent [*The Five Ways*, p. 2, cf. ch. iv *passim*].

Kenny's full argument is in his essay in *British Analytical Philosophy*, ed. B. Williams and A. Montefiore, pp. 131ff.

C

him as saying that he is now convinced that the second ontological proof is scarcely in *Proslogion* III but is rather in the
Reply to Gaunilo. Pailin comments that 'perhaps, in view of
this, Hartshorne will in future not be too hard on those who
failed to see in Anselm what Anselm himself never clearly distinguished'.[1] And Hartshorne is certainly hard on his opponents,
as anyone who has read his book *Anselm's Discovery* will admit.
But before we leave him we should, I think, see in more detail
what he really thinks Anselm himself failed to see.

On the basic issue of the existence of God Hartshorne distinguishes four possible positions, to each of which he assigns
names: (1) God's existence is logically impossible (positivism);
(2) God's existence is logically possible, but in fact false (empirical atheism); (3) God's existence is logically possible and in fact
true (empirical theism); (4) God's existence is logically necessary (neo-classical theism). The last is, of course, Hartshorne's
view and, as he sees it, Anselm's as well. However, Hartshorne
parts company with Anselm on the meaning of Anselm's definition. When God is defined as 'unsurpassable' (which Hartshorne takes as a convenient abbreviation for 'that than which
nothing greater can be conceived') what is meant is that God
can not be surpassed by anything other than himself, not that
he cannot continually surpass himself in the sense of continually
adding to his own perfection. Thus, while God's *existence* is
necessary, his *actuality* (by which Hartshorne means the character of his existence at any moment) is contingent. His actuality
is thus concrete, but his existence (that which is common to all
the instantiations) is abstract. And, while the existence of any
particular universe (or of any particular state of the universe)
is contingent, the existence of some universe or other appears to
be necessary.

Hartshorne gives special attention to an article by Professor
J. N. Findlay which appeared in *Mind* in April 1948 and which
caused some astonishment in the philosophical world.[2] In it
Findlay claimed to have produced an ontological argument for
the *non*-existence of God. Briefly, his argument was that only a
being who was unsurpassable in every respect could satisfy the

---

[1] art. cit., p. 105.
[2] 'Can God's Existence be disproved?'; reprinted in Plantinga, *The
Ontological Argument*, pp. 111ff.

requirements of the God of religion. It must possess every excellence and possess all these excellences in a necessary manner.
However, Findlay asserts, for people of what he describes as a
contemporary outlook, it will be clear that not only does no
such being exist but its existence is either senseless or impossible.
'It was indeed an ill day for Anselm', he writes, 'when he hit
upon his famous proof. For on that day he not only laid bare
something that is of the essence of an adequate religious object,
but also something that entails its necessary non-existence', or,
he adds in a footnote, '"non-significance", if this alternative is
preferred.'[1]

Findlay's argument does not seem immune to response and it
has in fact received a great deal of criticism, not least, as one
might expect, from Hartshorne. For Hartshorne, what Findlay
has disproved is empirical, but not neo-classical, theism, and
fifteen years after the first appearance of his article Findlay
admitted as much, writing as follows:

> I still think that it makes a valid point: that if it is *possible*, in
> some logical and not merely epistemological sense, that there is
> no God, then God's existence is not merely doubtful but *impos-
> sible*, since nothing capable of non-existence could be a God at
> all. . . . Professor Hartshorne has, however, convinced me that
> my argument permits a ready inversion, and that one can very
> well argue that if God's existence is in any way *possible*, then it is
> also *certain* and *necessary* that God exists, a position which should
> give some comfort to the shade of Anselm.[2]

Thus Findlay and Hartshorne are agreed that God's existence
must be either necessary or impossible; it cannot be a merely
contingent matter whether there is or is not a God. I would
agree with this last statement, but I would add that the necessity or impossibility must be ontological, not logical. Thus I do
not think that it can be derived from the ontological argument,
which, in spite of its name, is an argument in logic and not in
ontology. I do think God's existence follows from the *cosmological* argument, but that is matter for a later lecture.

The most original feature of Hartshorne's discussion is his
assertion that the God to whom the ontological argument leads

[1] Plantinga, p. 120.
[2] *Language, Mind and Value*, pp. 8f, cit. Plantinga, p. 121.

is not a changeless but a changing and continually developing God. If he is right, not only has Anselm's argument been consistently misunderstood by almost all philosophers after him—in his extremely polemical work *Anselm's Discovery* Hartshorne lists between forty and fifty of these, including such giants as Aquinas and Kant and ranging from Gaunilo to Bertrand Russell and Findlay—but even Anselm himself failed to understand what he had proved. There is indeed something paradoxical in the assertion that, while almost everyone since Anselm has radically misunderstood the nature of Anselm's argument, Anselm himself radically misunderstood the nature of God. It is a pity that Hartshorne's book appeared almost simultaneously with Dr M. J. Charlesworth's edition, with commentary, of the Anselm–Gaunilo writings, for it would have been extremely interesting to have the comments of either of these writers on the other. Charlesworth inclines to see *Proslogion* III as a complement to the basic argument of *Proslogion* II, added to defend the latter against the objection that it does not adequately exclude the possibility of God existing in a merely contingent way; while chapter II compares possible and actual existence, chapter III compares two kinds of actual existence, namely contingent and necessary, and is therefore logically superior to chapter II.[1] This goes most of the way to meeting Hartshorne's thesis that *Proslogion* III contains the real heart of the argument, but Charlesworth would not, any more than Anselm, admit Hartshorne's view of a developing God, who, while unsurpassable by anything else, is continually surpassing himself.

It should be added that, in summarising his discussion, Hartshorne admits that one basic objection to any ontological argument may remain in force, namely the objection that it is a mere assumption that 'greatest conceivable' and 'inconceivable as non-existent' are themselves consistently conceivable. He does, however, maintain that the other objections are dissolved and that therefore the whole question needs investigation *de novo*.[2] Whether his own doctrine of a developing God leads to fresh difficulties is not discussed. It is an interesting fact that Hartshorne has stimulated in the United States a revival of the process-theology which was started by A. N. Whitehead in 1929

[1] *St Anselm's Proslogion*, p. 73.
[2] *Anselm's Discovery*, pp. 301ff.

but which, perhaps because of the extreme unreadability—and perhaps even more extreme unlistenability—of his Gifford Lectures *Process and Reality*, made little impact outside rather narrowly academic circles. Let other Gifford Lecturers be warned by his example! It is at least interesting to find the doctrine of a developing God, which has usually been associated with a down-to-earth no-nonsense empirical outlook, emerging from such a sophisticated and alembicated mind as Hartshorne's. One fact remains clear, his almost incredulous contempt for the failure of one great thinker after another to perceive what, as he believes, Anselm really meant and of Anselm himself to see what he had himself really proved.

I shall conclude the present lecture with some mention of a careful and very detailed discussion of the ontological argument which is given by Dr Alvin Plantinga in his book *God and Other Minds*, published in 1967. Having stated the argument in the form given to it by Anselm in *Proslogion* II, he then considers Kant's alleged refutation of it and in particular the objection usually stated in the form that 'existence is not a real predicate'. As modern objectors of this type he instances C. D. Broad, A. J. Ayer and John Wisdom, but the three to whom he gives detailed attention are Broad, Jerome Shaffer and William P. Alston, the last of whom he discusses at considerable length. His conclusion is expressed in the following words:

> We have no reason to believe, therefore, either that existence in reality cannot be predicated of a being presupposed to exist in the understanding, or that Anselm's argument necessarily involves predicating real existence of such a being. I think the conclusion to be drawn is that we do not yet have a general refutation of Anselm's ontological argument.[1]

And again:

> No one has produced, it seems to me, a sense for the term 'predicate' such that in that sense it is clear both that existence is not a predicate and that Anselm's argument requires it to be one. Nor has anyone shown, it seems to me, that existential statements (or an appropriate subclass of them) are not necessary. Every general argument of this sort with which I am acquainted involves some unsupported premise that does not

[1] op. cit., p. 63.

seem self-evident and that Anselm would scarcely be obliged
to accept.[1]

Having thus, as he holds, refuted the refutations of Anselm's
proof, Plantinga goes on to examine in detail the proof itself.
'In this chapter', he writes, 'I shall not argue that no version of
the ontological argument can possibly succeed, but only that
none of the more obvious ways of stating it do in fact succeed.'[2]
Thus his final judgment on the ontological argument is agnostic; neither the objections to the argument nor the argument
itself has yet been stated in a form that is logically waterproof.
His examination is extremely minute and makes use of the
refinements of modern logic. His basic point is, to state it very
roughly, that, when Anselm compares a God, supposed for the
purpose of the argument to be non-existent in reality, with a
being precisely like God except that it has the added property
of real existence, he is in effect attributing to this being both real
existence and its absence, and thus introduces into his argument
a self-contradictory proposition. Plantinga makes a number of
suggestions of the way in which the argument might be patched
up, but condemns them all as unsuccessful.

> What we need [he writes] for a really thorough examination of
> this issue is a complete and accurate account of the predication
> of the properties of nonexistent beings. Unfortunately I am not
> able to give such an account. Nonetheless this last form of the
> ontological argument is as specious as the preceding one. No
> doubt there are other reasonable interpretations of this
> Anselmian argument; I can scarcely claim to have refuted the
> argument *überhaupt*. But until other interpretations are sug-
> gested, the verdict must be that the ontological argument is
> unsuccessful.[3]

[1] ibid., p. 64.
[2] ibid.
[3] ibid., pp. 81ff. Dr Jaakko Hintikka, in an essay 'On the Logic of the
Ontological Argument' (*Models for Modalities* (1969), pp. 45ff), maintains
that there are senses, not purely grammatical, in which existence clearly is a
predicate; nevertheless he holds that 'Gaunilo, Aquinas, and Kant . . .
appear to have been shrewder—or perhaps merely sounder—logicians than
St Anselm and Descartes' (p. 52). His definition is that '*x* is an existentially
perfect being . . . if and only if it exists, provided that anything at all exists'
(p. 46). It is not clear to me that this is equivalent to Anselm's definition
(i.e. that any being that satisfied Hintikka's definition would satisfy Anselm's
and that any being that satisfied Anselm's definition would satisfy Hintikka's)

Nevertheless Plantinga does not leave the matter there. He passes on to consider the rehabilitation by Hartshorne and Malcolm of Anselm's argument in *Proslogion* III, the argument that the existence of God is not merely a fact but a necessary fact, or, in other words, that God's non-existence is not merely false but self-contradictory and impossible. We have seen Hick's criticism of Hartshorne; Plantinga devotes his attention to Malcolm, and to much the same effect, for he accuses Malcolm of committing a fallacy in his use of modal logic. He sums up the matter as follows:

> It is a necessary truth that if God exists, then there is a being who neither comes into nor goes out of existence and who is in no way dependent upon anything else. But from this it does not follow, contrary to Malcolm's argument, that the proposition *There is a being who neither comes into nor goes out of existence and who depends upon nothing* is necessary; nor does it follow that *God exists* is necessary. Malcolm's reconstruction of the ontological argument therefore fails.[1]

The upshot of Plantinga's investigation, which is conducted with scrupulous care and professional expertise, is thus that neither the ontological argument nor the usual refutations of it

---

or indeed that it is equivalent to any other of the classical definitions of God, though Hintikka clearly thinks that it is. He writes:

> Our argument was couched in terms of one particular attempt to define God as the existentially most perfect being—'a being than which a greater (existentially greater!) cannot be conceived'. It can be shown, however, that no other characterisation along similar lines can succeed any better. By reviewing all the different characterisations that one may try to give of an existentially perfect being—or of any being, for that matter—in the sole terms of the predicates of identity and existence, the concept of knowledge, quantifiers, and propositional connectives, one can see that no one of them makes an essential difference to our attempts to prove the existence of a being so characterised. . . . Suffice it to say that it is a straightforward consequence of the adequacy of any reasonable system of epistemic logic that I know of. [p. 51]

Hintikka's argument is largely expressed in symbolic terms.

It may be interesting to add that, on one interpretation of the Löwenheim-Skolem theorem, even pure mathematics cannot be satisfactorily formalised without some appeal to the empirical realm (cf. J. A. Benardete, *Infinity* (1964), pp. 264ff).

[1] ibid., p. 94.

are strictly valid. And this would seem to represent the present state of the question. Gilson has seen the most significant fact about the ontological argument to be the fact that it emerged in a Christian setting, that is to say, a setting in which it is natural to identify God with Being.

> Thinkers like Plato and Aristotle [he writes], who do not ident-ify God and being, could never dream of deducing God's exist-ence from his idea; but when a Christian thinker like St Anselm asks himself whether God exists he asks, in fact, whether Being exists, and to deny God is to affirm that Being does not exist. That is why the mind of St Anselm was so long filled with the desire of finding a direct proof of the existence of God which should depend on nothing but the principle of contra-diction.[1]

As far as Anselm himself is concerned, perhaps the last word may remain with Hans Urs von Balthasar:

> Anselm does not distinguish between the natural and the supernatural, knowledge and faith, between the profane and the sacred; for he learned by faith that reason too was created for the sake of faith, nature for the sake of grace, and that both form, by their interconnection, a single revelation of the in-comprehensible love of the Trinity.[2]

[1] *The Spirit of Medieval Philosophy*, p. 59; cf. my *He Who Is*, p. 35 and appendix to 2nd ed.; *Existence and Analogy*, ch. ii.
[2] *Essays in Theology*, II: *Word and Redemption*, p. 83.

CHAPTER FOUR

TRANSCENDENTAL THOMISM—I

'The trouble with philosophers', *said Agathon*, *'is that you cannot find out whether they are usefully employed or not.'*
—Douglas Woodruffe, *Plato's 'Britannia'*, p. 91.

HAVING DISCUSSED IN the last lecture in some detail the ontological approach to theism, I propose now to consider the cosmological approach, that is to say the approach which takes as its starting-point the world which our senses disclose to us and of which, so far as our bodily constitution is concerned, we ourselves are part. Arguments of this type take two main forms, according as they are based upon the mere fact of the world's existence or upon the character which examination shows it to have; the two can, of course, be combined. A very impressive example of the combined method is provided by the late F. R. Tennant's massive work *Philosophical Theology*, published in 1928 and 1930, which I have discussed at length in my book *He Who Is*.[1] Tennant's argument reaches its climax in the chapter on 'The Empirical Approach to Theism', which bears the sub-title 'Cosmic Teleology'. Its key-word is 'purpose', and five fields of fact are examined in which purpose has been alleged to be evident. These range, from the epistemological adaptiveness of things to thought, to the purpose which some have discerned in the evolutionary process and in human morality. Again, William Temple, in his Gifford Lectures *Nature, Man and God* (1934), argued that the fact that the world has, in the course of evolution, given rise to minds that can

[1] One of the most recent discussions of Tennant's argument is given in Mr R. C. Wallace's article 'An Empirical Theology' in *Theology*, LXXIII (1970), pp. 73ff, 104ff, 168ff.

reflect on the very process out of which they have emerged provides strong justification for the belief that the world is itself the product of a transcendent Mind. I shall, however, restrict myself to the more metaphysical type of argument, though it is not always easy to fence it off strictly from more general considerations; of this the classical example is, of course, provided by the famous 'Five Ways' expounded by St Thomas Aquinas at the beginning of the *Summa Theologiae*.[1] These all have the same general form; starting from some very general character of finite beings, they argue to the existence of a being correspondingly unlimited, and this, the arguments triumphantly proclaim, is universally recognised as God. (The five characteristics in question are change, causation, contingency, gradedness and purpose.) There is something ironical in the fact that this absolutely basic part of St Thomas's system is that in which, above all others, this outstandingly lucid thinker seems to have become for once obscure. His most enthusiastic disciples disagree about the precise nature of his arguments and about what it is that each of them demonstrates. His critics condemn them as entirely fallacious. Dr Anthony Kenny, who has recently made an extremely minute dissection and assessment of them, certainly seems to have shown that, taken as strictly technical examples of metaphysical and logical argumentation, they are open to question at many points.[2] Comparison with other places in the Angelic Doctor's writings suggests that he may have been elaborating and decorating what is fundamentally a very simple and forceful insight for the sake of the 'beginners' for whom the *Summa* was professedly written. Dr Victor Preller has taken the heroic course of suggesting that, when St Thomas opens his discussion with the words 'The existence of God can be proved in five ways', he merely intends to summarise the arguments current in his time, without very seriously committing himself to any of them.[3] I have myself suggested that the five ways are not so much to be seen as five different arguments for the existence of God—if we take them as such there is the difficulty, among others, of seeing that they all lead to the same divine

[1] I, ii, 3.
[2] *The Five Ways* (1969). Cf. A. Plantinga's discussion of St Thomas's Third Way in *God and Other Minds* (1967), ch. i.
[3] *Divine Science and the Science of God* (1967), p. 24.

being and not to a celestial 'Council of Five'—but as five different ways of exhibiting the radically un-self-sufficient character
of finite beings and so of leading us to see them as dependent on
a transcendent self-sufficient creative Cause. 'Their function is
to exhibit to us five different characteristics of finite being, all
of which show that it does not account for its own existence. In
the last resort St Thomas has only one datum for an argument
for the existence of God, namely the existence of beings whose
existence is not necessitated by their essence; that is, beings in
which essence and existence are really distinct.'[1] I still think that
this is true, but I would wish to add that the real point now
seems to me to be that St Thomas has adopted implicitly an
extremely minimal definition of 'God'. I have in an earlier
lecture stressed the importance in any context of being clear
about the definition of God that one is using and of not sliding
from one definition to another in the course of the argument. It
is, I think, this, and not any real 'agnosticism' on the part of St
Thomas, that accounts for such well-known assertions as 'We
do not know what God is, but only what he is not and how other
things are related to him'.[2] After having proved that God exists,
St Thomas does in fact go on to prove a great many things about
him, even if these things are simply 'what must necessarily
belong to him as the first cause of all things'.[3] He argues that
God is immaterial, altogether simple, perfect, good, infinite,
immutable, eternal and one.[4] And, while fully recognising the
problem that is involved when we enquire how our finite minds
are to conceive the attributes of an infinite God, we can, I think,
see that the fact that St Thomas goes on to *argue* that God has
these attributes *after* he has proved that God exists shows that
these attributes could not have been included in the definition
of God which he had originally assumed. The definition of God
which he assumed was, I suggest, simply that of a transcendent
ground of finite beings, and everything beyond that is a matter
of rational deduction or of revelation. If this is so, then St
Thomas's conclusion of each of the five ways with the almost
casual remark that 'all men agree that this is God' (or a similar

[1] *Existence and Analogy*, p. 78.
[2] *S.c.G.*, I, xxx ad fin.
[3] *S.Th.*, I, xii, 12.
[4] I, iii–xi.

phrase) becomes less puzzling. It is not implausible that the prime mover, the first efficient cause, the absolutely necessary being and the rest are all identical with a transcendent ground of finite being, whatever that transcendent ground may later on be seen to be like. I have no desire to defend the details of St Thomas's Five Ways against the strictures of Dr Kenny, but I am disposed to maintain that when the Angelic Doctor puts the question 'Does God exist?' or 'Is there a God?', what he is asking is simply 'Has the world a transcendent cause or not?' To anticipate a little, I will add that this is the definition of God which I shall adopt in formulating my own argument.

I do not wish to imply that this is the only definition of God which a theistic philosopher could legitimately adopt; all that I maintain is that he should know what definition he is using and should stick to it. Mr H. P. Owen, to give one example, in his very fine work *The Christian Knowledge of God*, takes a much ampler definition which includes the chief attributes of God as Christians believe in him;[1] as he himself recognises, the task of arguing for God's existence is thus made the more difficult. And at the end of the day the results may be very much the same. One thinker may define God by the attribute A and go on to prove subsequently that God possesses the attributes B, C, D and E. Another may define God as possessing the attributes A, B and C and go on to prove that God possesses the attributes D and E. Both of them (if their arguments are valid) will have ended with the same God, one who possesses the attributes A, B, C, D and E. All that is essential, I repeat, is that extra attributes shall not be smuggled in without proof in the course of the argument.

In the palmy days of the logical positivist school it was widely held that all statements purporting to make assertions about God are simply meaningless and that therefore no question of their truth or falsehood could arise. They were neither logical tautologies nor registrations or elaborations of empirical observations; and therefore, by the requirement of the verification principle, they asserted nothing at all. More recently, in line with the indefatigable Professor A. G. N. Flew,[2] theological

[1] p. 1: 'a Being who is transcendent, creative, immanent, and personal'. Mr Owen goes on to fill out these attributes in considerable detail.

[2] 'Theology and Falsification', in *New Essays in Philosophical Theology* (1955), ed. A. G. N. Flew and A. MacIntyre; A. G. N. Flew, *God and Philosophy* (1966).

statements have been condemned as meaningless on the grounds that the people who make them refuse to admit that they could be falsified by any evidence whatever; in Flew's famous phrase, they die 'the death of a thousand qualifications'. What I feel needs saying about the earlier phases of the situation I have said in a small book called *Words and Images*; the more recent phases have been very faithfully dealt with by Dom Illtyd Trethowan in an article in *Religious Studies* for October 1966.[1] It would, I think, be otiose to refer to the great mass of writing that has appeared on both sides of the dispute. I will simply repeat what I said in a previous lecture, that, since meaningfulness means the capacity to be understood, the only way in which to discover whether a statement is meaningful is to see whether, in the linguistic context and community in which it is used, people can understand it. The question 'Has the world a transcendent cause or not?' is, I maintain, a perfectly intelligible question, admitting of the answer yes or no according to the evidence. I shall, however, show later on that for many modern theists the cosmological approach to theism does not consist in constructing an argument of syllogistic form, but in pointing to an awareness by us of finite being in relation to its transcendent cause.

It has been widely held that the cosmological argument for theism, like the ontological argument, was demolished by Immanuel Kant and that the Sage of Königsberg did in fact show that the cosmological argument itself depended upon the ontological. This view can hardly survive a careful reading of the relevant sections of the late A. E. Taylor's article on 'Theism' in the twelfth volume of the *Encyclopaedia of Religion and Ethics*.[2] The Kantian critique has, however, had a great influence, whether rightly or wrongly, on many apologists for theism, and it may be well to recapitulate the story.

The story begins in the seventeenth century with the distinction between the primary and secondary qualities of objects, first apparently made by Galileo but better known to English students from the writings of John Locke.[3] Secondary qualities, such as colour and smell, obviously depended to a great degree

[1] 'In Defence of Theism—A reply to Kai Nielsen', *Religious Studies*, II (1966), pp. 37ff.
[2] p. 278.
[3] *Essay concerning Human Understanding*, Book II, ch. viii.

on the sensory equipment of the percipient and indeed did not exist except when perceived; whereas primary qualities, such as shape, solidity and mass, were inherent possessions of the object, so it was held, and they existed whether they were being perceived or not. Thus, for Locke, substances existed with their primary qualities beneath the superficial array of secondary, qualities with which we perceived them. Berkeley had little difficulty in showing that Locke's primary qualities were just as subjective as were the secondary; indeed, that, in Locke's sense, there were no primary qualities at all. Physical objects thus became entirely subjective; *esse est percipi*, to exist is simply to be perceived. Berkeley tried to preserve their substantiality and continuity by holding that even when no one else perceived them God did; and that to exist in the mind of God was a sufficiently exalted status for any finite object to have. Later thinkers and in particular David Hume, eliminated God and, with him, the last vestiges of physical substantiality. Physical objects were simply concatenations of impressions in the mind, though Hume never managed to give a satisfactory account of the mind in which they were concatenated.

The story continues through Kant and Hegel, though the dominant British school of linguistic analysts, unlike their idealist predecessors, attach their allegiance, in so far as they have any respect for the past, to their fellow-Briton Hume. On the continent of Europe, however, the influence of Kant is still strong and it accounts for the existence of a school of Christian philosophers whom most English readers find both obscure and perplexing and whom they suppose mistakenly to derive their thought chiefly from Martin Heidegger.

Kant tried to preserve the objective character of physical objects by holding that, although the actual object of perception is the product of the very act in which it is perceived, so that we can never know things as they really are, there is nevertheless at the root of the phenomenal object a being-in-itself, a *Ding an sich* or *noumenon*, which is wholly real and non-subjective. It has always been difficult to see how Kant accounted for his knowledge that there is a *noumenon* at all, in view of his doctrine that all we can know is the *phenomenon* which the mind has constructed in the act of perceiving. Some have indeed thought that for Kant the *noumenon* (and probably God as well) was only a regulative principle for human thought and not a constituent element in reality. Now there is, I believe, a way in which the Kantian subjectivism can be countered and I shall discuss it later on. Many Christian thinkers, however, felt obliged to accept the basic Kantian position, at least in so far as it found its starting-point in the mind of the human percipient, and a very distinguished example is found in the person of Joseph Maréchal, S.J., who, in a tremendous work entitled *Le point de départ de la métaphysique*, whose publication began in 1927, set out on the formidable task of constructing a transcendental Thomism. His basic conviction was that, if we start from the 'conscious phenomenon' or 'object of thought' as it is initially and unavoidably given and analyse the object with all its constituent conditions, we find in it the objective existence of an absolute. It was at this point, a quite basic one, that Maréchal found the fundamental flaw in Kant. In the words of Otto Muck:

> For Kant, this relation to the unconditioned does not operate constitutively in the object known, but only regulatively, and thus the categories remain bound to phenomena and have no relation to the absolute order of the unconditioned. Knowledge remains phenomenal. Maréchal with the help of transcendental analysis, tries to show that the relation to the unconditioned is constitutive for the phenomenal object and that knowledge thus reaches the fundamental order of being. This means that the phenomenal object cannot be viewed as phenomenal in the exclusive sense.[1]

Maréchal thus feels obliged to adopt the 'transcendental method', that is the method which begins by investigating the conditions of the possibility of knowledge, but he is claimed by his followers as a transcendental *Thomist*. Critics such as Gilson, as we shall see later, hold that such a programme involves putting the cart before the horse. In any case, Maréchal, like St Thomas, insists on the *dynamic* character of knowledge; knowledge is not a mere pressure of the object on the knower, analogous to the impact of one material object on another. There is a real assimilation of the object to the knower; the knower *becomes* the object, not 'entitatively' of course but 'intentionally'. And, it is argued, 'noetic activity could not have the structure

[1] *The Transcendental Method*, p. 67.

which necessarily belongs to it if it were not orientated towards absolute being in such a way that this absolute is co-posited or co-apprehended in every mode of knowledge even though it is not explicitly in awareness.'[1] How far this absolute being is seen as demonstrably God, and if so what definition of God is assumed, it is not easy to make out. What, however, is clear is that Maréchal attempted to correct the Kantian view by arguing that absolute being is a constitutive and not merely a regulative principle of human knowledge. In Muck's words:

> The main point of Maréchal's five-volume work, especially the fifth volume, is clearly expressed viz. the overthrow of Kant's phenomenalism by showing, by means of Kant's method, that the phenomenal object is absolutely impossible unless it is contained in a knowledge which transcends the phenomenal method.[2]

One may perhaps wonder whether the same result might not have been attained by a shorter route.

On the whole, the reaction of French-speaking Catholic philosophers seems to have been conservative, though Maréchal would appear to have a good deal in common with such thinkers as Maurice Blondel and Louis Lavelle. M. Étienne Gilson, in his *Réalisme thomiste et Critique de la connaissance* (1939), discussed the writings not only of Maréchal but of several other representatives of 'critical realism', namely the 'immediate critical realism' of L. Noël, the 'realism of "I am"' of G. Picard and the 'realism of "I think"' of M. D. Roland-Gosselin. He sees them as being under the influence of Descartes as much as of Kant and has little use for the concept of a 'critical realism', that is to say an attempted realism taking its starting-point in a Kantian or quasi-Kantian critique of knowledge. 'In brief', he says, 'when it claims to signify anything other than *philosophical realism*, the expression *critical realism* is contradictory. The only case in which it is not is when it signifies nothing at all.'[3] M. Jacques Maritain, while agreeing on the whole with Gilson, holds that the term 'critical realism' can be given an acceptable meaning; he denies, however, that an authentic critique of

[1] ibid., p. 285.
[2] ibid., p. 45.
[3] op. cit., p. 78.

knowledge is a prerequired condition of philosophy.[1] Commenting on Gilson's book he writes: 'Between M. Ét. Gilson's position and ours there is no substantial difference.'[2] Both of them
are convinced that unless one frankly accepts the position that
it is of the very nature of the mind to grasp and assimilate extra-
mental being one will never be able to escape the toils of one's
own subjectivity.

Maréchal's disciples in the German-speaking world have been
much more thorough-going in their allegiance than the French.
They are also much more difficult to read. The most distinguished of them is undoubtedly Karl Rahner, whom Dr John
Macquarrie has acclaimed as the most outstanding of living
theologians.[3] He studied philosophy under Martin Heidegger
and, like many German theologians today, he shows in his
writing a marked influence of the idiom of existentialism. His
thinking is, however, far more in the line of Maréchal than of
Heidegger; this is also true of his fellow-Jesuit Emerich Coreth,
who, as we shall see, starts from a slightly different point.
Rahner's largest work *Spirit in the World* (*Geist im Welt*), written
in 1939, revised in 1957 and translated into quite extraordinary
English by William Dych in 1968, is an avowed attempt to
bring together Thomist epistemology and metaphysics on the
one hand and the transcendental method on the other. Coreth's
chief work, *Metaphysik*, consists of 584 pages in the German, but
has had the much happier fate of appearing in English in a
beautifully written and much shortened version by Joseph

[1] *The Degrees of Knowledge*, E. T. of 1959, ch. iii (French original, *Distinguer
pour unir* (1932)).
[2] ibid., p. xvi (French 4th ed., p. xxii); cf. ch. iii, 'Critical Realism'.
'Realism' here, where it is contrasted with 'idealism', has a very different
meaning from the medieval one, where it is contrasted with 'nominalism'.
[3] *Principles of Christian Theology*, p. ix. Cf. Charles N. Bent, S.J., *Interpreting
the Doctrine of God*, ch. iv; Louis Roberts, *The Achievement of Karl Rahner*,
passim; Peter Mann, O.S.B., 'The Later Theology of Karl Rahner', *Clergy
Review*, LIV (1969) pp. 936ff. The 'anthropocentrism' of Rahner's theology
or 'theological anthropology' has been attacked by H. Urs von Balthasar
(*Cordula, oder der Ernstfall*) and Rahner himself has criticised his former
pupil Johannes Metz for substituting a 'political' for a 'transcendental'
theology; cf. Peter Mann, O.S.B., 'The Transcendental or the Political
Kingdom', *New Blackfriars*, L (1969), pp. 805ff; LI (1970), pp. 4ff. This
controversy is, however, concerned with Rahner's dogmatic, rather than his
natural, theology, though the two are very closely related.
It should perhaps be noted that Heidegger himself has disclaimed the
title 'existentialist' and describes his position as 'fundamental ontology'.

Donceel, whose accuracy is certified by the original author. Rahner's basically Thomist outlook is shown by the fact that his book opens with a full quotation of the article of the *Summa* in which the Angelic Doctor expounds his doctrine that in perception the human intellect makes use of the 'phantasm' or, as a modern philosopher would say, the phenomenon, sense-datum or *sensibile*, as the medium through which it apprehends the intelligible being which is its proper object and that it turns to the 'phantasm' as the natural climate in which it functions.[1] Knowing, Rahner tells us, does not come about through a *contact* of the intellect with an object, but by their becoming *the same;* and for St Thomas conversion to the phantasm is the same as the abstractive illumination of the phantasm by the light of the agent intellect.[2]

The essential features of this line of approach to theism are excellently summarised by Fr Donceel in the following passage, in which he begins by contrasting with the transcendental method those more pedestrian types of approach which he describes pejoratively as 'demonstration':

> He who wishes to 'demonstrate' God's existence, starts from premises which are finite, contingent and relative, and hopes to arrive at a conclusion which is infinite, necessary and absolute. An impossible task. We cannot 'arrive' at God; the distance is infinite. We start from him and we end up with him. He is present implicitly in the premises and explicitly in the conclusion. We reach God right away or never at all.
>
> That we reach God right away can be shown by pointing to the fact that we know everything as finite and limited. But a limit can be known as limit only by him who is, in fact or in desire, beyond this limit. We are not beyond every limit in fact. But we are beyond every limit in desire, because we strive past it. Man is the being who is 'always already beyond' every knowledge, every truth, every beauty, every possession and pleasure. Of every object which he knows man affirms that it *is*. He keeps striving towards an object about which he can really say that it

[1] *S. Th.* I, lxxxiv, 7; *Spirit in the World*, pp. 1ff. Strictly speaking, one should distinguish between the *sensibile* or *species sensibilis* (the direct impression upon the external sense) and the *phantasma* or sense-image gathered into the 'internal senses' (the *sensus communis*, the imagination, the sense-memory and the so-called *vis cogitativa*). I have not found it necessary to make this distinction in the text.

[2] ibid., pp. 69, 266.

is, that it fully exhausts the fullness of this predicate. Only the Infinite comes up to this fullness, only God really *is*. All other objects are *this* or *that*.

Such is the meaning of the *excessus* of St Thomas, of the *dynamism* of Joseph Maréchal, of the *Vorgriff* of Karl Rahner and Emerich Coreth.

We can put it in another way by calling man the being which possesses an infinite horizon. The horizon which we see with our eyes is finite, we share it with animals. The horizon which we know with our intellect is infinite. It is the horizon of being. This horizon of being is the main topic of [Coreth's] work.[1]

Somewhat aside from Rahner and Coreth, as not employing their existentialist idiom, but nevertheless deriving his inspiration from Maréchal and sharing their ambition of constructing a transcendental Thomism, is the Canadian Jesuit Bernard Lonergan, whose monumental work *Insight*, of nearly eight hundred pages, was published in 1957. I shall attempt later on to indicate its special features, but before doing that I shall say something more about the three thinkers whom I have already mentioned.

We have seen that the basic disagreement of Maréchal with Kant is in Maréchal's assertion that the reference of the conscious phenomenon or object to a transcendent and unconditioned absolute beyond its horizon involves that the absolute is not, as for Kant, a regulative principle for knowledge but a constitutive principle of reality; in Francis P. Fiorenza's words: 'the analysis of the orientation towards the absolute in the affirmation of every judgment is the central and critical point of Maréchal's evaluation of Kant.'[2] Dr Fiorenza discerns a difference between Maréchal's disagreement with Kant and Rahner's, on account of the influence upon Rahner of Heidegger. 'Many aspects of Maréchal's position are close to Husserl and the Neo-Kantians, even though Maréchal does differ from them and Kant in so far as he attempts to deduce from the universal validity of man's judgment an ontological and metaphysical significance in the strict sense. Karl Rahner, on the other hand, differs quite distinctly from Husserl and the Neo-Kantians because he has

[1] Preface to E. Coreth, *Metaphysics*, p. 11.
[2] Intro. to K. Rahner, *Spirit in the World*, p. xxxvii.

assimilated Heidegger's critique of their position . . . [For Rahner] man's question concerning being presupposes a knowledge of Being and reveals the nature of man as a finite being, who questions about being.'[1] Fiorenza sees the basic difference between Kant and Rahner in their different replies to Kant's basic question: How is metaphysics possible if all human knowledge is necessarily referred to a sensible intuition? He continues:

> Rahner's answer to this question departs from the traditional scholastic and philosophical positions and offers a transcendental understanding of being. Since he is aware that all human knowledge is related to sense intuitions, he rejects those philosophical positions which maintain that a metaphysics of transcendence is possible because of a special innate idea or because of a specific and immediate intuition of a metaphysical object, be it an eternal truth or an objectively conceived absolute being. He denies explicitly that the absolute is known as some object or that the human mind could form an adequate objective concept of God. Instead he proposes a transcendental understanding of God, who is not known by man as an object of reality, but as the principle of human knowledge and reality. This fundamentally non-objective transcendental knowledge of God as the principle of knowledge and reality is central to Rahner's whole theology.[2]

In all knowledge, Rahner tells us, there is a pre-apprehension (*Vorgriff*) of being, in which the existence of an Absolute being is also affirmed simultaneously; this is implicit, unformulated and 'unthematic'. And, in Rahner's own words, 'this is in no sense an "*a priori*" proof of God's existence. For the pre-apprehension and its "whither" can be proven and affirmed as present and necessary for all knowledge only in the *a posteriori* apprehension of a real existent and as the necessary condition of the latter.'[3] Fiorenza points out that when Rahner goes on (as he does in his sequel *Hearers of the Word*) to account for this transcendental orientation of man to God, he explains it in terms of what, in his existentialist idiom, he calls a 'supernatural existential'. 'Man's relation to God', he writes, 'is not an abstract or "natural" openness to God, but is the result of God's

[1] ibid., pp. xlif.
[2] ibid., pp. xliiif.
[3] ibid., p. 181.

historical calling of man to himself in Christ and thereby constituting the historical nature of man.'[1] Here, I may interpose, I part company with Rahner; as will appear later on, I hold that, by his natural constitution as a creature, man has an inherent openness to God, though I would agree that the way in which God has in fact bestowed himself to man's openness is the concern of revelation and history, of *Heilsgeschichte*, salvation-history indeed.

To follow up this point would take us beyond the bounds of natural theology, but we may remark with Fiorenza that, unlike many of Maréchal's followers, Rahner prolongs his discussion from the realm of philosophy into the realm of history.

In the final phase of his metaphysical exposition it must be admitted that Rahner is not easy to understand. Nevertheless, two points seem to emerge. One is that, on the level of metaphysics, God is not known as the object of religion, *sub ratione deitatis*, but only as the absolute ground of finite being, *sub ratione primi entis*. The other is that, the finite being of which God is known as the absolute ground is not, at any rate in the first instance, the world which is the *object* of human perception but man himself who is its *subject*. Rahner indeed maintains that this follows from the very nature of human perception as mediated by the senses and of human mentality as 'turning to the phantasms', to use the Thomist phrase. He lays great stress upon St Thomas's assertion that, through our sense-involved perceptions, 'we know God as cause both by way of eminence (*per excessum*) and by way of negation'.[2] This 'and', Rahner tells us, 'joins *excessum* not with cause, but with negation (both . . . and), and so distinguishes it from the "as cause" as the presupposition for the fact that God is able to be known as the ground of the existent.' He continues:

> To know God as the ground of the existent does not mean: to know that God (as already known beforehand) is the ground of the thing, but: to know that the ground, already and always opened simultaneously in knowing the existent as being, is the Absolute Being, that is, God, and thus to know God for the first time. This explanation of the sentence is only a paraphrase of the statement that God is accessible to metaphysics only as the

[1] ibid., p. xliv.
[2] *S. Th.*, I, lxxxiv, 7 *ad* 3.

'principle of its subject', not as the subject. But if this explanation of the 'knowing God as cause' is the only correct one, then it is self-evident that the fundamental act of metaphysics is not some causal inference from an existent as such to its ground, which also would not have to be more than an existent, but the opening of the knower to being as such as the ground of the existent and its knowledge. But that is given precisely in the *excessus*.[1]

Rahner admits that this *excessus* cannot simply be identified with the *via eminentiae* because 'the *excessus* as the pre-apprehension of being as such is as a matter of fact a condition of the possibility of the way of eminence',[2] and the word 'pre-apprehension' is significant here, for, as we have seen, it denotes the unformulated and 'unthematic' awareness by the mind of itself in every cognitive act. Thus Rahner appears to be telling us that God is grasped not in his character as the ground of the *objects* of our perception but in his character as the ground of us who are the *subjects* of perception. And, since God is not himself a sensible object, Rahner maintains that, even when we examine the subjective element in perception in order to make this unthematic grasp of God explicit and thematic, we know God not as an *object* but only as the *principle* of our knowledge. He writes as follows:

> Although [the *excessus*] must open up the metaphysical realm, of itself alone it cannot immediately present any metaphysical objects in their own selves as objectively visible. For otherwise it would be the intuition of an object manifesting itself from itself and received by man as different. But such an intuition is essentially sensible, hence as such it gives no metaphysical object. Therefore, the *excessus* can only be the actuality of a formal principle on the side of the subject of the knowledge.[3]

And again:

> When man takes as the 'object' of his knowledge in metaphysics that which he affirms simultaneously in the pre-apprehension which makes possible his knowledge of [the] world, then he necessarily makes it a represented object in the only way in

[1] ibid., pp. 393f.
[2] ibid., pp. 394f.
[3] ibid., p. 396.

which he can have such an object at all: he represents it as a thing, as the things of the world are, because he can have no represented object at all without a conversion to the phantasm. But in so far as he again makes this representation of the meta-physical 'object' itself possible by a pre-apprehension, while the pre-apprehension already and always negates what is represen-ted, man has already and always negated the limitation of *esse* to mobile [i.e., changeable] being by this judgmental pre-appre-hension. Therefore in a judgment he can remove this limitation by a negation (*remotio*), and thus in a judgment think the meta-physical object through *excessus* and negation without the object as such being immediately represented.[1]

Thus, Rahner, tells us, negation and comparison, as means by which we pass from the experience of our senses to the primary being,

> are always founded upon the *excessus* as the pre-apprehension, as the act which pre-apprehends absolute *esse* merely in the apprehension of mobile being, and thus they give the meta-physical not in its own self, but only as the 'principle' of the real object of the one human knowledge, the world.[2]

Rahner is thus emphatic about the extremely limited know-ledge of God which we can acquire by purely natural and rational means.

> Although *esse* is in itself the full ground of every existent, never-theless, this fullness is given to us only in the absolute, empty infinity of our pre-apprehension or, what is the same thing, in common being with the transcendental modes intrinsic to it. And so it remains true: the highest knowledge of God is the 'darkness of ignorance.'[3]

And in his final section, on 'Man as spirit in the world', Rahner writes:

> The world as known is always the world of man, is essentially a concept complementary to man. And the last known, God, shines forth only in the limitless breadth of the pre-apprehen-sion, in the desire for being as such by which every act of man is borne, and which is at work not only in his ultimate knowledge and in his ultimate decisions, but also in the fact that the free

[1] ibid., p. 399.
[2] ibid., pp. 399f.
[3] ibid., p. 401.

spirit becomes, and must become, sensibility in order to be spirit, and thus exposes itself to the whole destiny of this earth....

Insofar as man enters into the world by turning to the phantasm, the revelation of being as such and in it the knowledge of God's existence has already been achieved, but even then this God who is beyond the world is always hidden from us. Abstraction is the revelation of being as such which places man before God; conversion is the entrance into the here and now of this finite world, and this makes God the distant Unknown. Abstraction and conversion are the same thing for Thomas: man.[1]

Nevertheless, for Rahner revelation both completes and fulfils this limited, obscure and still open natural awareness of God. "If man is understood in this way", he writes,

he can listen to hear whether God has not perhaps spoken, because he knows that God is; God can speak, because He is the Unknown. And if Christianity is not the idea of an eternal, omnipresent spirit, but is Jesus of Nazareth, then Thomas's metaphysics of knowledge is Christian when it summons man back into the here and now of his finite world, because the Eternal has also entered into his world so that man might find Him, and in Him might find himself anew.[2]

[1] ibid., pp. 406, 408.
[2] ibid., p. 408.

CHAPTER FIVE

TRANSCENDENTAL THOMISM—II

You ain't heard nothin' yet, folks.—Al Jolson.

W E MUST NOW turn from Rahner to his fellow-Jesuit Coreth.
For Emerich Coreth, as for Rahner, the programme of
metaphysics is provided by the transcendental method, which
he defines in the words of Kant: 'I call every knowledge transcendental which occupies itself not so much with objects, but
rather with our way of knowing objects, in so far as this is to be
possible *a priori*.'[1] And, as Lonergan remarks, in a fine review
of Coreth's original German work which is printed as an appendix to Donceel's translation and which bears the significant
title 'Metaphysics as Horizon', for Coreth the basis of the transcendental method, applied to any judgment, lies not in the
content of the judgment but in its *possibility*, and it functions by a
reductio ad absurdum:

> The main task of the metaphysician is not to reveal or prove
> what is new and unknown; it is to give scientific expression to
> what already is implicitly acknowledged without being ex-
> plicitly recognised.
> The proper tool in this mediation of the immediate is the
> rejection of the counterposition. Explicit judgments can contra-
> dict the latent metaphysics that they presuppose; but one has
> only to bring this contradiction to light, for the explicit judg-
> ment to be evident nonsense, and for its opposite to be estab-
> lished.[2]

The trouble with Kant, Coreth tells us, is that he did not start
far enough back. 'He did not go back far enough when looking
for the conditions of possibility of human knowledge. He stopped

[1] *Metaphysics*, p. 35.
[2] ibid., pp. 200f; this review is also reprinted in Lonergan's *Collection*.

at the finite subject, he did not reach an absolute horizon of validity, and thus he eliminated all possibility of metaphysical knowledge. Only if we can, against Kant and proceeding beyond him, show that our *a priori* knowledge is metaphysical knowledge of being, which opens for us the absolute horizon of being as such, shall we be able to validate metaphysics critically and methodically.'[1] Lonergan comments on the clean break which Coreth makes with the Wolffian tradition. 'By being is meant, not what can be, but what is. By general metaphysics is understood, not a study of some prior realm of possibilities, but an understanding of actual existents.'[2] Rahner would, of course, agree, but with him, as we have seen, the starting-point in the concrete realm was the human act of perception, in which the mind turns to the phantasms. For Coreth the starting-point is the conscious, concrete activity of the human subject asking a question. 'To doubt questioning is to involve oneself in a counter-position, and so questioning is beyond the doubter's capacity to doubt coherently.'[3] All kinds of questions can be asked, but to all of them the realm of being is presupposed as the condition without which there could be no questioning. And it is here that Coreth parts company with Kant in the operative moment itself, the moment in which questioning occurs. To quote Lonergan again:

> That operative moment lies in a contradiction not between content and content but between content and performance; but a Kantian context is a context of contents that does not envisage performance. Thus there is no explicit contradiction in the content of the statement 'We are under an illusion when we claim to know what really is'. On the other hand, there is an explicit contradiction in the reflective statement 'I am stating what really and truly is so, when I state that we are under an illusion whenever we claim to know what really and truly is so.'[4]

It is here, as Lonergan remarks, that Coreth's divergence from Kant differs from Étienne Gilson's; for Gilson, while he holds that Kantian idealism, like any other idealism, is false, does not hold that it is contradictory. He holds that it is in fact perfectly

---

1 ibid., pp. 36f.
2 ibid., p. 199.
3 Lonergan, ibid., p. 201; Coreth, pp. 45ff.
4 ibid., p. 204. I have added the quotation-marks for greater clarity.

consistent; its defect is that it cannot break through from the purely conceptual realm of ideas into the realm of concrete reality.[1] For Coreth, on the other hand, Kantian idealism involves a definite contradiction. 'This contradiction lies, not in the content uttered by the mind, but in the mind that utters the content, and not in a formal entity that merely thinks thoughts, but in a concrete intelligence that by its performance means and by its uttered contents denies that we know what really and truly is so.'[2]

By putting the question about questioning, Coreth claims to have shown 'that every question supposes, as a condition of its possibility, a previous knowledge about being; hence it supposes the *horizon of being*, outside which a question about that which *is*, is impossible.' (The metaphor of the 'horizon' is common to both Coreth and Rahner.) '*The material object of the intellect is every being. . . . The formal object of the intellect is being as being. . . .* The horizon of the question derives from a pre-knowledge that is never thematic [i.e. explicitly formulated] itself, but which conditions and determines every thematic question. . . .'

> This pre-knowledge of being [Coreth continues] is based upon our exercised or lived knowledge, through which we become aware of the unity of being and knowing. This exercised or lived knowledge never becomes thematic; likewise our pre-knowledge of being is never thematically given. Never do we know merely about being as being, without knowing at the same time about some being or at least without inquiring about some being. Being is never given as an object. But the pre-knowledge of being conditions and determines every inquiry about beings, it projects the horizon of being as the horizon of all possible inquiry.
>
> Being is never given as object, but only as the formal object in the subject. The formal object as object is not being, but beings, although we can inquire and know about them as such only in the light of our pre-knowledge of being.[3]

Coreth goes into very much more detail than Rahner in his discussion of the existence of God. But in much the same way he argues that 'in our every act of thinking there is co-posited

---

[1] 'An idealist philosophy is not necessarily incoherent; on the contrary, the more it is idealist, the more coherent it is' (*Le Réalisme méthodique*, p. 49).

[2] op. cit., p. 205 (Lonergan).

[3] ibid., p. 76.

and presupposed the primordial realisation of the necessity of absolute being'.

> This is not yet thematically a knowledge of the absolute being of God, since the absolute and necessary character of being is not yet contrasted with the finite and conditioned beings. At first we have only a general and undetermined knowledge, a basic unavoidable assertion: being as such cannot be, being as such is absolute. Within this assertion the knowledge about the absolute being of God is already co-posited, but it becomes thematic only when we have shown that no finite being is being itself, that every finite being is distinct from absolute being, since it possesses being only in a conditioned and restricted manner. However, since, insofar as it is, the finite being necessarily is, it presupposes, beyond itself, the absolutely necessary being, being itself.[1]

It is clear from this statement, as well as from many others, that Coreth's approach to theism is firmly *cosmological*; it is not based on any purely logical or conceptual argument, or on any alleged immediate awareness of God. In fact, for all the many obvious differences, his basic attitude has something in common with that of Austin Farrer in *Finite and Infinite*, with his stress upon the cosmological relation in which God and things are known together, God as their creator and they as his creatures.

> It is clear [writes Coreth] in what sense we admit an *immediate knowledge of God*. It is not in the sense of a thematic explicit knowledge, nor in the sense of an immediate intuition of God. Our explicit knowledge of God needs the mediation of the world, which we know and which we transcend in our knowledge. This knowing and transcending is possible only on account of an unthematic anticipation, through which we unconsciously reach out towards the Absolute. . . . It follows from all of this that the knowledge of God does not really represent a passage of our mind to something hitherto wholly unknown, but only an explicitation and development of our knowledge of the necessity of being. Thus it seems to be more correct not to speak of an immediate knowledge of God but only of an immediate knowledge of the necessary and absolute nature of being. To show that this necessary being is not the finite world of our experience, but only God, who infinitely surpasses this world, requires further steps in our argumentation.[2]

[1] ibid., p. 171.
[2] ibid., pp. 174f.

In developing these further steps Coreth is much more explicit than Rahner. His definition of God, though not given in so many words, is clearly that of a transcendent ground of the world, though he has approached this ground not by a consideration of the objects of our experience—the 'external world'—but of our own perceiving subjectivity. 'The necessary being', he writes, 'is distinguished from the finite beings because the latter are many, conditioned, and finite, thus presupposing being itself as one, unconditioned and infinite. In the following proofs we further explain the relation between the many and the one, the conditioned and the unconditioned, the finite and the infinite. . . . Thus we have basically—although not exclusively—three demonstrations of God, corresponding to three ontological principles of identity, causality and finality.'[1]

'In the first proof', Coreth writes, referring to his earlier discussion of the 'horizon of being', 'we have shown that the principle of identity, which underlies our every act of thinking as a condition of its possibility, presupposes the primordial affirmation of the necessity of being. The second proof', he continues, 'shows that, according to the principle of causality, every finite and contingent being demands the Absolute Being as its first cause.' He develops this argument along traditional lines, beginning with the assertion that 'a being is contingent whenever it stands *in the flux of becoming*, when it begins and ceases to exist, thus showing that it is not necessary', and he adds two further criteria of contingency, namely *temporality* and *finiteness*.[2] While asserting that the criterion of *becoming* can be applied to many, though not all, of the objects of our experience, he sees it as applying most obviously to ourselves. 'We experience in the most direct manner the contingency of our own Ego. We ourself have not always existed. We have emerged from non-being, we have been thrown into existence, we know that we were not, that we are not necessarily in existence, that we have not entered into existence by ourself.' The distinction here made is not unlike that made by Farrer in a very different context of argumentation between *usiological* arguments, based upon finite beings in general, and *anthropological*, based upon the particular being which each of us knows most immediately, namely

[1] ibid., pp. 175f.
[2] ibid., pp. 176f.

himself.[1] It should be added that this awareness of our own contingency to which Coreth here appeals is quite different from
the unthematic, precognitive self-awareness of oneself as subject
which he has previously discussed; what he is now concerned
with is the self-awareness derived from introspection. It should
also be added that Coreth shows no concern with the type of
objection that has been urged against causal arguments for
theism by philosophers of the linguistic school, namely that it is
not self-evident that contingency in the sense of not-always-
existing is identical with contingency in the sense of metaphysical non-necessity, that causality is a concept that applies
only *within* the empirical realm and cannot be extrapolated
beyond it, and so on. The fact that Coreth can argue in sublime
indifference to such objections as these is a striking sign of the
total lack of communication that persists between the empirically and linguistically minded philosophers of the Anglo-Saxon
world and the existentialist and phenomenological philosophers
of the Teutonic. They simply do not speak the same language.
I am far from admitting that the objections of the linguistic
empiricists are unanswerable, but they are very widespread and
influential in English-speaking countries and they will need to
be taken note of by writers of the transcendentalist school if these
latter are to obtain a hearing.

To return to Fr Coreth. His third argument, based upon
finality, begins by asserting that 'we can know and enquire
about God only because our intellect, although immersed in the
world of experience, transcends this world towards the absolute
and infinite being. . . . Such a striving', he goes on, 'which
constitutes the very essence of our mind, cannot head towards
nothingness. Its end must at least be possible. . . . But if the
absolute being is possible, it is also necessarily real. In the
present case, and only in it, may we conclude from the possibility to the reality, provided only that the possibility in question is not a mere logical possibility, but the real possibility of
being.' Coreth would thus not accept against his argument the
objections commonly levelled against that of St Anselm. 'We
do not conclude', he insists, 'from a conceivable, non-contradic-
tory *concept* of God to his reality. This would be an invalid conclusion. But we start from the real activity of the spirit, which is

[1] *Finite and Infinite*, part III.

possible only if it aims at a really possible end, the absolute being.'[1] To substantiate this defence would require a much fuller examination of the earlier part of Coreth's book than is possible here. He does, however, link up his theistic argument with his original starting-point in the following passage:

> The above proof might be formulated in a simpler and briefer way as follows: The question presupposes the possibility of an answer. But our question is an unlimited one, since we may inquire about everything and continue to inquire beyond any possible limits. By its very nature, the question aims at the infinity of all that which is knowable. Therefore, the act of inquiring presupposes the possibility of an infinite answer, which puts an end to all questions. But neither a finite being nor the totality of all finite beings can supply an infinite answer and put an end to an unlimited inquiry. Therefore, the question presupposes something infinite, which, insofar as it is knowable, may supply an infinite answer. But, as we have shown, the possibility of the infinite necessarily implies its reality. Hence the act of inquiring presupposes the reality of the absolute, infinite being.[2]

It is not difficult to think of the flaws which a philosopher trained in the linguistic empiricist school will claim to detect in this passage. How many senses have been given to the words 'infinite' and 'unlimited' in the course of the argument? What, precisely, is 'the question' about which so much has been said? In what sense does it 'presuppose' something infinite as providing a possible answer? Must not the answer to a question be a proposition? If so, is the 'infinite' a proposition? And will it satisfy Fr Coreth's needs if it is? Has it been shown that the possibility of the 'infinite' necessarily implies its reality, and what, in this context, does 'necessarily implies' mean? Such awkward questions will inevitably be asked and they are not easy to answer. And yet I am sure that Coreth—and Rahner as well—are making a very important point, however vulnerable may be the language in which they express it and however tortuous and circuitous the path by which they approach it. It is the point made by the old cosmological argument, that if only we look at finite creatures in the right way we shall see them as

[1] ibid., pp. 178f.
[2] ibid., pp. 179f.

created and upheld by that transcendent cause to which we give
the name 'God'. Coreth himself says that 'other proofs of God
may be devised . . . from the finalistic order and harmony of the
world, from the finite subject–object relation, hence also from
the ontic truth and goodness of beings, further from the absolute nature of moral obligation, from the transcendence of
human society and history, from the religious experience both
of the individual and of humanity as a whole, and so on.'[1]
Nevertheless, having added that such a proof may use either
the principle of causality or the principle of finality or merely
argue simply from the conditioned to its condition, he writes as
follows:

> All demonstrations of God's existence are ultimately based upon
> the *transcendence of the spirit*. It is only because and insofar as the
> finite spirit operates in the horizon of being as such, because it
> possesses an essential relation to the absolute and infinite being,
> that in every one of its spiritual activities it always already
> transcends the conditioned towards the unconditioned, the
> finite towards the infinite. Thus whenever we wish critically to
> reduce a proof of God's existence to the ultimate conditions of
> its possibility, we must, by means of transcendental reflection,
> render thematic the essential transcendence of the human spirit.
> Or the other way around: Whenever through reflection we
> make explicit the metaphysically transcendent nature of the
> human spirit, we have a proof of God's existence—or rather we
> have *the* proof of God's existence, which is the ground and
> foundation of all the other demonstrations.[2]

I have emphasised in an earlier lecture the importance of
being clear and consistent in one's explicit or assumed definition
of the word 'God'. Obviously the God whose existence Coreth
claims to have proved is an infinite and transcendent ground of
our human existence, and, at this stage of the argument, nothing
more. He goes on, however, to argue that because Absolute
being *is* the ground of finite beings we can therefore have a
knowledge of him of a strictly analogous kind. 'When the transcendent movement of our spirit heads for the Absolute, we may
drop and transcend the limitations, through a *negation of the*

[1] ibid., p. 180.
[2] ibid., pp. 180f.

negation, thus intending the pure positivity of an unlimited perfection. Each such unlimited perfection is realised in the absolute being of God, they are all infinitely unified in him. Hence we must attribute to God all pure perfections of being.'[1] On this basis Coreth then argues that God is the infinite fullness of all the infinite possibilities of being, that he is absolutely simple, absolutely transcendent of the material, spatiotemporal and all finite orders, he is absolute Spirit, pure activity and life, infinite knowledge, infinite willing, infinitely free and absolute person. 'Hence philosophy can really reach a *personal God*.'[2] Thus, whether transcendental Thomism is genuinely Thomist or not, it here reaches the same God as St Thomas.

One final point should be added before we leave Fr Coreth. He does not, like Rahner, invoke the notion of a 'supernatural existential' in order to make room for a more than merely natural knowledge of God on the part of man. He does, however, maintain that, by his very nature, man can put the question whether God has something to say to him or not.

> Even when known by us, God remains unknown. Even when we know him, we do not understand him. And thus the question stays with us. But from a question about God it turns into a question *to* God. We inquire whether he might not come down to meet us, whether he himself might not by himself answer our questions and reveal himself to us in a way which goes beyond all our human knowledge. . . .
> If God speaks to us and reveals himself to us, he will do so in a way which we may understand. Hence if God is freely to reveal himself, he will have to do it in the world, in history. And we, being aware of such a possibility, should stand open and be ready for it, for a possible word of God to man in the world and in history.[3]

It is here that Fr Coreth leaves us, on the outermost limit of natural theology and the hithermost limit of the Christian revelation. And it is here that, in gratitude and admiration but with some residual puzzlements and reservations, the Gifford Lecturer must leave Fr Coreth.

[1] ibid., pp. 182f.
[2] ibid., p. 188.
[3] ibid., p. 196.

D

I have already referred in some detail to Bernard Lonergan's review of Emerich Coreth; I must now turn to his systematic statement of his own metaphysical and epistemological position.[1] This is to be found in his formidable volume *Insight*, which consists of nearly eight hundred pages of medium-sized type. No more than Rahner or Coreth is Lonergan easy to read, but the difficulty in his case is of a very different kind. He is, in contrast to the other two writers, hardly ever obscure, but his work is at the same time extremely voluminous and extremely compressed. Taking short cuts in Lonergan is very much like taking short cuts in South London; one is very much tempted to do it, but if one yields to the temptation one almost invariably gets lost and has to retrace one's steps. He is certainly in the line of Maréchal's correction and reconstruction of Kant, but he is to all appearance totally uninfluenced by Heidegger, and in the index to *Insight* there is not a single reference to the German existentialist. His method is transcendental, in that he bases metaphysics upon epistemology and not *vice versa*, he discusses knowledge first and only then goes on to discuss being; and he adopts the method of proving positions by showing the counterpositions to be self-contradictory. His work is divided into two parts of roughly equal size; the first, entitled 'Insight as Activity', answers the question 'What is happening when we are knowing?', the second, entitled 'Insight as Knowledge', answers the question 'What is known when that is happening?'. That is to say, the first part is concerned with the *activity* of knowing and the second with its *object*. The title of his book indicates its fundamental thesis; it is that knowing always consists in penetrating beneath the immediately apprehended surface of an object into its intelligible *being*. Insight is *in*-sight, seeing *into* the observed object; and in his earlier work *Verbum: Word and Idea in Aquinas* he generally uses the word 'understanding', which, like the Latin words *intelligentia* and *intellectus*, carries the same suggestion: 'standing under', *legere intus*. Lonergan rejects explicitly what he describes as 'the mistaken supposition

[1] Cf. Conn O'Donovan, 'Masters in Israel: I. Bernard Lonergan', *Clergy Review*, LIV (1969), pp. 666ff; Charles N. Bent, S. J., *Interpreting the Doctrine of God*, ch. V; *Spirit as Inquiry: Studies in Honour of Bernard Lonergan*, Continuum, II (1964), no. 3; Hugo Meynell, 'The Lonergan Phenomenon', *Month*, CCXXX (1970), pp. 11ff; Desmond Connell, 'Father Lonergan and the Idea of Being', *Irish Theological Quarterly*, XXXVII (1970), pp. 118ff.

that knowing consists in taking a look'.[1] In the course of his argument, he traces the operation of the enquiring human mind from one level to another, from commonsense awareness of the world, through the various types of mathematical, scientific, aesthetic and moral experience, up to the level of metaphysics; and at each level of abstraction there is always left an 'empirical residue' which raises further questions and leads the mind on to further heights of enquiry. Like Gilson, Lonergan refuses to remain in the order of conceptual thought and insists on the place of the judgment; furthermore he sees the judgment as not merely affirming the unity of concepts but as asserting existence in concrete reality. Time after time he makes use of the double notion of 'intelligent grasp and reasonable affirmation', thus bringing concept and judgment together.

The greater part of his book is devoted to the knowledge by man of what he calls 'proportionate being', meaning by this term being which is proportionate or correlative to the finite human intellect. He asserts that in a certain sense his whole discussion has been directed by the notion of 'transcendence', in the simple meaning of 'going beyond': science 'goes beyond' common sense, metaphysics and ethics 'go beyond' science. He summarises this movement in the following words:

> Clearly, despite the imposing name, transcendence is the ele-
> mentary matter of raising further questions. Thus, the present
> work has been written from a moving viewpoint. It began from
> insight as an interesting event in human consciousness. It went
> on to insight as a central event in the genesis of mathematical
> knowledge. It went beyond mathematics to study the role of in-
> sight in classical statistical investigations. It went beyond the
> reproducible insights of scientists to the more complex function-
> ing of intelligence in common sense, in its relations to its psycho-
> neural basis, and in its historical expansion in the development
> of technology, economics, and politics. It went beyond all such
> direct and inverse insights to the reflective grasp that grounds
> judgment. It went beyond all insights as activities to consider
> them as elements in knowledge. It went beyond actual know-
> ledge to its permanent dynamic structure to construct an
> explicit metaphysics and add the general form of an ethics. It
> has found man involved and engaged in developing, in going
> beyond what he happens to be, and it has been confronted both

[1] *Insight*, p. 635.

with man's incapacity for sustained development and with his need to go beyond the hitherto considered procedures of his endeavour to go beyond.[1]

However, beyond this elementary notion of transcendence there is another, which Lonergan sees as of profound significance. 'Finally', he writes, 'one can ask whether human knowledge is confined to the universe of proportionate being or goes beyond it to the realm of transcendent being; and this transcendent realm may be conceived either relatively or absolutely, either as beyond man or as the ultimate in the whole process of going beyond.' 'The immanent source of transcendence in man', he asserts, 'is his detached, disinterested, unrestricted desire to know', but 'man's unrestricted desire to know is mated to a limited capacity to attain knowledge.' 'The possibility of transcendent knowledge, then, is the possibility of grasping intelligently and affirming reasonably a transcendent being.' 'But before we can affirm reasonably, we must grasp intelligently; and before we can grasp transcendent being intelligently, we have to extrapolate from proportionate being.'[2] Thus Lonergan goes on to enquire into the legitimacy of this extrapolation.

The object of our unrestricted desire to know, he argues, can be nothing else than being itself. Therefore, the idea of being is nothing else than the content of an unrestricted act of understanding. The primary component of such an act will be the unrestricted act's understanding of itself; its secondary component consists in the understanding of everything else because it understands itself. Can there be, and if there can be is there, such an unrestricted act? In a long argument, based on an analysis of the notion of causality and its relevance to the matter of our own aspiration to the transcendent, Lonergan gives an affirmative answer. The application of the notion of causality beyond the empirical realm and its adoption for metaphysical purposes will, of course, scandalise all true-blooded linguistic analysts; Lonergan's use of it is, however, very impressive. I cannot attempt to justify it here, but it may be well to give Lonergan's own summary of his argument:

> First, the universe of proportionate being is shot through with contingence. Second, mere contingence is apart from being,

1 *Insight*, pp. 635f.
2 ibid., pp. 635, 636, 639, 640, 641.

and so there must be an ultimate ground for the universe, and that ground cannot be contingent. Thirdly, the necessary ultimate ground cannot be necessitated in grounding a contingent universe, and it cannot be arbitrary in grounding an intelligible and good universe. It cannot be necessitated, for what follows necessarily from the necessary is equally necessary. It cannot be arbitrary, for what follows arbitrarily from the necessary results as a mere matter of fact without any possible explanation. But what is neither necessary nor arbitrary yet intelligible and a value, is what proceeds freely from the reasonable choice of a rational consciousness.[1]

At this point a less conscientious writer might think his task was finished. Not so, however, Lonergan. 'By asking what being is', he writes, 'already we have been led to the conclusion that the idea of being would be the content of an unrestricted act of understanding that primarily understood itself and consequently grasped every other intelligibility.'[2] Two questions arise about God, he tells us, namely what is God and whether God is. He then proceeds, in an argument of no less than twenty-six stages, to show that this idea of being is identical with the idea of God, as theists understand him. He still holds, however, that further argument is needed to show that God exists, if we are not to fall into the fallacy of St Anselm and Descartes:

> For when we grasp what God is, our grasp is not an unrestricted act of understanding but a restricted act of understanding that extrapolates from itself to an unrestricted act and by asking ever further questions arrives at a list of attributes of the unrestricted act. Accordingly, what is grasped is not the unrestricted act but the extrapolation that proceeds from the properties of a restricted act to the properties of the unrestricted act. Hence, when the extrapolation is completed, there remains the further question whether the unrestricted act is just an object of thought or a reality.[3]

It is revealing to see the reasons why Lonergan rejects both the Anselmian and the Cartesian form of argument:

> The Anselmian argument . . . is to be met by distinguishing the premise, *Deus est quo majus cogitari nequit*. One grants that by appropriate definitions and syntactical rules it can be made into

[1] ibid., pp. 656f.
[2] ibid., p. 657.
[3] ibid., p. 670.

an analytic proposition. But one asks for the evidence that the terms as defined occur in concrete judgments of fact.

The Cartesian argument seems to be from the concept to the existence of a perfect being. That would be valid if conceiving were looking and looking were knowing. But that view involves the counter-positions; and when one shifts to the positions, one finds that the conceptions become knowing only through reflective grasp of the conditioned.[1]

Again, Lonergan says:

What has to be added to mere conception is not an experience of God but a grasp of the unconditioned. Affirming is an intrinsically rational act; it proceeds with rational necessity from grasp of the unconditioned; and the unconditioned to be grasped is, not the formally unconditioned that God is and that unrestricted understanding grasps, but the virtually unconditioned that consists in inferring God's existence from premises that are true.[2]

In Lonergan's terminology, the 'virtually unconditioned' is something that is in itself conditioned by conditions which are in fact fulfilled. Thus, as he goes on to say, the existence of God is known as the conclusion to an argument, and he adds that all such arguments are of the following general form:

If the real is completely intelligible, God exists. But the real is completely intelligible. Therefore, God exists.

Lonergan is emphatic that the acceptance of the proof involves more than an acquaintance with the laws of logic. 'Proof is not some automatic process that results in a judgment, as taking an aspirin relieves a headache, or as turning on a switch sets the digital computer on its unerring way.'

All that can be set down in these pages is a set of signs. The signs can represent a relevant virtually unconditioned. But grasping it and making the consequent judgment is an immanent act of rational consciousness that each has to perform for himself and no one else can perform for him.[3]

And again, after two pages of persuasion, he repeats:

Such, then, is the argument. As a set of signs printed in a book, it can do no more than indicate the materials for a reflective

[1] ibid., pp. 670f.
[2] ibid., p. 672.
[3] ibid.

grasp of the virtually unconditioned. To elicit such an act is the
work that the reader has to perform for himself.[1]

And he adds further considerations to fortify the reader who has
been brought up on the dogma that the existence of God cannot
be proved.

In the last resort, then, it would seem that Lonergan is interpreting the function of his arguments in the same manner as that
in which, in my book *Existence and Analogy*, I have interpreted
St Thomas's Five Ways, namely as persuasive discourse intended to help us to grasp the fundamental dependence of finite
beings on infinite being as their ground.[2] There is, however, an
apparent difference, in that for Lonergan what is grasped as the
'virtually unconditioned' does not, if we are to take his words
literally, appear to be finite being in its dependence on infinite
being, or infinite being as the ground of finite being, but the act
of inferring God's existence from true premises. Here I am
frankly puzzled, but I suspect that the difference is due to the
fact that Lonergan, while repudiating the Kantian view of God
as merely a regulative principle of our thinking, appears to discover God as a constitutive principle of our perception of finite
being rather than as a constitutive principle of finite being itself.
In any case he alleges that his conception of God as the unrestricted act of understanding coincides both with Aristotle's
conception of God as the unmoved mover who is *noesis noeseos*
and also with St Thomas's conception of God as *ipsum intelligere*,
ipsum esse and *summum bonum*, but with the significant rider that
Lonergan's own ultimate is not being but intelligence.[3] He sees
the Five Ways as 'so many particular cases of the general statement that the proportionate universe is incompletely intelligible
and that complete intelligibility is demanded'.[4] There can
nevertheless be no doubt for anyone who has read his book
Verbum that Lonergan believes himself to be a faithful inter-
preter of the Angelic Doctor, while holding that Thomism is a
living and developing thing and not a lifeless museum-piece.

This has been a long discussion, and even so it has done little
justice to either the depth or the range of Lonergan's thought. I

[1] ibid., p. 674.
[2] op. cit., pp. 77ff.
[3] *Insight*, p. 677.
[4] ibid., p. 678.

have said nothing about his final chapter, in which he gets to grips with the problem of evil and expounds the heuristic structure of his solution, working up to the famous paragraph which opens with the words 'In the thirty-first place . . . '. Nevertheless I hope I have succeeded in giving some impression of the approach to theism pursued by a thinker who, in these days of specialisation, seems to have taken almost all knowledge for his province and who has attempted, without any submission to the wiles of Heideggerian existentialism, to develop the principles of Thomism in a way that recognises the force of the Kantian critique and at the same time survives its blows. If, as one of Lonergan's admirers has alleged, 'the trouble with *Insight* is that it requires not summarising but expansion' and that 'it is much less a book to be read than a programme to be followed',[1] the inadequacy of the present account may be, if not excusable, at least explicable. I should, however, add that Fr F. E. Crowe, who can claim, if anyone can, to be an authoritative exponent of Lonerganism, has produced a masterly résumé of *Insight* in less than a page of the *New Catholic Encyclopaedia*.[2]

[1] Conn O'Donovan, S. J., *The Clergy Review*, LIV (1969), p. 675.
[2] XIV, pp. 389ff, s.v. 'Understanding (Intellectus)'.

CHAPTER SIX

THE CASE FOR REALISM

To a philosopher no circumstance, however trifling, is too minute.
—Oliver Goldsmith, *Citizen of the World*, xxx.

THE MOST OBVIOUS characteristic of the approach to theism typified by Joseph Maréchal, Karl Rahner, Emerich Coreth and Bernard Lonergan is its length. The busy reader may well recall the complaint of Andrew Marvell to his mistress:

> Had we but world enough, and time,
> This coyness, Lady, were no crime,

and reflect that, while the world no doubt is extensive enough, time, for us mortals, is limited and that, therefore, unnecessary verbosity is at best inconsiderate and at worst immoral. In the case of Fr Coreth, Fr Donceel has indeed shown that the essential features of the thought of a transcendental Thomist can be compressed into a reasonable space; nevertheless, I do not think that the prolixity of these writers is accidental or purely temperamental. It is, I think, almost inevitable in a thinker who feels bound to justify the validity of knowledge before he allows himself to indulge in the luxury of knowing. For, once you have refused to assume the reliability of your apprehension of beings other than yourself and have postulated that the objects of your perception are *prima facie* states of your own mind, you are launched on the endless process of trying ineffectually to escape from the prison of your own subjectivity. To change the metaphor, you are involved in ever more complicated gymnastics in your attempts not to saw off the branch on which you are sitting.

There can, of course, be no harm in investigating and analysing the structure of the human mind and the process of human knowledge. St Thomas did this in the thirteenth century, and M. Jacques Maritain has done it in our own time at considerable length in his book *The Degrees of Knowledge*. What differentiates these thinkers from those of the transcendental school and enables them to avoid the missiles which, in the later chapters of *Réalisme thomiste et Critique de la connaissance*, M. Gilson has directed against all forms of idealist epistemology, is the fact that they embark on the construction of their critique—or, it would be better to say, their doctrine—of knowledge and perception *after* they have allowed themselves to know and perceive, and do not attempt to perform the frustrating, and in the last resort impossible, task of doing it *before*. Their purpose in developing their epistemology has not been to discover *whether* it is possible for them to know beings other than themselves but *how* it has been possible to do this already. The influence of Descartes and Kant has been so strong in the modern world that it takes a very courageous and persistent thinker to question the basic assumption of idealism. Nevertheless, in 1934 William Temple could write: 'If I were asked what was the most disastrous moment in the history of Europe I should be strongly tempted to answer that it was that period of leisure when René Descartes, having no claims to meet, remained for a whole day "shut up alone in a stove",'[1] while Lord Russell in 1927 had written even more irreverently: 'Kant deluged the philosophic world with muddle and mystery, from which it is only now beginning to emerge. Kant has the reputation of being the greatest of modern philosophers, but to my mind he was a mere misfortune.'[2] No one, to my knowledge, has so ruthlessly, and at the same time so good-humouredly, exposed the self-frustrating character of idealist epistemology than has M. Gilson, and I shall allow myself the pleasure of quoting at some length from the brilliant little work *The Realist Beginner's Handbook* (*Vade Mecum du débutant réaliste*), which forms the last chapter of his book *Le Réalisme méthodique*. But before doing this I must warn anyone who is unfamiliar with the technical terms of philosophy that in the present context the words 'idealism' and 'realism' have meanings far removed from those of ordinary discourse. 'Idealism' means the view that the objects which we perceive are simply *ideas* inside our minds, while 'realism' means the view that we perceive *real beings* outside them. There is nothing

[1] *Nature, Man and God*, p. 57.
[2] *An Outline of Philosophy*, p. 83.

starry-eyed about idealism nor anything cynical about realism, as we shall use these terms. Nor has 'realism' here, where it is contrasted with 'idealism', anything in common with the medieval usage, in which it is contrasted with 'nominalism'.

The first step on the path of realism [writes M. Gilson] is to recognise that one has always been a realist; the second is to recognise that, however much one tries to think differently, one will never succeed; the third is to note that those who claim that they think differently, think as realists as soon as they forget to act a part. If they ask themselves why, their conversion is almost complete.

Most people who say and think that they are idealists would prefer to be able not to be such, but they cannot find out how. People tell them that they will never get outside their thought and that anything beyond thought is unthinkable. If they consent to seek a reply to this objection they are lost from the start, for all the idealist's objections against the realist are formulated in idealist terms. . . .

We must begin by distrusting the term 'thought'; for the greatest difference between the realist and the idealist is that the idealist thinks, whereas the realist knows. . . .

[For the idealist] the spirit is what thinks, while for us the intellect is what knows. . . . An idealist term is generally a realist term which designates one of the spiritual conditions of knowledge, but is now considered as generating its own content.

The knowledge of which the realist speaks is the lived and experienced unity of an intellect with an apprehended reality. This is why a realist philosopher always presses towards the very thing that is apprehended, without which there would be no knowledge. The idealist philosophers, on the other hand, since they start from thought, very soon choose as their object science or philosophy. When he genuinely thinks as an idealist, the idealist embodies perfectly the essence of a 'professor of philosophy'; while the realist, when he genuinely thinks as a realist, fulfils the authentic essence of a philosopher; for a philosopher talks about things, but a professor of philosophy talks about philosophy.

Having fired his opening shots, Gilson now develops his attack:

Just as we do not have to go from thought to things (knowing the enterprise to be impossible), so we do not have to ask ourselves whether something beyond thought is thinkable. It may well be that something beyond *thought* is not thinkable, but it is certain that all *knowledge* implies something beyond thought. The fact that this something-beyond-thought is given to us by knowledge only *in* thought does not prevent it from being something-beyond; but the idealist always confuses 'being given in thought' and 'being given by thought'. For one who starts from knowledge something-beyond-thought is so far thinkable that it is only this kind of thought for which there can be a 'beyond'.

Gilson is emphatic that we have a primary perception of something other than our own selves:

The realist will be committing an error of the same kind [as the idealist] if he asks himself how, starting from the ego, he can prove the existence of a non-ego. For the idealist, who starts from the ego, this is the normal, and indeed the only possible, formulation of the question. The realist must be doubly wary: first because he does not start from the ego, and secondly because for him the world is not a *non-ego* (that would be nothing at all), but an *in-se*. An *in-se* can be given in knowledge; a *non-ego* is what the real is reduced to for an idealist, and it can neither be grasped by knowledge nor proved by thought.

For Gilson, the idealist problem, how we can compare the content of our mind with the reality outside in order to know to what degree the former accurately depicts the latter, simply does not arise. It is an insoluble problem which idealism has created for itself; for the realist, there is no such thing as a *noumenon* in the idealist's sense of the term:

Knowledge presupposes the presence of the thing itself to the intellect, and we do not have to postulate, behind the thing that is in the thought, a mysterious and unknowable duplicate, which would be the thing of the thing that is in the thought. Knowing is not apprehending a thing as it is in thought but, in thought, apprehending the thing as it is.

Gilson is not ignorant of the objection that is brought against the realist doctrine from the occurrence of dreams and hallucinations, but he is clear that it is only because perception is in general authentic that we can identify dreams and hallucinations as such. For the consistent idealist, there can be nothing to differentiate illusions from reality.

Taine performed a great service for good sense when he defined a sensation as a *true hallucination*, for he showed where logic necessarily lands idealism. Sensation is what a hallucination becomes when this hallucination isn't one. We must not let ourselves be impressed by the famous 'errors of the senses' or be surprised by the enormous hoo-ha that the idealists make of them; idealists are people for whom the normal can only be a particular case of the pathological.

Gilson refuses to admit the accusation that realists are committed by their doctrine to posing as infallible; quite the contrary:

> We are simply philosophers for whom truth is normal and error is abnormal; this does not mean that truth is any easier for us to achieve than is, for example, perfect health. The realist does not differ from the idealist in being unable to make mistakes, but primarily in the fact that, when he does make mistakes, it is not because thought has erred through being unfaithful to itself but because knowledge has erred through being unfaithful to its object. But, above all, the realist makes mistakes only when he is unfaithful to his principles, while the idealist avoids them only in the degree in which *he* is unfaithful to *his*.

And finally, it is the idealist, not the realist, who takes the mystery out of existence and claims to know everything that there is to know:

> To say that all knowledge consists in grasping the thing as it is does not in any way mean that the intellect grasps the thing as it is infallibly, but that it is only when it does so that there is knowledge. Still less does it mean that knowledge exhausts the content of its object in one single act. What knowledge grasps of an object is real, but the real is inexhaustible, and even if the intellect had discerned all its details it would still be up against the mystery of its very existence. It was the idealist Descartes who believed that he could grasp the reality infallibly and at one fell swoop; Pascal, the realist, knew how naive this pretence of the philosopher was. . . . The virtue proper to the realist is modesty concerning his knowledge, and even if he does not always practise it, he is committed to it by his profession.[1]

Gilson, is, I believe, entirely correct in locating the source of our present philosophical malaise in Descartes' idealism, but I think that something more than idealism is involved, namely sensationalism. And here again I must utter the warning that

[1] *Le Réalisme méthodique*, pp. 87ff.

the word 'sensationalism' has a different meaning from that which it bears in contemporary lamentations about the evil influences of television and the popular press. Sensationalism here simply means the doctrine that, in an act of perception, the object perceived is purely and totally an object of sense, a coloured patch, a loud squeak, a musty smell, a bitter taste, a feeling of warmth and so on. Now such a doctrine is certainly idealist in tendency, for it is difficult to see how colours, noises and the rest can exist when no one is perceiving them. Nevertheless, it is possible, with some sophistication, to evade the idealist suggestions of sensationalism to some degree. Thus Locke held that it was only the secondary qualities, so called, that had a purely intra-mental existence and that the primary qualities, such as extension, impenetrability and mass, could exist even when unperceived, though it was not entirely clear whether the primary qualities which we perceived were identical with the primary qualities in the extra-mental substances or were only accurate counterparts of them. And even Descartes, for whom the perceived objects were entirely intra-mental, held that they presented themselves to the mind purporting to be pictures of extra-mental objects, though he had to construct an argument for the existence of God before he could accept their claims as veridical. It was Berkeley's demolition of primary qualities that rendered sensationalism purely idealist; and nothing that Hume, with all his hard-headedness, could contrive could rehabilitate extra-mental reality. All he could do was to disintegrate the mind into a succession of unconnected mental states. There was, however, an attempt at the beginning of the present century to devise some kind of non-idealist sensationalism; the leading figures in this movement were G. E. Moore, Bertrand Russell, C. D. Broad and H. H. Price.[1] One suggestion was that sense-data could exist unperceived with the same characteristics that they had when someone was perceiving them, though it was of course only when someone was perceiving them that they and their characteristics could be perceived. Another suggestion was that the unperceived object was a *sensibile* rather than a *sensum*, though apart from the fact of being perceived it was exactly the same whether it was being perceived or not. It may be doubted whether these two views differ except verbally. Yet another view

[1] Cf. R. J. Hirst, s.v. 'Sensa', in *Encycl. of Philosophy*, VII, pp. 407ff.

was that there existed a vast number of elementary perceptive acts, each having a mental and a physical pole, and that when they were grouped according to the mutual relations of their physical poles they constituted physical objects and when they were grouped according to the mutual relations of their mental poles they constituted minds. By and large, however, sensationalism tended to be idealist, and its never-failing supports were the subjective character of sense-data and the occurrence of hallucinations. For if one man saw a penny as circular while another saw it as elliptical, and if one man saw pink rats when another saw no quadrupeds at all, it seemed impossible to hold that either the penny or the rats had any existence except as modifications of the minds of their observers. The natural outcome would seem to be solipsism, the view that nobody and nothing exists except myself; and, although, as C. D. Broad observed, solipsism, like another vice whose name begins with the same letter, is more often imputed than committed,[1] sensationalist philosophers have usually rejected it by an act of faith rather than by any argument. Russell, indeed, has a story of a lady who wrote to him saying that solipsism seemed to her to be so reasonable a position that she was puzzled that so few people held it.[2] It is also related that a young man commenting on an address by G. K. Chesterton, concluded his remarks with the statement 'Personally, I have only one conviction which I hold with certainty, and this is of the reality of my own existence.' (The reply of the Sage of Beaconsfield was brief: 'Cherish it.')[3] Solipsism is a justifiably uncommon position, for we are conscious of the existence of other persons and other things before we become conscious of the existence of our own selves. Tennyson's

> ... baby new to earth and sky

who,

> What time his tender palm is prest
> Against the circle of the breast,
> Has never thought that 'this is I',

provides an example:

> But as he grows he gathers much,
> And learns the use of 'I' and 'me',

---

[1] *Examination of McTaggart's Philosophy*, II, p. 259.
[2] *Human Knowledge: its Scope and Limits*, p. 196; *Outline of Philosophy*, p. 302.
[3] Maisie Ward, *Return to Chesterton*, p. 130.

> And finds 'I am not what I see,
> And other than the things I touch.'[1]

And indeed the answer both to solipsism and to sensationalism is that, strange as it might seem *a priori*, we are aware of the existence of beings outside our own minds more immediately than we are aware of the existence of our own selves. This is true whether we consider the development of perception in early life (Tennyson's baby) or our normal adult perceptive acts. We can, of course, by deliberate introspection, perceive our own selves in a very elusive and fugitive manner, and I am far from holding that this self-perception is hallucinatory; we can also, I think, very plausibly deduce the existence of a subject of perception from the fact that objects are perceived, though I would doubt whether we can *deduce* the continuous persistence of that subject. Nevertheless, the primary deliverance of perception is the extra-mental being. I use the word 'extra-mental' deliberately, for it could be held as a logical possibility (and I think some phenomenologists hold this) that we do perceive objects but that these objects are only modifications of our own minds. What in fact makes many philosophers reluctant to admit that we perceive extra-mental beings is the subjective character of what have been variously called sensa, sense-data, sensibilia, sensible species or phenomena: the colour of the patch, the shape of the coin, the intensity and pitch of the squeak and so on. But this is in turn due to the assumption that the datum of perception is a purely sensory object (even if it is also held, along Kantian lines, that the mind has had some part in its manufacture), and that, if the intellect comes into the act of perception at all, it is by using the sense-object as the ground for an inference, whether that inference be immediate and spontaneous or subsequent and deliberate. According to this view, perception, in the strict sense of direct awareness of a real object, is simply identical with sensation; the intellect in no way *apprehends*, it merely *infers*.

Now against this assumption I wish to put forward the view, which has a very respectable ancestry though its existence has been ignored by most modern philosophers, that the non-sensory and intellectual element in perception does not consist simply of inference, but of apprehension. According to this view,

[1] *In Memoriam*, XLV.

there is (at any rate normally, for we are not here concerned with mystical experience) no perception without sensation (*nihil in intellectu quod non prius in sensu*,[1] to quote the scholastic tag), but the sensible particular is not the terminus of perception, not the *objectum quod* (to use another scholastic phrase) but the *objectum quo*, through which and in which the intellect grasps, in a direct but mediated activity, the intelligible extra-mental reality, which is the *being*, the real thing. It is this latter, intelligible being that is the *objectum quod*.

I have argued this thesis at some length in my book *Words and Images*[2] and I will only recapitulate the main points here. We can readily admit that all sensible qualities are subjective—are secondary qualities, in Locke's sense—but the real world remains; for, although it is perceived and known *through* our sense-experience, its contents are intelligible beings which are not just sensed by the senses but grasped by the intellect. Berkeley was entirely right in maintaining against Locke that all sensible qualities are subjective; he was wrong in supposing that the world has no qualities except sensible ones. It is, in fact, amusing to see the precise point in his *Dialogues between Hylas and Philonous* at which this supposition has slipped in.[3]

My primary perception, then, is of some extra-mental being, of some being that is not myself or any aspect or modification of myself. In saying that I perceive some extra-mental being I do not mean that I necessarily perceive it *as* extra-mental, for in order to do that I must already have an awareness of my own mind. I am aware of the being simply *as a being*, as something existing, as something *in itself*, as an *in-se*. This may be accompanied by a mysterious and fugitive awareness of myself as the subject and not the object of the act, an unthematic and implicit admission that I am at the near end of the act, so to speak; but usually this is so implicit as to be unrecognised. There may, also, of course be a secondary act of reflection upon the primary act, as a result of which I am fully conscious that I am aware of the extra-mental being, but this is even less common. When this does occur I am brought face to face with the mystery of mind

---

[1] Cf. St Thomas Aquinas, *De Veritate*, ii, 3, obj. 19 *et ad* 19.
[2] ch. ii, 'The Senses and the Intellect'.
[3] ibid., p. 35. The reference is to the first dialogue (Everyman edition, p. 226).

and the not less mysterious character of intellectual apprehension. For to know a being is not to achieve some kind of external contact with it analogous to the impact of one material object on another. It is to achieve a real union with the being, to get it 'into one's mental skin' or, from another aspect, to become identified, however imperfectly, with it. This is what is implied by the scholastic assertion that in knowledge the knower *becomes* the thing known, not entitatively but 'intentionally'. This is, I repeat, highly mysterious, but it is a fact. It pertains inchoatively, on the level of pure sensation,[1] even to sub-human animals, but it is on the level of intelligence or spirit that this capacity to penetrate other beings, not physically, but none the less really, reaches its full manifestation, and it comes to its climax in the mutual communication of spirits with one another. In us humans, compounded as we are of spirit and matter, it is not only mysterious but extremely complex. There is nothing in the intellect that was not first in the senses, the mind spontaneously turns to sensory representations, but, simply as mind, as intellect, as spirit, it can (intentionally) 'become' all things. *Nihil in intellectu quod non prius in sensu; mens convertit se ad phantasmata; mens quodammodo fit omnia:* these well-worn tags are not statements of a theory about knowledge, they are a description of what knowledge is.

Now one can, as we have seen, build up an argument for the existence of God on the basis of this inbuilt urge of the human mind to take all beings as its object and to press beyond the horizon of the material world towards the realm of subsistent being itself. This is the programme of the transcendental Thomists among others, and we have seen that Karl Rahner takes as his starting-point in *Spirit in the World* the article in which St Thomas argues that, in the present life, the human intellect can know nothing without 'turning to phantasms'. Fr W. Norris Clarke, in a very impressive essay on 'The Self as Source of Meaning in Metaphysics', has similarly, but more briefly, argued that 'what we are really doing . . . when we make [the affirmation of an ultimate infinite Source of all being, God,] on philosophical grounds (not religious faith or mystical experi-

---

[1] Words such as 'sensation', 'sensitive', 'sensible' and 'sensuous' in the present context simply refer to the five senses and their meaning has little in common with that which they have in ordinary speech.

ence) is going all the way to the limit in committing ourselves
to the intellect's radical drive toward intelligibility, and asserting that there *must be* a completely self-sufficient, and therefore
infinitely perfect, single (because infinite) ultimate cause or
existential explanatory principle for all finite being (presuming
that we have already shown that no finite being can meet the
demand for existential self-sufficiency by itself).'[1] This final
qualification is significant, and it suggests that an argument
from the dynamic urge of the human intellect cannot dispense
with argument based upon the general contingency of finite
being. One of the advantages of Fr Norris Clarke's procedure is
that, if it is valid, it provides a very rich content for the God at
which it arrives. I shall, however, not follow this course myself.
I shall take as my starting-point the existence of extra-mental
being, in the sense that I have given to that term, prescinding
from the act by which it is perceived and the properties of the
percipient, and I shall argue from it to the existence of a God
whose content will, in the first instance, be very minimal indeed.
Later on I shall try to give it more substance. In taking this line
I intend no disparagement of the procedure followed by Fr
Clarke or even that of the transcendental Thomists; there may
well be more than one way of approaching the divine mystery.

Fr Norris Clarke has himself deprecated the demand, commonly made by linguistic empiricists, that if we are legitimately
to argue for the existence of God we must start off with a clearly
expressed and exhaustive concept of the being which we are
seeking. He writes as follows:

> The proper philosophical approach to discovering or proving
> the existence of God is not to ask, 'Can I prove the existence of
> God?' . . .
>
> The proper mode of procedure is to start with the world of
> one's experience and ask concerning the necessary conditions
> of possibility for explaining its existence and nature. The first
> step is to show that this whole finite world cannot contain with-
> in itself the sufficient reason for its own existence. . . . The
> principle of sufficient reason or intelligibility is the dynamo of
> one's whole intellectual life and to it one should have made a
> fundamental commitment. . . .
>
> One now proceeds by heuristic concepts, somewhat as is done

[1] *Review of Metaphysics*, XXI (1968), p. 609.

in mathematics when undertaking to solve a problem. 'Let X be the real entity which is needed to solve this problem, possessing whatever properties or attributes are required to fulfil this function.' Then the properties of this not directly known or experienceable X are gradually filled in by postulates, one by one, as the indispensable requirements for a solution of the problem appear. . . .

One can, of course, start off with a vague nominal definition of what one hopes to reach, drawn not from the problem itself but from some outside pre-existing religious or philosophical belief held by men. But it is clearly impossible and unreasonable to ask for a clear detailing of the properties of the X that solves a problem before actually working out the solution to the problem.[1]

There is a further point made by Fr Clarke, the importance of which should become evident as we proceed. It is that the principle involved in arguing for the existence of God is the principle of sufficient reason and that this cannot be simply reduced, as many scholastic and other philosophers have tried to reduce it, to the principle of contradiction.

It is indeed unintelligible to assert that something can come into existence completely out of nothing with no cause at all. Still this is in no way a logical contradiction or reducible to one, since it never asserts that being is nothing or that nothing is being. The principle of contradiction is static, like all logic; the principle of sufficient reason and its immediate corollary of causality are dynamic, like all existential explanation.[2]

Metaphysics is thus something more than logic: as M. Gilson has repeatedly pointed out, it was the basic error of idealists to identify them. That is why they interpreted the self-consistency of their systems as proofs of their truth. It is, on the other hand, the occupational disease of linguistic analysts to deny the existence of metaphysics altogether. Thus, from opposite poles of the philosophical firmament both these schools fail to recognise metaphysics as a study in itself, having its own proper concern and its own method.

Perception, I shall thus maintain, is an activity in which sense and intellect are both involved. This does not mean that in an act of perception there are really two acts performed by two

---

[1] 'Analytic Philosophy and Language about God', in George F. McLean ed., *Christian Philosophy and Religious Renewal* (1967), pp. 64f.

[2] ibid., pp. 48f.

distinct subjects, a sense which senses and an intellect which understands. There is one subject, the human being, who in one act of perception senses by his sense and apprehends by his intellect, the sensible impression being the *objectum quo* and the intelligible extra-mental thing the *objectum quod*. This is the heart of the epistemology of St Thomas Aquinas and of such modern Thomists as M. Gilson and M. Maritain. It is, in my opinion, basic to any adequate account of knowledge, and, provided it is accepted, its elaboration and ornamentation seem to me to be secondary and optional; this does not mean that these latter are uninteresting or trivial, but it does mean that the central doctrine can stand without them. As for the notorious 'errors of the senses', I am content with M. Gilson simply to admit, with all due modesty, that we are not infallible. As I have written elsewhere:

> It is quite wrong to talk about hallucinations as is often done, as if they were due to well-behaved perception of misbehaved objects; they are due to disorder in perception itself. If a drunkard 'sees rats that are not there', this does not mean that there is a special species of rat, the *rattus inexistens*, which the drunkard has a peculiar capacity for observing, co-ordinate with but less common than the more familiar *rattus rattus* and *rattus norvegicus*; it means that there is no such thing as the drunkard's rat at all, he only 'thinks there is'. Misperceptions are not due to awareness of a 'wild' sense-datum; it is the awareness that is wild, otherwise the percipient would not suppose he was perceiving an object at all.[1]

And what is true of the drunkard's hallucinations is, I would hold, true of our less spectacular errors of perception in their degree.

To return now to the point from which I digressed, the primary object of our perception is extra-mental being, existing *in se*; and, although further consideration may have much to add to this, it must never deny this basic datum. It is here, as I see it, that phenomenology tends to go astray, though as Fr J. M. Bocheński has pointed out, we must distinguish between phenomenological method and phenomenology as a doctrine.[2] The

[1] *Christian Theology and Natural Science*, p. 239; I have substituted 'an object' for 'a sense-datum' in the last line. Cf. also my *Existence and Analogy*, pp. 53ff; *Words and Images*, pp. 70ff.
[2] *The Methods of Contemporary Thought*, p. 16.

method consists in refraining from attending to anything except the purely phenomenal aspect of the object; there is no room for the notion of an *objectum quo*. To quote Fr Bocheński:

> The given object ('phenomenon') has ... to be subjected to a two-fold reduction: first the *existence* of the thing must be disregarded, and attention concentrated exclusively on *what* the object is, on its 'whatness'; second, everything inessential has to be excluded from this 'whatness', and only the essence of the object analysed.[1]

Bocheński makes two important points. First:

> it should be noted that the phenomenological reduction is not the same thing as a denial. The elements excluded are only set aside and abstracted from while attention is concentrated on what remains. The eidetic reduction similarly does not imply a value-judgment on the aspects that are excluded: to use the phenomenological method does not rule out the possibility of using other methods later on and of considering the aspects that have been ignored for the time being. The rule of reduction is valid only for the duration of the phenomenological exercise.[2]

Secondly, Bocheński points out that, whereas 'at first sight phenomenological observation seems to be something quite simple, and to consist merely in keeping one's intellectual eyes open, and where appropriate putting oneself in a suitable position for getting a good view of the object by making various external movements',[3] the phenomenological method in fact involves a technique which needs to be mastered. 'The leading rule of phenomenology is "back to the things themselves", where by "things" is meant just the given'[4] and this involves a three-fold self-restraint or 'reduction': first, a detached and 'objective' attitude, concentrated solely on the object or 'phenomenon'; secondly, an abandonment of all theory, hypotheses and arguments derived from outside sources; thirdly the abandonment of all 'tradition', of all views that have ever been held on the object in question. The intention is to arrive at the pure *essence* of the object, in abstraction from both its existence and contingency.

[1] ibid., pp. 16f.
[2] ibid., p. 17.
[3] ibid.
[4] ibid., p. 16.

The immediate reaction to which one is tempted is to wonder whether the phenomenological method does not exclude from consideration the most important characteristics of experience. Just as a training in linguistic analysis seems frequently to condition the disciple to be unable to attend to the meaning of sentences while developing a remarkable capacity for observing their behaviour and dissecting their structure, so it might appear that the complete phenomenologist would be incapable of attending to anything but the most spectral and superficial aspects of the world. This, of course, the phenomenologists deny. 'It is imperative to see *everything* that is given, as far as that is possible. . . . Further, phenomenological observation must be *descriptive*. That is to say, the object must be taken apart, and its elements then described and analysed.'[1] Nevertheless, the whole process is so artificial and doctrinaire that the suspicion remains that, in the attempt to achieve pure and perfect objectivity, a great deal may be excluded that ought to be preserved and that much of what is preserved may be distorted. It might seem more reasonable not to impose upon perception an externally dictated technique but rather to assist the mind to perform its natural operations more comfortably and unimpededly. Any other programme lays itself open, among other objections, to the question *Quis custodiet custodes ipsos*? There is more than a suggestion in the phenomenological method of the type of Hindu yoga in which normal awareness of the world is suspended and it is seen only as *maya* or *phenomenon*. From the point of view of our present concern, the drawback of the phenomenological method is that it tends to exclude from consideration the very aspect of perceived being upon which we most need to concentrate our attention, namely its existence as an extra-mental *in-se*. The leading rule of phenomenology may indeed be 'Back to the given', but since its intention is to abstract from both the existence and the contingency of the object, the one thing it ignores in the given is precisely its givenness. As Bocheński has remarked, the use of the phenomenological method does not rule out the use of other methods later on and the consideration of the aspects that the phenomenological method has ignored. It is such another method that I propose to use, a method that concentrates upon the sheer *givenness* of perceived being.

[1] ibid., p. 23.

CHAPTER SEVEN

CREATURE AND CREATOR

Il n'y a de création que dans l'imprévisible devenant nécessité.
—Pierre Boulez, *Revue Musicale*, 1952.

I SAID AT the end of the last lecture that the approach to theism which I propose to develop takes its basis in the sheer *givenness* of the extra-mental beings which we perceive through our senses. I now add the assurance that I do not intend to fall into the fallacy of arguing that, as a matter of pure grammar, givenness implies a giver. It may be useful to begin by comparing the line which I am following with that worked out by Austin Farrer in his great work *Finite and Infinite*. Like myself, he argues that if only we perceive finite beings correctly we shall perceive them as created and sustained by infinite and transcendent being; and his argument, which is extremely systematic and complex, is intended to help us so to perceive them. Farrer does not attempt, as scholastics such as Garrigou-Lagrange do,[1] to argue from the existence of finite being to the existence of infinite being syllogistically, using the principle of contradiction, but to help us to see God-and-the-creature-in-the-cosmological-relationship; we shall either grasp God in his creatures or we shall not grasp him at all. Farrer divides his arguments into two types: *usiological* arguments, based on finite beings as such, and *anthropological* arguments, based on the particular kind of finite beings that we ourselves are, namely human beings, men.[2] However, the function of his anthropological arguments is not ultimately to call our attention to characteristics which are possessed by men alone among finite beings, but, by putting

[1] *Dieu, son Existence et sa Nature* (1914).
[2] Cf. my discussion of Farrer in *Existence and Analogy*, ch. vii.

before us the type of finite beings with which we are most familiar (namely ourselves), to call our attention to a universal character of finite beings as such; otherwise he would seem to be suggesting, as I fear some existentialists do, that, while human beings need God as their creator, the existence of non-human beings needs no particular explanation. The long and extremely elaborate central section of his book is devoted to establishing the substantiality of the human self as basic to his argument, but this emphasis upon the self has a quite different function from that which it has in the systems of the transcendental Thomists. For Farrer the self is simply the *object* of knowledge with which we are best acquainted;[1] for the transcendental Thomists it is the *subject* whose yearning to overpass the horizon of finite being witnesses to its concern with the infinite. Mr H. P. Owen's position is much the same as Farrer's. 'Our knowledge of God', he writes, 'is direct in so far as it is non-discursive, but indirect

[1] In the preface to the second edition of *Finite and Infinite*, published in 1959, sixteen years after the first edition, Farrer offered the following reflections on his approach:

I told myself that I had to reconstruct the doctrine of substance; by which I meant, that I could not be content to derive the structure of being from the grammar of description; I must unearth it where it could be genuinely apprehended. And where was that? Initially, anyhow, in myself, self-disclosed as the subject of my acts.

My starting-point was correct, and my procedure materially sound; but my methodology was ill-considered. I talked of a genuine apprehension, where the structure of one's own existence was concerned. . . . What was I doing, in fact, but finding a certain abstract, artificial and diagrammatic account of my active being applicable or luminous? . . . The fatal gap between language and reality yawns again. . . .

Never mind, for the gap can be closed, and at the place where I proposed to close it. For language is otherwise related to our acts, than it is to anything else. Speech is the very form of our linguistic activity, and linguistic activity is but a specialised type of intentional action in general; which, as it were, attains to explicitness in the spoken mode. . . . Every grammar is a grammar of speech, but speech is human being, and uniquely revelatory of the rest of it. And as I trust I was able to show in this book, we both do and must think of the being of all things through an extension of our self-understanding.

The paragraph I have just written would require a treatise to expound [pp. ixf].

Farrer suggests reference to his Gifford Lectures, *Freedom of the Will*, especially chapters vii, ix and x. His later work *Faith and Speculation* (1967), although described (p. v) as purging out the old Aristotelian leaven from the voluntarist metaphysics of *Finite and Infinite*, does not give explicit attention to the point made above.

in so far as it is mediated. .... Its apprehension is always given in and with the Godhead's created signs; and among these signs [the mind's] own nature and operations are the most significant.'[1] But ultimately the self is in the same boat as everything else:

> It must be remembered that to say that apart from God the world is finally unintelligible is to say that *everything* is finally so. An ultimate query is placed against every fact, and every explanation of every fact. It is easy to lapse into thinking that because the cosmological question is a metaphysical one—because it comes after finite explanations have been given—it refers either to the world 'as a whole' or to the 'beginning of the world'. But it refers to everything at every moment. In itself everything at every moment is enigmatic.[2]

Thus for Owen neither the world as a whole nor the human self has any special ontological status as an index of the divine existence. The self is simply the finite being with which we are most immediately acquainted:

> The unitary and unifying self is not merely a postulate of reason; it is a reality of which each person is conscious. Certainly he is not conscious of it as an entity which is separable from its acts, and which can be known apart from them. Rather he is conscious of it as something which underlies, pervades, and unifies its acts. He is conscious of himself, not as a pure ego without empirical content, but as an ego qualified by this or that activity of thinking, willing, or feeling. .... Similarly we are aware of ourselves as both the subjects and the objects of causal activity.[3]

Now I do not wish in any way to quarrel with the stress which, for their own purposes, both Farrer and Owen place upon the human self as the datum for theistic argumentation. Furthermore, I agree with Owen that theistic argumentation is not 'rational demonstration', in the sense which he gives to that term, the very strict sense in which it covers ontological and syllogistic arguments. He certainly does not intend to suggest that belief in God is not to the fullest degree rational. Furthermore, I agree with him that God is known primarily by intuition or 'contuition', that, in the words already quoted, 'our

---

[1] *The Christian Knowledge of God*, p. 143.
[2] ibid., p. 87f.
[3] ibid., p. 129.

knowledge of God is direct in so far as it is non-discursive, but indirect in so far as it is mediated. . . . Its apprehension is always given in and with the Godhead's created signs.' I am, however, not so sure that 'among the signs [the mind's] own nature and operations are the most significant', though I admit that, starting from them, Owen builds up an extremely impressive argument. Just because I hold (as Owen does too) that God is the ground of existence of *every* finite being I prefer to start from beings that we know more objectively and at the same time less intimately than we know ourselves, beings of which the radically un-self-sufficient character can be directly apprehended in its true metaphysical status and is in no danger of confusion with those psychological states of insecurity and anxiety to which existentialists attribute direct ontological status but which psychologists interpret as manifesting a morbid rather than an authentic reaction to our cosmic environment. My starting-point will therefore be taken in any one of the extra-mental beings which we perceive through the mediation of our senses as a real thing, an *in-se*.

Now there are, I claim, two basic characteristics of such a being of which I can take note when I perceive it, though my awareness of them may be initially implicit. The first is its *reality*, the second its *contingency*. By its reality I mean its character as having concrete existence. Whatever causal relations it may have to other beings, it is not just a state of my mind or a figment of my imagination, nor is it an appearance or aspect of the absolute. It is something in itself, a being, an *ens*, an *in-se*. It confronts me, as the chestnut-tree confronted Antoine Roquentin in Sartre's novel *La Nausée*, in all its obstinate indifference to me and my desires, in its ontological self-centredness, its *densité*, as some of the French writers would say. Although in my perception of it, I can get it into my own mind and, as the scholastics say, can *become it* (not entitatively but intentionally), it has nevertheless a hard core of impenetrability and resistance; it *exists*. And this existence with which it confronts me is not just a bare, passive 'thereness', the 'existence' which in the symbolism of *Principia Mathematica* is denoted by an inverted capital letter E; it is energy, activity, the fundamental activity without which no other activity is possible. And, however much I can 'become it' in knowing it, its basic individuality resists me because *it is itself and not I.* I cannot absorb its entitative being into myself.

But, real as it is, it is also contingent. It is unnecessary; there is in its own nature neither reason nor cause why it should exist at all. Neither logic nor metaphysics would have been violated if it had not existed; *it might not and need not have been.* At this point a caution is needed to exclude possible verbal confusion. I am not here giving to the word 'contingent' the meaning which, as we have previously seen,[1] some writers have given it, as indicating simply that a being has not always existed or will not always exist; nor am I using the word 'necessary' to denote simply that a being has always existed and will always exist. In the sense in which I am using the words, 'contingent' might be rendered by 'non-self-existent' or 'non-self-explanatory', and 'necessary' by 'self-existent' or 'self-explanatory'. If it be objected that I am now confusing metaphysical existence with logical explanation, I shall reply that, when we are concerned not just with the properties or the behaviour of anything but with its existence, logic and metaphysics are inseparably connected. If we say that there is no logical necessity that a being should exist, we imply that, if it does exist, it must either be the ground of its own existence or have the ground of its existence in something else. And, in spite of the very telling criticisms which some writers such as Dr Kenny have levelled at St Thomas's formulation of the first three of his Five Ways, it seems to me that the Angelic Doctor quite validly makes this essential point.

Whether we should describe the passage from the recognition of contingent being to the affirmation of necessary being as an 'argument' seems to depend both on the precise sense which we give to the word 'argument' and on the circumstances of the particular case.[2] It is certainly possible for the mind to grasp

---

[1] Cf. p. 51 *supra.*

[2] Professor Peter Geach, in a very original and forthright essay on 'Causality and Creation' in his volume *God and the Soul* (1969), takes a somewhat different view from mine. He writes:

Some people have argued that we cannot demonstrate God's existence in the sense of proving it from premises, but only in the sense of pointing out, to a metaphysical eye that has somehow been got open, the dependence of finite being on the Infinite or of contingent being upon the Necessary Being. I cannot make any sense of this metaphysical vision; neither, I suspect could Aquinas—I find no mention of it in his

both the contingency of the material object of perception and the necessity of its ground in one mental act, a contuition of God-and-the-world-in-the-cosmological-relation. On the other hand, it may well be that before this act takes place some kind of interior or exterior dialogue is needed; however, the purpose of this dialogue is to enable the mind to grasp what the contingency of contingent being really is rather than to conduct it through a formal argument from contingent being to necessary being. We can, of course, formalise the process in a conditional syllogism in the *modus ponendo ponens*, as follows:

(Major premiss)   If there is contingent being, there is necessary being;
(Minor premiss)   But there is contingent being;
(Conclusion)   Therefore there is necessary being;

but this is really misleading. For it is only through perceiving contingent being that we can be brought to affirm the major premiss; and the minor premiss having thus been given, the

---

works. . . . Certainly this understanding of 'necessary' and 'contingent' is quite alien to his thought; for him contingent beings are beings liable to corrupt, break up, or the like, and necessary beings are beings with no such inner seeds of their own destruction; souls and angels belong to the latter class, and so, he thought, do the heavenly bodies. . . .

My own view is that at least the first three of the five 'ways' both were intended to be logically conclusive and may possibly, on suitable restatement, in fact be so. The general arguments against using deduction can, I think, be quite easily refuted; whether the first three 'ways' are valid can be determined only by considering them, not by including them in some blanket condemnation. But I am afraid logic is not yet in a position to pronounce decisively on their validity, because the formal logic of causal propositions, which was studied a little in the Middle Ages, has made no progress to speak of since then [p. 77].

Geach was writing before the publication of Dr Kenny's book *The Five Ways*, in which the desired detailed examination of St Thomas's 'ways' is made; as far as I know the intriguing reference to the formal logic of causal propositions has not been followed up, though Geach briefly touches on the matter in a review of Kenny's book (*Philosophical Quarterly*, XX (1970), pp. 311f). In his own book Geach writes: 'I shall say something by way of preliminary to a formal logic of causal propositions; may others push the work on' (p. 78). He denies that the objections to the idea of proving God's existence by deductive methods are valid, and writes as follows:

Whatever Kant and some neo-scholastics have thought, syllogistic is only a small fragment of logic; and objections that rule out a syllogistic proof of God's existence do not necessarily rule out deductive proofs.

It is in fact very easy to show that a valid deductive causal proof of

conclusion is given too.[1] Everything thus depends on our
capacity to apprehend the objects of our perception as they
really are, in their radical contingency. This is something which
appears to be extremely difficult for many modern people to do,
as compared with people of previous ages, but, as I have argued
elsewhere,[2] this would seem to be due far more to the atrophy
of a normal human faculty than to the emancipation of the
human mind from the shackles of superstition and confusion.
Of such a highly revered modern philosopher as Wittgenstein
it is recorded that, in a paper on ethics, 'he said that he sometimes had a certain experience which could best be described
by saying that "when I have it *I wonder at the existence of the world.*
And I am then inclined to use such phrases as 'How extraordinary that anything should exist' or 'How extraordinary

---

God's existence could not possibly be purely syllogistic. We might
suspect this, for such a proof could hardly avoid making essential use of
e.g. the fact that some causal relation is transitive and aliorelative, and
thus over-stepping the bounds of syllogistic. However, the matter admits
of formal proof ... If ... the universe of discourse involved in the
premisses is the familiar universe of mutable things, no syllogistic mani-
pulations can bring out a conclusion asserting the existence of something not belonging to that universe—an immutable God. You cannot
possibly defend both the exclusively syllogistic character of logic and the
deductive nature of natural theology; and the sooner this is realised the
better [pp. 79ff].

Geach then emphasises the qualitative difference made by the introduction of relative terms, such as 'cause of', into our reasoning and outlines the
logical form of a deductive argument for theism. 'The idea that creation
involves insuperable logical difficulties, as compared with ordinary making,'
he writes, 'thus turns out to be unfounded' [pp. 84f]. He sums up as follows:

There is a lot more hard logical work to be done in these areas: but I
hope I have said enough to show how empty the claim is that we know
enough about the logic of causal propositions to see that there can be no
causal deductive proof of God's existence. It may even be rational, as I
am inclined to think it is, to accept some such proof as valid before a
satisfactory logical analysis has been worked out: mathematical proofs
were valid and rationally acceptable long before logicians could give a
rigorous account of them. But especially in the face of scepticism, a
highly rigorous analysis of the proofs is an urgent task; and after all
some accepted ways of mathematicians have turned out not to be
logically acceptable. And a necessary preliminary to such analysis is a
fully developed logic of causal propositions, which we need anyhow to
deal with many non-theological reasonings [p. 85].

1 Cf. my *He Who Is*, pp. 72ff.
2 e.g. *The Christian Universe*, ch. iii.

that the world should exist.'"[1] In his early work the *Tractatus Logico-philosophicus*, he wrote 'Not *how* the world is, is the mystical, but *that* it is', though he added: 'For an answer which cannot be expressed the question too cannot be expressed.'[2] My own comment on this would be that, since the question *can* be expressed, the answer must be expressible too. Mr H. P. Owen well remarks that, although 'no Christian can accept Wittgenstein's previous statement that "God does not reveal himself *in* the world" ... the fact remains that he feels obliged to raise the cosmological question as one to which he is driven after his analysis of scientific language is complete.'[3]

At this point it may be useful to make a few remarks about Dr Milton K. Munitz's very original work *The Mystery of Existence*, in which he argues that 'Why is there a world?' or 'Why does the world exist?' is a perfectly proper question, but is an inherently unanswerable one. His basic assertion is that, owing to the all-inclusive character of the world, *to exist* is its fundamental activity.

> The term used to describe [the world's] mode of 'activity' should be irreducible to any other; it should not be replaceable by some other term. ... The mode of functioning that is appropriate to the world is—to exist. Instead of saying 'The world worlds' or 'The world carries on as a world', we say 'The world exists'. To exist is all that the world can do; this is what it is 'fit' to do; or—to use traditional terminology—the essence of the world is its existence.[4]

For Munitz, therefore, the world has very much the character that traditional theism ascribes to God. I cannot here give a full discussion of his argument, but it is noteworthy that for him the starting-point of the argument is the world as a whole and not simply any constituent of it. The reason which he gives for this is that if we simply ask 'Why does anything exist?' the various entities which 'anything' would cover are of vastly different types and so, presumably, is their 'existence': 'Would the term "anything", for example, include the number "three", or the

[1] N. Malcolm, *Ludwig Wittgenstein: A Memoir*, p. 70.
[2] op. cit., secc. 6.44, 6.5.
[3] *The Christian Knowledge of God*, p. 88.
[4] op. cit., p. 94.

possibility that my chair might collapse in the next five minutes, or the smile of the Cheshire cat?'[1] He does not consider the possibility of starting, as I have done, with the existence of extra-mental material beings, and it is not easy to see what would be his conclusion if he did. It is part of his argument that the world is the *totality* of finite being, and that what is true of it will therefore not be necessarily true of its parts. And the reason why he holds that the question 'Why does the world exist?' is unanswerable is that there is simply nothing else in terms of which the question could be answered. Clearly this objection will not hold against the question 'Why does this or that extra-mental material being exist?' Thus, his discussion, though it is extremely able and interesting, does not bear directly on the line which I have been following.[2]

Another American writer, Dr Wallace I. Matson, gives a widely ranging discussion of the various traditional arguments

[1] ibid., p. 45.

[2] Professor Peter Geach (*Three Philosophers* (1961), p. 111) interprets Aquinas as implicitly defining God as the Maker of *the world*. 'This notion,' he writes, 'as we shall see, raises problems; some theologians would wish to avoid them by proving God's existence from the existence of some casually chosen thing, not from the existence of the world. . . . I think they are wrong as to the feasibility of such a proof, and it is fairly easy to show that Aquinas would not have agreed with them.' Thus on the nature of the basic question of theism Geach (who clearly considers himself in agreement with Aquinas on this point) lines up with Munitz and not with me, though, unlike Munitz, he holds that the question can be answered and can indeed be answered affirmatively. It is, he holds, by treating the world as 'a great big object' that Aquinas locates God not as the first cause in a sequence of intra-mundane causes but as transcendent to the whole finite order. He writes:

> What would have appeared to Aquinas not worth discussion at all is the idea that, though we can speak without contradiction of the world as a whole, we cannot raise concerning it the sort of causal questions that we can raise concerning its parts. Why should we not raise them? It would be childish to say the world is too big for such questions to be reasonable; and to say the world is all-inclusive would be to beg the question—God would not be included in the world [p. 113].

Aquinas's approach, as Geach understands it, is clearly different from mine, but his discussion, which makes use not only of scholastic but also of modern logic, deserves more attention than it has received. He writes:

> Natural theology can show us some of the main attributes of God, and expose some of the grosser errors about him. But serious study of natural theology requires a rigorous philosophical training, for which few have leisure, talents, or inclination. Moreover, the divergent views of great philosophers who have pursued this study show that there is still risk of grave error [p. 125].

for the existence of God; he concludes that they are all unconvincing and that this is just as well, since, in his view, 'the essential and proper function of God in the higher religions is that of the ideal, something to be aspired to'.[1] However, he pays no attention to the form of cosmological argument which I have been developing, which asserts the possibility of a *contuition* of God with and in our apprehension of extra-mental material being. I certainly do not want to claim from such writers a support which they would not be willing to give, but, in view of the widespread assumption that ultimate questions about the universe and its constituents are invalid and are indeed only pseudo-questions, such works as these are not without significance. Indeed, the very fact on the strength of which positivists dismiss the ultimate questions as meaningless—namely that they do not admit of an answer in the framework of scientific explanations—is precisely the fact on the strength of which a theist will assert that they need an answer in non-scientific and metaphysical terms. It is at least striking that the theist is attacked not for being unable to answer certain ultimate questions, but for presuming to answer them when the positivist has refused to allow them even to be raised. One is tempted to enquire which of the two is refusing to face the facts.

I have been taken to task by Dr Munitz for saying that what is primarily needed for a philosophical approach to theism is that we should grasp finite beings as they really are, in their contingency and dependence. Why, he asks in effect, should I suppose that my grasp of them is more accurate than that of the atheist or of the positivist, who can see nothing in them other than themselves? This is the type of complaint that invites a *tu quoque*. Why should the atheist or the positivist suppose that his grasp of them is more accurate than mine? On which of us does the *onus probandi* lie? Academic mud-slinging, however, gets one nowhere; and I will only repeat that the theist, in developing the cosmological approach, does at least claim to give an answer to an intelligible and urgent question. In the last resort, and prescinding from the possibility of direct divine intervention, it seems to me that the primary need is the cultivation of the attitude of wonder. To quote what I have written elsewhere:

[1] *The Existence of God*, p. 248.

E

In order to penetrate the phenomenal skin of the perceptual world in order to grasp either physical objects or human persons or the God who is the creator and sustainer of both, we must learn to contemplate them with humility and wonder and not merely to record their sensible qualities and analyse their relationships. The element of wonder is of the highest importance here, and we must note that the wonder which is associated with contemplation does not consist of wondering what the answer to certain questions may be—for example, wondering how many electrons there are in the outer ring of the dysprosium atom—but simply of wondering *at* finite beings themselves.[1]

And my contention is that, if we do wonder at the things which we perceive, we are able to recognise both their own contingency and also the presence of necessary being as the only intelligible ground of their existence as concrete and contingent realities.

It is, of course, well known that many modern philosophers hold that the terms 'necessary' and 'contingent' (i.e. non-necessary) can be rightly predicated only of propositions and never of things, and they will add that the only necessary propositions are those that express logical tautologies. This objection seems to me to be purely irrelevant. The necessity which I am denying to the objects of my experience is not the logical necessity that belongs to a tautological proposition, and I do not

[1] *Words and Images*, p. 80. Dr H. D. Lewis has written as follows about this element of 'wonder':

The wonder which is basic to religion, and in which it begins, comes with the realisation, usually sharp and disrupting, that all existence as we know it stands in a relation of dependence to some absolute or unconditioned being of which we can know nothing directly beyond this intuition of its unconditioned nature as the source of all other reality....

I believe that, in fact, it lies in the background of most of our thinking, although more dimly in lives that have a secure routine of pleasing preoccupation with features of present existence, as happens often in civilised communities. ... But however hard to disentangle from the folds of the anthropomorphic garb in which it appears, it is only with some dawning in the minds of men of this realisation of all existence being rooted in unconditioned being and a sense, humbling and elated at the same time and in many ways akin to aesthetic joy, of the complete but unexpected appropriateness by which the world comes, with a peculiar inevitability of its own, to have a sustaining wholeness, that religion proper begins—this is the wonder that gives it birth, having as its core some awareness of the beyondness we name the transcendent [*Our Experience of God*, pp. 107f].

think that anyone (except perhaps some supporters of the ontological argument) ever supposed that it was. The contingency
of the objects of our experience has nothing whatever to do with
the question whether the predicate of a proposition is logically
contained in the subject. This is why I hold, with Fr Norris
Clarke, that theistic argumentation rests not simply on the
principle of contradiction (a logical principle) but on the principle of sufficient reason (a metaphysical one). When I ask why
any particular being exists I am not led to do so because I cannot derive the existence of the object from its definition; I should
never expect to do that in any case. I wonder why it exists, because my immediate apprehension of it is of something which
need not be there; and this 'need not' is a metaphysical, not a
logical, 'need not'. That there are certain analogies between
logical and metaphysical entities is not surprising, for we can
hardly suppose that a world might be metaphysically existent
and logically incoherent, but this provides no ground for denying the metaphysical relevance of the notions of contingency
and necessity.

It will not do to dismiss this approach, as I have heard it
dismissed by a very well-known philosopher who should have
known better, by saying that, if you explain the world by saying
that God made it, you are then left with the question 'Who made
God?' For the theistic argument, whether it is good or bad, is
simply that the only way to explain the existence of being that
is *not* self-existent is to postulate the existence of being that *is*
self-existent; and it is clearly ridiculous to ask for an explanation
of the existence of that which is self-existent. The concept of self-
existent being may indeed be a puzzling one. We may find it
difficult or impossible to think what it is like, but the argument
does not require us to do this. We may indeed find it strange
that there should be such a thing as self-existent being, though
if our capacity for wonder is functioning properly we shall see
that what is really strange is that there should be anything else.
This is perhaps the truth behind the assertion of Hartshorne
and Findlay that the existence of God is either necessary or
impossible.[1] The ontological argument cannot decide between
these alternatives; it takes the concrete existence of contingent
being to do that.

[1] Cf. p. 53 *supra*.

In claiming that we can apprehend the existence of necessary being in our wondering apprehension of contingent being we may appear to have reached a very minimal conclusion. It is, however, backed up by St Thomas's assertion that we do not know *what* God is, but only *what* he is *not* and *how* his creatures are related to him.[1] Might not some other approach have paid higher dividends? That may well be so, and I would repeat once more that, in adopting one particular approach, I have not either explicitly or implicitly ruled out others. I have, however, had one special reason for following this line of argument. Modern philosophers of the dominant school of linguistic empiricism have maintained that it is impossible for us to know anything other than the finite world and its constituents, and indeed that the very notion of a transcendent realm is incoherent or meaningless. From the opposite angle a very influential school of theologians have asserted that reason and our other natural powers cannot give us any genuine knowledge of God and that we can know him, if at all, only by his intervention *ad hoc* and *ad hominem* in revelatory acts which are entirely uncoordinated with any of our natural powers; man has no point of contact, no *Anknüpsfungspunkt*, with the divine. It has therefore seemed worth while to enquire whether there is any feature of the world which provides such a point of contact. That its size is minimal—and does not Euclid tell us that a point has position but not magnitude?—will not matter; this can be dealt with later. The question is whether it exists at all. And I have argued that such a point of contact is in fact to be found in the sheer element of contingency in all the beings which our senses disclose to us. It is indeed minimal, but it is also universal. It locates the finite world and all its constituents on a foundation of self-existent being on which they are themselves totally dependent. What this relation between the world and its transcendent ground implies for either or for both we must go on to enquire.

When, in the *Summa Theologiae*, St Thomas has, as he claims, demonstrated the existence of a being which, in his own words, 'everyone understands to be God'[2]—when, that is, he has argued

---

[1] *S.c.G.*, I, xxx; cf. *S.Th.*, I, xii, 12.
[2] *S. Th.*, I, ii, 3. In a recent article on 'Immanent Transcendence' (*Religious Studies*, VI (1970), pp. 89ff) Dr Leslie Stevenson has argued that cosmological arguments for theism as usually stated involve a logical fallacy, in

that the world of our experience has a transcendent self-existent ground—he goes on to argue, in the next nine questions, that this self-existent being is simple, perfect, good, infinite, immutable, eternal and one. This may at first sight be surprising in an author who, as we have seen, also tells us that we do not know what God is, but only that he is and how he is related to his creatures. The answer must be, that, in St Thomas's view, the attributes just listed, impressive and august as they are, do not in fact state 'what God is' but only 'how he is related to his creatures'. This assertion will be less puzzling if we recall that critics have often complained that the God of the philosophers, and especially the God of the Thomist philosophers, is a very austere and frigid deity when compared with the God and Father of Jesus Christ. And indeed the passages in which the Angelic Doctor argues that God is simple, perfect, good and all the rest do not, by the very place which they hold in his treatise, profess to do more than provide a certain explicitation or 'unpacking'—a very partial unpacking at that—of what is involved in the affirmation of the existence of a transcendent self-existent ground of contingent being. That this is very limited and tenuous will not worry St Thomas, for whom revelation gives us a knowledge, and indeed a self-communication, of God that reason and our other natural powers cannot achieve. I shall not follow through St Thomas's discussion in detail, but shall merely put the question whether there is anything that we can say about the transcendent self-existent ground of contingent being beyond the bare fact that it is contingent being's transcendent self-existent ground? I suggest that we can say this at least, that it must possess the attributes of thought, will and power, and

---

that they pass illicitly from the assertion that every finite being has a transcendent ground to the assertion that all finite beings have the *same* transcendent ground (I am stating his objection in my words, not in his). I think that this objection, taken simply in itself and without reference to any further considerations, is valid. It might, however, be replied (1) that the supposition that there are two or more self-existent beings each of which is the transcendent cause of a different set of finite beings (or perhaps different sets of which are the transcendent causes of different sets of finite beings) leaves their own co-existence unexplained, (2) that the contuition of finite beings with their transcendent cause manifests the latter as being absolutely ultimate and not as one who shares his ultimacy with others. Such replies as these receive welcome support from considerations of the nature of morality (Cf. H. P. Owen's impressive work *The Moral Argument for Christian Theism*) and from revelation.

that it must possess these in a supereminent degree. For to maintain contingent being in existence involves a decision that there shall be contingent being and what kind of contingent being there shall be; and this implies what, however analogically, we can validly describe as an activity of thinking and willing. And the bringing of this decision into effect implies the exercise of what, however analogically, we can validly describe as an exercise of supreme power. Taken together, these attributes of thought, will and power justify us in describing the transcendent self-existent being as personal and in applying to it the personal pronoun 'he'. We would certainly seem to be justified in describing him as omnipotent, if we remember that the basic meaning of 'omnipotent' is 'powerful over everything in a supreme degree', for we could hardly conceive a higher degree of power than is exemplified in giving to contingent beings not merely this, that or the other quality but their very existence. (St Thomas himself tells us that God cannot do what is self-contradictory or inconsistent with his own nature, though he neatly adds that 'it is better to say that such things cannot be done than that God cannot do them'[1].) Whether we can convincingly go on, as St Thomas does, to argue that this personal God is good and that he is, not only numerically but also constitutionally, one I shall not consider here, nor is it very important in the last resort to anyone who believes that our rational enquiry about God is supplemented or accompanied by God's movement towards us in revelation. What I have been concerned to do is to find the chink in the armour of naturalistic atheism through which the spear of theism can find entry. That the chink is tiny does not matter; it can be enlarged later on. To vary the metaphor, it is the first step that counts. My contention is that the sheer contingency of the objects of our experience demands explanation in terms of transcendent self-existent being, and I am fortified in this conviction by the fact that the opponents of theism do not offer an alternative answer but contrive excuses for evading the question. It may, however, be useful to pay attention at this point to one commonly urged objection, for in answering it we shall further clarify the theistic position. This is the objection that, by the theist's own admission, God and his creatures are altogether different from each

[1] *S. Th.*, I, xxv, 3c.

other and that it would seem to follow from this that no term which can be applied to creatures can, even in a supreme degree, be intelligibly applied to God. If, for example, we take account of God's transcendence by saying not merely that he is good but that he is infinitely or self-existently good, does not the qualifying adverb 'infinitely' or 'self-existently' demolish any intelligibility that was previously possessed by the epithet 'good'? To answer this it is necessary not merely to affirm that God and his creatures are altogether different from each other but to consider what that difference is. And when we do consider this we shall see that, so far from isolating God and his creatures from each other, their difference paradoxically places them in the most intimate relation.

For, when we say that the fundamental difference between God and creatures is that God is self-existent while creatures are non-self-existent, we are not merely making a logical or semantic comparison between the two concepts of self-existence and non-self-existence. We are implying that, because the creatures in spite of their non-self-existence do in fact exist, they are the objects of the incessant creative activity of the self-existent God. This creative relationship is, of course, entirely asymmetrical; they depend on him, and not he on them. Some of the implications of this fact and some of the problems that it raises are discussed at length in my book *Existence and Analogy* and I have summarised the more recent treatments of the doctrine of analogy in the introductory essay to the revised edition of my earlier work *He Who Is*. For our present purpose I will merely quote the following passage:

It is vital to the whole position which I have been maintaining to insist that in natural theology we are not merely instituting comparisons between two orders of concepts but considering created and uncreated being as the former actually exists in dependence on the latter. That is to say, we are not merely concerned with the question 'How can an infinite, necessary and immutable Being be described in terms that are derived from the finite, contingent and mutable world?' but with a question that is anterior to this and without which this cannot be properly discussed at all, namely 'How is the possibility of our applying to the infinite Being terms that are derived from the finite order conditioned by the fact that the finite order is dependent for its very existence on the fiat of the infinite and self-existent Being?'[1]

These words were written in 1949 and I would wish to modify them in only one detail, in accordance with a point which I have made earlier in these lectures when discussing the question of Theology and Language.[2] I there asserted that one is already loading the question if one puts it in the form 'How can terms which in their normal and natural application refer to finite beings refer analogically to God?' and I suggested that the primary datum is that the terms apply *both* to finite beings and to God and that the relevant question is how this dual application is to be explained. Furthermore, I anticipated the argument of the present chapter by saying that the explanation is that God and finite beings are in a definite causal relation. 'Only the notion of a God who is related to the world—and who is related to it in a very particular way—can make the fact of this dual applicability of terms intelligible.' The justification of this assertion will, I trust, now be clear. God is supreme thought, will and power; and it is because he establishes his creatures in existence by exercising his will and power in accordance with his thought that they embody, in their infinitely lower mode of dependent being, the perfections which in him are self-existent and unlimited. God is therefore really manifested in his creatures, limited, obscure and mysterious as that manifestation is. It is this ontological relation between God and his creatures that makes it possible for both to be spoken of in the same language. In Farrer's phrase, we know God-and-the-creatures-in-the-cosmological-relation; and it is because of this that we can speak of them in the same breath.

Thus, to summarise the discussion of the present lecture, I will reaffirm that there are solid rational grounds, based on our perception of extra-mental material beings, for holding that they owe their existence to the incessant creative activity of transcendent self-existent being, in which thought, will and power are combined to a supereminent degree and which therefore is properly to be described as personal and, without distorting the traditional use of the term, as God. I have stressed in addition that many theists would say that the very limited

[1] *Existence and Analogy*, p. 116.
[2] Cf. p. 33 *supra*.

information about God which is acquired in this way is supplemented by revelation, that is to say by a deliberate self-communication by God to men. Such a self-communication may indeed be expected on the part of a personal God, though just because he is personal its occasions and its modes cannot be predicted; it will be given 'at sundry times and in divers manners'. Furthermore, it may well be doubted whether such self-revealing activity will be altogether absent from any occasion in which a man contemplates God's creatures in such a way as to discern his presence in them as their creator; it is difficult to suppose that a personal God will restrain himself as a purely passive and quasi-inanimate object for human inspection. If on certain occasions he appears so to restrain himself, this will be due to his own deliberate choice. There are such occasions in the lives of most believers, and experts in the spiritual life assure us that it is good for us that this is so. Dr John Macquarrie has even suggested that something like this dark night of the soul may be a phenomenon in the lives of human societies and cultures no less than in those of individual believers.[1] If this is true, it merely serves to emphasise that a personal God will make himself known to men as and when he sees fit. He will be as active in concealing himself as in openly manifesting himself. It will thus follow that the purely natural knowledge of God as the transcendent ground of finite beings, which has been the subject of this lecture, is only one element in the experience in which we apprehend God through his creatures. This is indeed what I suggested at the beginning of the first of these lectures,[2] when I quoted Dom John Chapman's assertion of the inevitably abstract character of natural theology. Nevertheless, a great deal is to be learnt by considering this particular element by itself; in particular such consideration can help to assure us that religious experience is not a purely psychological phenomenon having no object outside the mind of the experient, but is a genuine knowledge of a real and transcendent divine being. Provided that we remember that abstractions are abstractions, they can be of the greatest use in aiding our thinking about concrete reality. And when all is said and done concreteness is itself an abstraction; only the concrete is concrete.

[1] *Principles of Christian Theology*, p. 148.
[2] p. 1 *supra*.

CHAPTER EIGHT

BEING AND TRUTH

To be, or not to be : that is the question.
—William Shakespeare, *Hamlet*, III, i.

I PROPOSE AT this point to interrupt the steady course of my exposition in order to examine an approach to religious belief which has received widespread attention during the last few years and which, if it was adopted, would undermine not only traditional theism but also any attempt to construct a systematic and reasoned metaphysic. This is the approach which was introduced by Dr Leslie Dewart in 1967 in his moderately sized book *The Future of Belief* and was elaborated two years later in a massive work entitled *The Foundations of Belief*. The former book was described by Dr Harvey Cox, in words which the publishers quoted in their banner, as a mature, highly erudite and utterly radical book which could be epoch-making. The fact that it urged, in the name of Catholic Christianity, nothing less than the abandonment of nineteen centuries of Christian thought makes the question of its truth or falsehood of some importance. In the preface to the second work Dr Dewart wrote as follows:

> In *The Future of Belief* I addressed myself to the question: can the Christian faith be deemed truly to develop and unequivocally to evolve . . . even if it is assumed that this faith is *supernatural* and that its object is *revealed*? The question to which I address myself here, however, is more fundamental yet: can the Christian faith be said truly to develop and unequivocally to evolve, on the assumption that this faith is *true* and that its object is *real*? . . . My earlier publication was synecdochically devoted, in effect, to the future of *Christian* belief, whereas the present one is elliptically concerned with the foundations of *religious* belief.[1]

[1] *The Foundations of Belief*, pp. 12f.

Nevertheless, the former work contains enough about religion in general to make its discussion not irrelevant to the special concerns of a Gifford Lecturer.

Dr Dewart begins by defining his subject as 'the problem of integrating Christian theistic belief with the everyday experience of contemporary man,'[1] and I agree with him that this is among the most fundamental theoretical problems which challenge Christianity in the present age. He rightly sees this as much more than a problem in public relations. Nevertheless, he is entirely uncritical in his acceptance of 'contemporary experience' as the norm which is to be applied; it is 'the mode of consciousness which mankind, if not as a whole at least in respect of our own civilisation constituting man's cultural vanguard, has reached as a result of its historical and evolutionary development,' and to demand any renunciation of this mode of consciousness would be to show 'an unrealistic and misguided lack of appreciation of the nature of man—if not also of that of the Christian faith'.[2] This involves much more than *aggiornamento* on the part of the Church: 'it is the contemporary experience *as a whole* that is incongruous with Christian belief *as a whole*.'[3] And it must be stressed, as the basic assumption of Dewart's discussion, that there is no question of altering or criticising 'contemporary experience'; that is the norm by which the Church and the Faith must themselves be judged. To dispute this would be to fly in the face of historical necessity. We must be quite clear about this at the start.

When enquiry is made as to how this condition of incongruity has arisen, a simple answer is given; it is because the Church has hung on to Hellenistic categories of thought and these are not the categories of thought of the present day. When we go on to ask what must take their place, the answer is that we must adopt an existentialist–phenomenological outlook, and Dewart expounds this in detail. The three points of his programme are thus contemporaneanism, dehellenisation and phenomenological existentialism.

Now I wish to make it plain that I am just as concerned as Dewart is with the problem of integrating Christian theistic

---

[1] *The Future of Belief: Theism in a World Come of Age*, p. 7.
[2] ibid., pp. 9, 10.
[3] ibid., p. 17.

belief with the everyday experience of contemporary man, though I would prefer to describe it as the problem of integrating the everyday experience of contemporary man with Christian theistic belief. And in saying this I do not wish to suggest that the forms in which Christian belief has been expressed in the past, in the realms alike of thought, of liturgy and of social action, need no development and adjustment if it is to be relevant to the situation of contemporary man. I believe that the task is in fact much more difficult and needs to be more radical (in the proper sense of that word) than Dewart himself recognises. For to Dewart there is only one adjustment that needs to be made, namely the adjustment of the Christian religion to the contemporary world, the latter being taken as exempt from criticism. As I see the matter there are three, not just two, things that need to be brought together, namely the Christian religion itself, its traditional forms of expression and the contemporary world; and the last two of these need to be criticised in the light of the first. This raises problems that are difficult enough in all conscience, and I do not claim to have cut-and-dried answers to them. Not the least of these is the problem of the relation of the Christian religion itself—the revealed thing given by God in Christ to the Church—to the expression of it in a given cultural setting and cultural epoch. It is perhaps fortunate that that problem falls outside the scope of Gifford Lectures. It does, however, seem to me to be clear that it is one of the duties of any religion claiming a basis in the transcendent order of reality—a duty which, alas, religious bodies have often failed adequately to perform—to criticise and assess the assumptions, aims and methods of contemporary society. What shocks me most about most of our so-called radical thinkers is their sheer social conformity, though it is the last thing of which they conceive themselves to be guilty. Ready though they are to condemn the Church for its social conformity in the past—about which we can in any case do nothing—they swallow hook, line and sinker the outlooks of their contemporaries. Some of Harvey Cox's most perceptive critics—not necessarily Christian critics at that[1]—have seen that his glorification of 'technopolis' is basically the adornment with a Christian label of the American way of life. Dewart is more subtle, but his outlook is much the

---

[1] Cf. the Jewish writer Richard L. Rubinstein in *The Secular City Debate*.

same. If we enquire how it is that such an obviously intelligent and committed Catholic has fallen into this kind of relativism, we shall see that it is at least partly due to the philosophical doctrine which he has adopted, according to which truth is itself a historically conditioned concept. This stands out very clearly in what might otherwise have been an extremely valuable discussion of Marxism. He pertinently observes that atheism as a cultural phenomenon is indigenous to Christian societies, and we might expect that he would explain this, when it was not due to less respectable causes, as at least partly due to the failure of Christians to live in accordance with their professed beliefs. On the contrary, he sees it as resulting from the fact (for such he holds it to be) that for Christianity it is not either belief or disbelief that really matters but a conditional attitude to both. 'I recall it', he writes, 'in confirmation of the conditional nature of Christian belief and its relativity to disbelief. ... In the Judaeo-Christian tradition ... the steady purification of the concept of God has increasingly facilitated the emergence of that peculiar disbelief which, being born of the same religious experience as belief, can fairly be called—in contradistinction to the atheism born of inconsiderateness, unreflectiveness, inexperience, or sheer obstinacy in refusing to admit the possibility of God—*religious atheism*.'[1] Both Christianity and Marxism, Dewart tells us, share a relative atheism, but that of Marxism is relative to its humanism while that of Christianity is relative to its theism. Dewart sees, indeed, some problems in his view of the nature of Christian theism:

> From the relative nature of Christian theism follows its aptitude for development, readjustment and cultural polymorphism. It is not given once for all. It is, therefore, dynamic, evolving and self-transforming. But how could Christian theism be all these things and nevertheless *true*?[2]

The answer which he gives to this question is, as we shall see, that truth itself is changing and relative.

At this point Dewart plunges into a discussion of the development of Christian dogma. 'The fact of which we have recently become aware', he writes, 'is not that Christian doctrine has begun to develop in recent times, but that it has *always* existed

[1] *The Future* . . ., p. 75.
[2] ibid., p. 76.

in a process of development. It is only the awareness of this fact that is new.'[1] His explanation of this is simply that human awareness in general has become aware of its own historicity and evolutionary nature, and the Church is sharing in this contemporary experience, though lamentably lagging behind because of its attachments to the past. It is here that he introduces his phenomenological existentialism, with its new doctrine of the nature of knowledge. From early Greece to early modern times human thought—and this means especially Christian thought—was dominated by the belief that 'the psychism of the animal consists in the intentional appropriation ("intussusception") of beings other than itself (cognition), and in the correlative intentional self-disposition of itself towards beings other than itself (appetition).'[2] The difference between man and the lower animals was held to be that man grasps an intelligible object immaterially instead of a merely sensible object materially. In contrast, what Dewart describes as 'contemporary thought' (which appears to exclude not only modern scholastics but linguistic empiricists and indeed everyone except existentialists and phenomenologists) sees the difference between man and animals as transcending the order of mere knowledge altogether. For man, what is primary is consciousness; this, 'though it objectifies the self in the same manner as it objectifies the non-self, gives us an awareness of a being which does not merely *happen* to be a self; rather, what is typical of it is that it produces this experience: *myself*, that is *my self's be-ing*.'[3] I shall not attempt here to discuss the validity of Dewart's epistemology as such; that has been done both sympathetically and critically by Dr Elmar Kremer in *The Ecumenist*.[4] I am, however, concerned with its consequences. One of these is that truth is purely relative to man's state of development, another is that it is conditioned by his cultural and social context. 'Truth', we are told, 'is not the adequacy of our representative operations, but the adequacy of our conscious existence.'[5] 'The nature of

[1] ibid., p. 78.
[2] ibid., p. 80.
[3] ibid., p. 82.
[4] Vol. V (1967), pp. 25ff. Cf. Hugo Meynell, 'Shaking the Foundations', *Month* 2nd N.S. I (1970), pp. 150ff and the reply by Michael Simpson, S.J., 'Settling the Foundations', ibid., pp. 336ff.
[5] *The Future . . .*, p. 92.

truth does not merely permit truth to develop, but indeed requires that it do so. For truth itself consists in a certain intensive
development of man's original relation to reality given by the
fact that, being a reality, he participates in being. ... Hence
the only valid 'criterion' of truth is that it create the possibility
of more truth.'[1] Dewart is emphatic that this involves something
more than the translation of truth into new linguistic and conceptual forms or the acquisition of a deeper insight into truth
already possessed or the apprehension of more truth. It is truth
itself that changes, that is historically and socially conditioned,
so that what is true at one time and in one context will not be
true at another. It is in this sense that Dewart holds that Christian dogma can develop, and it is for this reason that he demands the dehellenisation of dogma. For what was wrong with
the traditional 'hellenised' Christian dogma was not merely
that it was conceived and expressed in forms that are obsolete
and unevocative to present-day people; it was that its notion of
truth was perverted.

I do not want to pick a quarrel with existentialism as such or
with any particular type of it; it may have much to teach us. I do,
however, wish very seriously to question Dewart's notion of
truth, and this for several reasons.

In the first place, this view of truth is inherently self-
destructive. As Dr Armand Maurer wrote in *The Ecumenist*:

> The doctrine of the historicity of truth espoused by [Dewart's]
> book faces the further difficulty that, if it is true, it must have
> come into existence as a part of man's process of self-awareness
> and self-making, and hence it is relative to his situation in a
> certain moment of history. Like all truths, it must be histori-
> cally relative, not timeless and supracultural. And yet the doc-
> trine says more than this; it pretends to be a philosophical truth
> valid for all times and cultures. In short, total historisation is
> not tenable, for the doctrine of historicity cannot be formu-
> lated without denying itself.[2]

Thus Dewart's view of truth makes all discussion futile, for if it
is true no reasons can be advanced or rebutted in favour of it or
of anything else. It is conceivable that we need to develop a new
approach to philosophical problems which will be more dynamic

[1] ibid., p. 111.
[2] no. cit., p. 25.

than traditional scholasticism and will give a more central
place to the notion of personality; indeed I think that this is so.
But if once we start to tamper with the idea of truth itself,
philosophising, like every other intellectual activity, is reduced
to mere parrot-talk.

Secondly, I find it very difficult to think that existentialism of
Dewart's type is really the philosophy for the present age. Certainly, not many English-speaking philosophers would think so.
I am as ready as anyone to maintain that philosophy has more
to do than simply to clarify,[1] but the imprecision and impression-
ism of the more philosophical parts of Dewart's book almost send
me screaming into the arms of the linguistic analysts. It is
difficult to imagine scientists, technologists or educated non-
specialists making very much of it. Dewart's own view of truth
makes it impossible, as we have seen, to give reasons for supposing that his philosophy is true, and one would be inviting him
to violate his own principles if one asked him to give *reasons* why
it should be congenial to contemporary man. One might, however, have expected him to make the alleged congeniality
apparent; as Wittgenstein might have said, to *show* what cannot
be *proved*. This he simply fails to do.

It is important to notice that Dewart does not blame traditional Christian thought, as Karl Barth might have blamed it,
for expressing itself in philosophical terms, but for expressing
itself in terms of the *wrong* philosophy. It was the great fault of
Hellenism, Scholasticism or Thomism (the three terms are,
surprisingly, used as more or less equivalent, and Thomism is
accused of holding a good many views that St Thomas certainly
did not hold) that it adopted a Parmenidean doctrine of the
identity of being and intelligibility. Dewart's own position (for
which, as I have said, no grounds are or, on his own principles,
could be urged) is expressed as follows:

> If reality is not assumed to be constituted by intelligibility—or
> by any (possible or actual) relation to mind—reality can no
> longer be identified with that-which-is (which is the usual
> meaning of *being, ens*). To be sure, reality will still be as a matter
> of fact intelligible. But its intelligibility will now be a matter of
> *fact*, not of *necessity*. Being is intelligible, but not *as such*. Things
> can be understood, and can be conceived as being, because if

[1] Cf. the symposium edited by Professor H. D. Lewis, *Clarity is not Enough*.

they in fact exist they will also have a history—and this history makes them relatable to mind. Essences, therefore, what things are, are always created, whether created by another or self-created (in the case of consciousness).[1]

I think most readers will feel that something more than Dewart's affirmation is needed before they accept the doctrine that being is intelligible by sheer accident, but his own philosophy will preclude him from offering any reasons for his belief. It is, however, not surprising that he goes on to assert that God should not be conceived as a being.

He makes it plain that this last assertion is not to be understood as meaning that God is not a being as other beings are, that God is *above being* or is *super-being*, in the sense in which the pseudo-Areopagite, for example, might have said this. (After all, the pseudo-Areopagite was steeped in Hellenism!) 'What it means', he writes, 'is literally what it says, that God is not a being at all. . . . Unless we retain the Greek philosophical outlook, the ordinary facts of Christian experience are sufficient to establish that we do *experience* God, but that we do not experience him as *being*. This proposition should be obvious and commonplace to the philosophically unprejudiced Christian believer. In fact, since it is a matter of simple observation it should be one of the starting-points of a Christian philosophical enquiry that would rise to the empirical level of methodology to which philosophy has been developed in our time.'[2] In other words, nothing is real except as we experience it, and it is obvious that we experience God. I find it very difficult to think that so simple an apologetic as this is going to impress a world that, as Dewart assures us, has at last 'come of age'.

There is a great deal in this first book of Dr Dewart's that is penetrating and enlightening and that does not need his very questionable philosophy for its expression. With the reflections which he goes on to make about the present condition and future prospects of the Roman Catholic Church we are not concerned here. The real weakness of the book, in my opinion, derives from the unmitigated phenomenological existentialism which he accepts as providing the ultimate ground of Christian theism. I do not think it is capable of doing the job which he

[1] *The Future* . . ., p. 174.
[2] ibid., p. 175.

lays upon it and I do not think that it has any particular appeal to either the scientific experts or to people in general in the technological age in which we live. It is, after all, a common-place among historians of science that the hellenistic outlook was one of the determining factors in the development of modern science and that it is more than a coincidence that science came to birth in the European setting and not in that of India or China, highly civilised as those societies were. A. N. Whitehead in a famous passage described 'the inexpugnable belief that every detailed occurrence can be correlated with its antecedents in a perfectly definite manner, exemplifying general principles' as 'the greatest contribution of medievalism to the formation of the scientific movement' and asserted that 'it must come from the medieval insistence on the rationality of God, conceived as with the personal energy of Jehovah and with the rationality of a Greek philosopher.'[1] It is perhaps interesting to notice that Dr John Macquarrie, who shares with Dewart and myself an admiration for Fr Karl Rahner and who has explored as thoroughly as any recent theological writer the resources of existentialism as a medium of Christian understanding, has come to stress the necessity that the existentialist and phenom-enological standpoint should be balanced by, and integrated with, a genuinely ontological element.

Dewart's second work, *The Foundations of Belief*, claims, as I have said, to carry his thesis from a Christian setting to that of religion in general. While immensely longer, it does not seem to add anything much to the main themes of the earlier book, though it does to some extent clarify them. We are told afresh that we must get rid of the idea that truth consists in the corres-pondence of thought with being, and we are explicitly told that God must be thought of not as being but as reality. This process is again described as 'dehellenisation', and it must be stressed that in Dewart's usage both 'true' and 'real' have very different meanings from those which 'hellenisation' had given them, though precisely what these new meanings are it is not alto-gether easy to discover.

To begin at the end, it is argued in Appendix 2 that neither the Neo-Thomism exemplified by Maritain and Gilson nor the 'transcendental Thomism' of Maréchal, Marc, Lotz, Karl

[1] *Science and the Modern World*, ch. i.

Rahner, Coreth and Lonergan will serve Dewart's purpose. First they are not really Thomism (though Dewart would readily forgive them for that) and secondly they cling to the discarded notion of truth. It is unfortunate that Dewart was apparently unable to refer to a long criticism by Bernard Lonergan of his earlier work,[1] for Lonergan is as anxious as he to dehellenise dogma, though not to understand dehellenisation in the same way. This article disposes once and for all of the impression that was apparently prevalent at one time in some circles that Lonergan is fundamentally in agreement with Dewart.

Dewart states explicitly that 'the concept of consciousness is not only more adequate than the concept of knowledge: it is also more comprehensive'.[2] He repudiates both 'the epistemological position that truth is the adequation of the mind to things and . . . the metaphysical position that being is intelligible as such'.[3] Dewart is willing to admit that 'when knowledge is true it is perfectly possible truly to describe the relation of the mind to being as one of conformity',[4] but he is also convinced that this is not what makes it true. (In any case, the phrase 'when know-ledge is true' leaves us wondering what 'untrue knowledge' would be like!) 'Truth and falsity', we are told, 'thus pertain neither to subject as such nor to object as such. They pertain to the relation in which we render ourselves present to ourselves and to the world. In a word, they belong to consciousness.'[5]

And again:

> Truth is, thus, the meaningfulness of the facts. We might even say that truth is the meaning of the facts, provided this were not construed as if the meaning were in the facts. Truth is the mind's 'making out' the meaning of the facts; it is making the facts to have meaning. Truth is not the meaning found within the facts; truth is the meaning which is put upon the facts because they are understood.
>
> Although the reality of the relation of truth is not given *in any manner* [italicisation mine] by the reality of the object of know-

[1] 'The Dehellenisation of Dogma', *Theological Studies*, XXVIII (1967), pp. 336ff.
[2] *The Foundations* . . ., p. 243.
[3] ibid., p. 246.
[4] ibid., p. 317.
[5] ibid., p. 270.

ledge, nevertheless, the relation of truth is the relation of consciousness [not intelligence, my comment] to its object, being.[1]

Now what Dewart calls 'knowledge' is, no doubt, very important,
though I should, I think, disagree with him as to how it is to be
obtained, but I cannot see how we can afford to dispense with
knowledge in the common or garden sense of the correspondence of thought with thing. Dewart's book, of over five hundred pages, contains, I suppose, several thousand sentences in
the indicative mood, all of which he presumably wishes the
reader to accept; does he hold that the thoughts which they
express correspond with reality or not? If they do not correspond with reality, does he (a) wish and (b) expect us to accept
them or not? I raised this point (though I was not the only
critic who raised it) in connection with Dewart's earlier book.
He nowhere attempts to answer it, and he has apparently not
even understood it. For he complains[2] that I ascribed to him
the claim to possess an understanding of the nature of truth
which is final, conclusive and irreformable. The precise opposite is the case. What I criticised him for was holding a view of
truth which made it impossible for him on his own principles
to assert consistently that anything that he said conformed to
reality. There is, in fact, much in both books which I should be
very glad to accept; what I cannot see is why, on his own principles, he should expect me to accept it. He modestly remarks:
'If my understanding of the nature of truth is at all correct, it
will be superseded, it will be improved upon. Its very truth will
contribute to its supersession; and it will be superseded precisely
because it enjoyed a measure of truth.'[3] The question which I
want to put to him here is: are these sentences true, and if so
in what sense of truth? And this question is provoked by every
statement in his book. Fr F. C. Copleston has dealt as mildly as
possible with Dewart's view of the nature of truth,[4] but he has
felt obliged to remark: 'Statements such as "truth is the orientation of the mind towards that condition which it does not have,
namely truth"[5] are somewhat odd. And I cannot help feeling

[1] ibid., p. 299.
[2] ibid., p. 303.
[3] ibid.
[4] *Clergy Review*, LV (1970), pp. 298ff.
[5] *The Foundations . . .*, p. 328.

that some painstaking logical analysis would help to clarify the situation and facilitate discussion.'

The importance of this for our present purpose is that there is an evident and close connection between Dewart's doctrine of truth and his doctrine of God.

The human intellect [he announces] has developed itself to the point where it has found it necessary to redefine itself, its consciousness and the object of its consciousness. Does it not seem *prima facie* likely that man should also redefine the object of belief? In the light of this hypothesis, the question I have asked is legitimate. It means: does the interpretation of religious experience, on the assumption of the philosophical foundations of contemporary Hellenic-Western thought, not require us to reconceptualise the reality which has been traditionally conceived as the Supreme Being, God?...

The task to which philosophy is called today is, therefore, not the dismantling and re-construction, but the transcending of... every metaphysics, and even the transcending of its ghost, which still haunts phenomenological ontologies themselves....

It should be possible to understand philosophically that which, at first 'physically', and later metaphysically, has been traditionally called God, not only while avoiding the pre-critical inadequacies of metaphysics (which phenomenological ontologists have already done), but also transcending the ontological reduction of reality; I mean the unwarranted reduction of reality to that reality, being, which is given in empirically given being as such.[1]

Being and reality are thus to be distinguished; later on we are told that, while all being is reality, not all reality is being. And, very significantly, God is the kind of reality which is not being; he does not 'exist', he is 'present'. Here is Dewart's statement of the matter:

A reformulation of the problem of God which sprang from an adequate critique of *meta*-physics would have to reject also the *pre*-metaphysical assumption of metaphysics, namely, that God is being or else nothing at all. It is illegitimate to ask 'whether God exists' (or 'whether there is an objective, and not merely a subjective, reality which corresponds to our religious experience'), because we cannot reasonably assume that religious experience is adequately conceptualised *a priori*, that is, in terms

[1] ibid., pp. 356, 359, 363.

of a God who may or may not exist (or of a reality which may be either objective or subjective). The question of God must be so put as to allow the possibility of conceiving God *a posteriori*. That is, a philosophical enquiry into God of the critical calibre which has become possible for philosophy today, should not merely refrain from asking whether an actually existing reality corresponds to the concept of God, as if the real problem were not the mystery of the nature of a reality (usually called God) about whose actual reality there can be scarcely any reasonable doubt, but as if it were simply whether there is an extramental substance to an idea which almost anybody is reasonably clear about.[1]

This is, we must observe, very different from the Thomist 'agnosticism' which holds that, while we can know of God *quia est*, we cannot know *quid sit*. But to return to Dewart:

Contemporary Christian philosophy must also refrain from assuming *any* concept of God—though, on the other hand, it must remember that the concept of God has a history, and that it emerged in history as an evolving interpretation of religious experience. Thus, the question of the foundations of belief in God today is for philosophy: should ontology be 'rehabilitated', or should it be transcended? Granted that the concept of being must be 'dismantled', do we proceed to reconstruct, re-fashion and re-new—and even rehabilitate—the traditional belief in some sort of Supreme Being, or do we not rather proceed to re-develop the traditional belief into belief in a reality beyond being itself?[2]

Two conditions, we are told, are necessary for the investigation, though the answer which is expected to the question seems to be predetermined: first, 'the reality to which religious experience relates must be empirically accessible' and 'somehow empirically signifiable'; secondly, 'if the critique of metaphysics is valid, a transcendent being is a contradiction in terms and, therefore, metaphysical theism is invalid.'[3]

All is not lost, however, to Professor Flew and his colleagues:

This does not imply that the reality to which religious experience relates is not a transcendent reality, if the common assumption of atheism and metaphysical theism—that there is no

[1] ibid., pp. 393f.
[2] ibid., p. 394.
[3] ibid., p. 395.

empirical reality other than being—is questioned. For the reality
which answers to religious experience may be transcendent,
even if it is not being. In other words, the possibility to be
explored is that the reality of God may be transcendent precisely because it transcends being.[1]

Here the plot has really thickened. This reality which is both
empirical and transcendent but is other than being is not to be
understood, as a follower of the pseudo-Areopagite might
understand God, as 'above being' in the sense of transcending
his creation. Dewart prefaces his account of 'the meta-meta-
physical concept of God' with an investigation of the notion of a
reality which is non-being. This is extremely obscure, even if we
keep in mind Dewart's peculiar notion of truth, and the ob-
scurity is, if anything, increased by the Appendix in which he
tries to clarify it. He starts from the, not entirely unquestionable,
assertion that 'by reality in today's ordinary language we usually
mean that which transcends consciousness, that which is
other than oneself'.[2] Reality, we are told, is 'whatever the self
can have real relations towards', whether it is being or not.[3]
The common assumption that being and reality are identical is
blamed on our Indo-European language systems; Hellenism is
apparently raising its ugly head again, though we are not told
this, perhaps because the Indian languages are not obviously
Hellenistic. The trouble is, of course, with the subject–predicate
form of sentence and the double function (copulative and existential) of the verb 'to be'. Chinese is alleged to follow a quite
different pattern both in language and in thought. I am not
competent to criticise this exposition, but some of Dewart's
statements surprise me. In Chinese it is apparently significant
that verbal sentences do not always have a verb in our sense of
the term, but do they always in Latin or even in English ('Caution! Wild Bull!')? 'The verb does not necessarily have a subject, and its function is always that of attributing an act.'[4] 'The
existential sentence in Chinese is usually composed of an impersonal verb, *yu*, and an object', so that 'it would be correct to
assert that in Chinese one does not say "Something is" but "Has

[1] ibid., pp. 395f.
[2] ibid., p. 397.
[3] ibid., p. 399.
[4] ibid., p. 415.

something". But it must be kept in mind that the "has" is impersonal, that there is *nothing* which "has" it.[1] But do not the French say *Il y a* and the Germans *Es gibt*? However, all that Chinese is introduced to do is to show that 'it is perfectly possible to conceive a reality which is relative to being but is other than being';[2] it is admitted to have its own weaknesses.

Passing now to the question of God, Dewart refuses to see any theistic implication in the contingency of the world. To draw any consequences from the world's existence would be to import an *a priori* principle and to violate the principle of empiricism. 'What is a fact may be asserted universally without the implication that it is more than a matter of fact.'[3] Nevertheless, 'man becomes self-problematic because he finds it difficult to reconcile his self-consciousness as being with his being an absolutely contingent fact.'[4] Thus, 'our experience of being reveals that which transcends being, though it reveals it in relation to being.'[5] This transcendent reality is God, but we must not ascribe existence to him; that would imply that he was a being. 'Presence' is the word to use. 'Religious experience, then, does not reveal a transcendent being: what it reveals is that being exists in the presence of a reality which transcends it.'[6] Once again we are faced with great difficulty in understanding what Dewart is asserting. God does not *exist*, but he is (or can be) *present* in our consciousness and he cannot be present anywhere else. 'It is not only true . . . that God must be a reality which transcends man's transcendence: it is also true, in a way, that God has no reality outside human experience.'[7] Is this really coherent? And is there any reason to suppose that it is true? Not perhaps in the old-fashioned sense of 'true'; but that is not Dewart's sense of 'true' in any case. Some things are at least clear. For Dewart, God is not the creator of the universe. And all this talk that God is not a being that exists but a reality that is present is not intended to exclude the attribution to the exalted Deity of words that are also applied to his lowly crea-

[1] ibid., p. 416.
[2] ibid., p. 420.
[3] ibid., p. 431.
[4] ibid., p. 433.
[5] ibid., p. 441.
[6] ibid., p. 443.
[7] ibid., p. 470.

tures. It is intended to indicate that God is not the creator of the universe or the ground of its existence; he is found only in the minds of men, and presumably only some men at that.

This has serious implications for man himself. 'The death of man's "natural" (i.e. biological) life is truly final; it is the total and irrevocable termination of existence.'[1] 'The best index of man's dignity is that only he ceases to exist by dying.'[2] Does this mean, we might ask, that after death man enjoys some other form of life, some other 'reality' than 'existence'? Not at all. 'One of the best indications that reality is not convertible with being is man's spontaneous refusal to believe that the end of his existence, death, is the end of his reality. This makes a great deal of sense. What does not make sense is to interpret this datum in the self-contradictory terms of the "immortality of the soul" or of a "life after death".'[3] In plain terms, man is inherently and (unless instructed by Dr Dewart) inescapably deluded about his own destiny. If this is the case, we must no doubt make the best of it, but we have been given very little ground for believing it except Dewart's own conviction about the stage that has now been reached in the growing-up of man and the evolution of truth.

It is with no feeling of pleasure that one passes a very adverse judgment on Dr Dewart's massive and laborious work. Its weaknesses cannot, however, be glossed over, in view of the fact that he puts it out not simply as a speculative work for academic consideration and assessment but as providing the justification for a total revolution in the Church's faith, spirituality, worship and structures. That these need a considerable *aggiornamento* need not be denied, but it would be disastrous, and would simply provide ammunition for the vested interests of conservatism, if it appeared that *aggiornamento* implied the sheer relativism and anthropocentrism of Dr Dewart's meta-metaphysics. It is indeed surprising to see how often at the present day anthropocentric philosophies of existentialist or phenomenological type set themselves forward as peculiarly congenial to a world dominated by science and technology. That there is a genuine theistic anthropocentrism (if that is the word to use) is indeed

[1] ibid., p. 376.
[2] ibid., p. 494.
[3] ibid., p. 375.

true and it reaches its highest expression in the Christian anthro-pocentrism which is based on the doctrine of the Incarnation. And that doctrine asserts the becoming-man of a God who is the creator of the whole universe, not one who is present only to the consciousness of man. William Temple's Gifford Lectures of 1934, *Nature, Man and God*, may appear old-fashioned to some, but I am sure that he was speaking to twentieth-century man in his assertion that the scientific picture of the universe was to be accepted in its broad details, while the most significant thing about it was the fact that, in the course of evolution, it had given rise to minds which, emerging in it, could nevertheless reflect upon it and investigate it, thus embracing in their scope the very process out of which they had come. Temple would not have described himself as a Thomist, but he certainly under-stood that *mens quodammodo fit omnia*. 'I am greater than the stars', he once said, 'for I know that they are up there and they do not know that I am down here.' It is an odd characteristic of thinkers of the school of Dr Dewart that, while they profess to be extremely sensitive to the outlook of a world that has been transformed by science, they show remarkably little interest in anything that science has in fact discovered. One is tempted to suggest that their retreat into human subjectivity is the result of an unconscious fear of the world in which they live.

CHAPTER NINE

THE OPENNESS OF BEING

Nothing is given to one unless one has the capacity to find it as given.
—Pratima Bowles, *Is Metaphysics Possible?*, p.71.

THE ARGUMENT OF the seventh lecture had as its datum our perception of extramental material beings as both real and contingent, and it was asserted that their existence with this character demands for its explanation the existence of a transcendent self-existent ground, in which are united knowledge, will and power and which is therefore rightly to be described as personal and given the traditional name 'God'. It was also asserted that it is misleading to conceive this passage from the perception of contingent being to the affirmation of transcendent being as consisting simply of discursive argumentation and that such argumentation is indeed nothing more than the explicitation of a primary awareness of the creature as dependent upon its creator or, in Austin Farrer's words, of the 'cosmological idea', 'the scheme of God and the creature in relation'.[1] This awareness, it was admitted, is less common and is more difficult to achieve today than it was in the past, and it is closely linked with the capacity for contemplative wondering. Nevertheless, without it argumentation for theism almost inevitably has that character of circularity of which its critics accuse it, and—what is more serious from the religious point of view—it all too easily leaves us with the concept of a remote and glacial deity. In the very act of affirming God's existence it tends to lose that hold upon the intuition of God and finite being together without which the argument could never begin.

I also argued that it is possible, and is indeed likely, that a personal God will not merely restrict himself to the status of a

[1] *Finite and Infinite*, p. 16 *et al.*

passive and unresponsive object for our consideration and investigation, like the inanimate members of the physical world,[1] but will communicate himself to us in deliberate revelationary activity, whether that activity is subsequent to our rational recognition of him or whether it is an occasional, frequent or possibly even an invariable accompaniment of it. I intend therefore in the present lecture to consider the question of man as a possible recipient of divine revelation, while recognising that it would be improper in the context of Gifford Lectures to appeal to the content of any particular alleged revelation as providing authority for the view to which we may come.

It has, of course, been held by an impressive body of theologians, of whom Karl Barth was, at any rate for most his life, the most distinguished member, that man has, so far as the exercise of his natural faculties is concerned, no power whatever of attaining to any genuine knowledge of God, and that any alleged knowledge of God so attained will be so debased and distorted as to be worse than useless. Thus Gustav Aulén has written:

> If the cosmological argument concludes on the basis of cause and effect that there must be a first cause, and then calls this cause God, Christian faith must answer, from its point of view, that this pseudonymous 'first cause' has nothing in common with the God of faith. Nor can the teleological argument which attempts to find a wise providence on the basis of a purposeful adaptiveness of the world prepare a way to the God of faith. The 'God' who is demonstrated in this way has only the name in common with the God of faith.[2]

'Nothing in common', 'only the name in common'—these are fairly downright expressions, and go far beyond asserting that man's rationally based knowledge of God is limited or obscure; they imply that, in so far as the word 'God' means the object of devotion of Christians, rational theology does not speak about God at all but about an entirely different being. Austin Farrer in

---

[1] I am in fact doubtful whether we ought to describe even inanimate objects as in all respects passive in our perception of them. There is, however, an immense difference between any contribution that they can make and that made by animate, and still more by rational, personal beings. Cf. my *Existence and Analogy*, pp. 182ff.

[2] *The Faith of the Christian Church*, p. 27.

a well-known passage has commented tellingly on this position:

> There is a superstition among revelationists, that by declaring themselves independent of any proof of God by analogy from the finite world, they have escaped the necessity of considering the analogy or relation of the finite to the infinite altogether. They are completely mistaken; for all their statements about God must be expressed and plainly are expressed in language drawn from the finite world. No revelationist supposes these statements to be perfectly literal; God is not a man and human language requires to be read with some tacit qualification before it applies to him. . . . This problem of analogy is in principle prior to every particular revelation. For the revelation has to be thought about to be received, and can be thought about only by the aid of words or finite images; and these cannot signify of God unless the appropriate 'mode of signification' functions in our minds.[1]

Farrer's remarks are explicitly concerned with the capacity of human language to describe God, but they are equally relevant to the capacity of the human mind to apprehend God, for we can only speak of that which, to some degree at least, we apprehend. Even if we conceded to the revelationists that we can know nothing whatever about God except what he deliberately and explicitly reveals to us, we should still have to maintain that we are able to recognise and understand the revelation when it is given. And if the revelationists replied, as I think many of them would, that we have no such natural ability but that when God reveals himself he gives, simultaneously with the revelation, the power to recognise and understand it, we should again have to assert that, even if that be the case, the human mind must have a natural capacity to receive this power. At some stage or other the finite must be *capax infiniti*. Unless there is some *Anknüpfungspunkt*, however small, between God and man in human nature, unless man has, by nature, some *potentia oboedientialis*, some receptive capacity, however minimal, for the supernatural, God will be unable to communicate with man because, even if God speaks, man will be unable to hear him. I would agree that in the Catholic textbooks the relation between the natural and the supernatural, between nature and grace, between reason and revelation, has often been conceived in far

[1] *Finite and Infinite*, pp. 2f.

too rigid and impersonal a manner. We may perhaps prefer to say, with Karl Rahner, that man, in his concrete existence, has been endowed by God with a 'supernatural existential'.[1] But, unless we admit that at some level of his being man has a point of contact with God, not only will natural theology be impossible but so will theology of revelation as well. We cannot become 'hearers of the word' unless we have ears to hear the word when it is spoken. (*Hearers of the Word* is, we may recall, the title of Rahner's work on what he describes as 'the ontology of the *potentia oboedientialis* for Revelation'.[2]) I shall therefore, in the present lecture, argue three points: first, that finite being as such has a capacity, which it cannot actualise by its own powers, to be elevated above its natural level by God; secondly, that this capacity has a special and highly important character in the case of a rational being such as man; thirdly, that in the case of man it includes, though it is not exhausted by, an ability to recognise and apprehend God's word if and when God speaks to him. I must, however, at this stage, make two remarks in clarification of my position. First, while I disagree with those I have described as 'the revelationists' when they deny that we can have any knowledge of God by our natural powers, I agree with them that God can make himself known by revelation. Secondly, I hold that our capacity to apprehend divine revelation is only one aspect of a capacity to be elevated into the life of God. And, while it will be impossible to conduct this argument without some mention of revealed religion and while it may well be true that the general line of argument would not suggest itself to someone who was ignorant that there are religions which claim to be revealed, the argument will make no appeal to the authority of any alleged revelation.

First, then, as to the capacity of finite being to be elevated by God above its natural level. Finite being is, as we have seen, characterised by the mysterious—it might indeed seem paradoxical—combination of reality and contingency. Philosophers and theologians have never found it easy to hold these two factors in true balance and proportion. Some have tended to minimise the factor of reality—this is exemplified by those forms of

[1] Cf. K. Rahner, 'Concerning the Relation between Nature and Grace', in *Theological Investigations*, I, pp. 297ff *et al*. Cf. also pp. 233 *infra*.

[2] op cit., p. 3. The original German title is *Hörer des Wortes*.

Hinduism which look upon the world as illusion and by the Platonic tradition in Europe. Others have tended to minimise the factor of contingency—this is characteristic of the prevalent scientific humanism, which takes the existence of the world as an ultimate and irreducible fact, and of the linguistic empiricism which still dominates Anglo-Saxon philosophy. Against both these tendencies I have argued that a full recognition of both factors, based upon a contemplation of the world in an attitude of wonder, can lead us to grasp the beings in which they are combined as totally and radically dependent upon the creative activity of a transcendent, self-existent and personal God. While exerting concrete existence and manifesting the special characteristics of the particular beings and kinds of being that each of them is, they are metaphysically incomplete and exist at all only because they are the objects of incessant creative activity on the part of God. They are centres of real existential energy, but this energy is finite and received; they have real determinate natures, but their natures are inherently limited and restricted in their sphere. And just because their being is both received and limited, it is inherently open to fresh influxes of creative activity from God. The view of the world that derives from these considerations is radically and uncompromisingly dynamic, and it stands in sharp contrast with the view that was typical of the ancient world. Greek philosophy, when it did not dissolve the world into a featureless Heraclitean mush in which 'all things flow', thought of every being as a limited incapsulated entity, all of whose potentialities were included in it at the start, even if their development took time and was conditioned by their environment; the kitten might become a cat, but in doing this it was only becoming more perfectly what it had really been all the time. It made little difference whether the forms of the various species of being were conceived as laid up in an ideal realm and as imitated with varying degrees of success by the individuals on earth, or whether they were conceived as existing only in the individuals. In any case, if you only knew enough about their nature you would know all they could possibly become; it was all really there from the start. Over against this ultimately cramped and static view Christian philosophers developed the doctrine that finite beings are maintained and energised by the incessant creative activity of a personal God, who is himself infinite plenitude of activity (*actus purus*) and who is continually pouring being into his creatures, *semper infundens bonitatem in rebus*. We need not enquire here how far this view was a direct derivative from the Judaeo-Christian tradition, though we may note in passing that, while one school of Christian thinkers, such as Étienne Gilson and Jacques Maritain, find its origin in the name of God revealed to Moses at the burning bush, others, such as Karl Barth and Gustav Aulén (to say nothing of such out-and-out anti-hellenists as Leslie Dewart) see it as the radical contamination of Christianity by Greek metaphysics. In any case I would maintain that it is capable of rational justification and is therefore the proper subject of rational theology. We may note that, while the various systems of pagan philosophy gave various answers, more or less convincing as the case might be, to the question why the world is the sort of thing it is, they never made a serious attempt to answer the much more important and fundamental question why there is a world at all.

To return to our present concern, the view that all finite beings depend for their very existence as well as for their particular natures on the incessant creative activity of God implies that, while they are relatively autonomous, in that God conserves in each its own particular pattern of finite activity, they are, by the very fact that they are dependent and not self-existent realities, open to fresh influxes of creative activity from God, which will not destroy their spontaneity but will elevate and enhance it. Nor is there any antecedently specifiable limit to such influxes; anything that a finite being receives will be finite, but there is no greatest finite quantity. As the scholastics say, grace does not destroy nature but perfects it. By their very dependence upon God, finite beings are inherently open to him; an absolutely autonomous and incapsulated finite entity would be a contradiction in terms. A created universe—and there can be no other—is necessarily not only a finite but also an open one. Nature has, simply as nature, a *potentia oboedientialis* for the supernatural, whether or no (and this is not the business of natural theology) God has in fact equipped it with a 'supernatural existential' in the Rahnerian sense.

Once it has been recognised that God's relation to creatures as their creator consists not in projecting them into a condition of isolated and unrelated self-sufficiency but in incessantly energising them as the real and at the same time open entities that they are, it will be seen how delicately poised their existence is. I have, in an earlier work entitled *Via Media*, attempted to expound the paradoxical notion of 'dependent reality' and to contrast it with other views of finite being that philosophical and religious systems have held. Here I will merely stress that it is only too easy to lose the balance in either direction, falling either into an over-emphasis on the element of dependence, thus depriving creatures of any real substantiality and spontaneity, or into an over-emphasis on their reality, forgetting that this reality is itself a gift from creator and making the creatures virtually into finite gods. It is indeed not easy to see all the implications of the openness of creatures to God, as long as we remain on the level of subhuman and subrational existence; the matter will become clearer when we go on to consider those implications in the case of man. We may, however, observe that, while it is difficult to see how subrational creatures can, without losing their particular individualities, be elevated into the life of their creator (and this is what, where rational creatures are concerned, the word 'supernatural', in the strict sense, has come to mean in Catholic theology), they conspicuously manifest on the natural level a character of incompleteness, of reaching beyond themselves for their fulfilment, which is in line with their dual aspect as genuine and at the same time open realities. One need not agree in every detail with Pierre Teilhard de Chardin in order to see significance in the way in which, throughout the ladder of nature at every level, entities do not just go on their way as isolated individuals but find their fulfilment, and are taken into progressively higher orders of activity, by entering into organic association with others to which they are inherently open and in union with which their own activity is enhanced and elevated. Fundamental particles grouped into atoms, atoms into molecules, molecules into cells, cells into multicellular organisms, these again grouped into social complexes, until we come at last to man and the noosphere. This openness of creatures to one another and their openness, in association with others, to higher levels of existence and activity is, of course, not the same thing as their openness to their creator, but it is an analogue of it and a tendency towards its realisation. At any

F

stage in the process the balance between individuality and openness can be lost, and the process can come to a halt with either, on the one hand, a collapse and deliquescence of the individual into non-existence or, on the other, a loss of openness and a retreat into a static and incapsulated condition in which the possibility of further development and advance has vanished. Many examples of both these types of dead end can, of course, be found in the course of biological evolution. The most terrible example of the incapsulated condition occurs on the human level, if a man loses his openness not only to his fellow men but also to God.

Here we have moved on to our second point, which is concerned not with finite beings in general but with man. The special feature is that man, as a rational and personal being, is capable of actualising his openness to a rational and personal God in a way that is impossible to beings devoid of rational personality. I have said that man is capable of actualising his openness to God, but it would be more accurate to say that he is capable of having it actualised for him. By the nature of the case the initiative must come from God, by whose will and power man's very openness to him is conferred and maintained. However, I would not denote man's part in this simply by the adjective 'passive', for this has much too static and negative a suggestion to be an adequate term for the relation of a conscious and rational person to the personal being by whom his very existence is continually bestowed; I would prefer the adjective 'receptive'. But however we designate it, its distinctive feature is its personal character. Man, unlike (as far as we know) any other inhabitant of the material world, is made in the image of God. The personal creature is open to the personal Creator; *cor ad cor loquitur*.

Now the intercourse of personal beings, even on the finite and created level, is characteristically one of conversation, of the mutual communication of thought and knowledge; this is why language plays such an important part in human society. And even when two human beings achieve such a degree of union that at the points of its highest realisation, language gives way to silence, the element of communication, indeed of self-communication, so far from vanishing remains and is enhanced. Indeed, if I have been right in asserting that the essence of knowledge is that the knower in a mysterious way, 'intentionally' as the Thomists say, *becomes* the object known, it is impossible to conceive even the lowest and most uncommitted modes of human communication as leaving the knower and the known entirely external to each other. All the more then, when we consider the possibility of God revealing himself to man, is it impossible to think of God as making a purely external impact upon man or as simply offering him items of information.

Many theologians in recent years have indeed asserted that divine revelation is given in acts rather than in words, but this assertion has, I think, often been unhelpful, since they frequently seem to have conceived of God's acts as having an even more external character than words could have. They have sometimes suggested that God's revelatory acts are such sheer bolts from the blue, such explosions of divine invasion totally unrelated to anything in the situation to which they are addressed, that they are not only unaccompanied by any intelligible utterance but are also insusceptible of intelligible description or interpretation. Oddly enough, this view has tended to appear in just those theological circles in which, as regards theology in general, the notion of the Word of God holds a very central position. This radical opposition between revelation conceived in terms of acts and revelation conceived in terms of words is, I believe, in any case perverse, since it mistakenly thinks of both the acts and the words of God as having a primarily external relation to the creature, as consisting in an impact rather than in an intimate transformation and vivification. Behind all this there lies a fear, laudable enough if one were to grant its presuppositions, that to admit that there could be any real self-communication of God to man, any real elevation of man into the life of God, any 'deification' of man (to use the term that has become classical in Catholic theology[1]) would be to blur the distinction between the Creator and the creature and to slip into a position virtually indistinguishable from pantheism. It is, however, the presuppositions that need questioning, for they consist, I believe, in a false, or at any rate a very inadequate, understanding of the relation between the Creator and

---

[1] It is, of course, maintained that this 'deification' involves no loss of creaturely status. Cf. my *Via Media*, ch. iv, 'Deified Creaturehood: the Doctrine of Grace'.

the creature. This relation has only too often been thought of solely in terms of a comparison of the respective natures or essences of God and man, to the neglect of the concrete existential activity uniting them. It makes little difference whether the comparison is made in quantitative or in qualitative terms. Sometimes we are told that God is infinite and man is finite, sometimes that God is *das ganz Anderes*, the 'wholly other', and both these assertions are true. They neglect, however, the basic fact in which the mutual otherness of God and man consists, namely that man is totally dependent for his existence on the incessant creative activity of the self-existent God. And the importance of this, as I have previously emphasised, is that, while it involves the greatest conceivable contrast between God and man, it simultaneously places them in the most intimate connection. Extrinsecism as regards grace does not logically necessitate extrinsecism as regards nature, though I think the converse is true. It is logically possible to hold that man as a creature is interiorly energised by God but that God never augments the bare minimum without which man could not exist as man at all; but it is not, as I see it, logically possible to hold that man is raised by God to a supernatural union with him and to hold at the same time that on the natural level man is entirely isolated from God, for grace must have some foothold in nature in order to act at all. It is, however, fairly clear that in practice the two extrinsecisms are likely to go together. One of the most striking examples known to me of extrinsecism on the level of nature is to be found in Dr Harvey Cox's book *The Secular City*, in which, after quite correctly pointing out that the monotheism of the Bible rejects any suggestion that the world is itself divine and thus repudiates all forms of pantheism and nature-worship, he interprets this as meaning that the world has no connection with God whatever and that therefore no traces of God's activity are to be validly discerned in the world. Apparently Cox conceives creation as the projection of the world by God into a condition of total isolation from him. I cannot think that this position is rationally coherent, as Cox appears to hold that God has at least managed to communicate to this isolated world the information that it is isolated from him.[1]

---

[1] Cf. my *Theology and the Future*, pp. 162ff, for a fuller discussion of Dr Cox's position.

In much recent theological writing the concept of the supernatural has been either disowned or else pushed right into the
background. In Dr J. A. T. Robinson's famous book *Honest to
God* it is disowned in scornful tones, usually under the still more
contemptible form of 'supra-natural'. Dr George A. Lindbeck,
writing about the Second Vatican Council, refers to 'the negative fact that only rarely in the hundred thousand words which
the council produced is the classical distinction between the
natural and the supernatural introduced. The pattern of
thought', he adds, 'is sometimes present, particularly in the
Declaration on Religious Freedom, but not once are the terms
themselves used in the major documents.'[1] I do not think, however, that we can afford to do without the distinction, though I
think that Catholic theology has tended in the past to formulate
it in a very rigid and unsatisfactory manner, especially in the
textbooks, and that it needs a good deal of reformulation and
development.

The textbook doctrine has tended to see man's natural constitution as rounded off and complete in itself, and as concerned
entirely with his life in this world and sustained by the forces
of nature. On top of this there has been superposed a supernatural constitution, in virtue of which man is orientated to
the supernatural end of the vision of God and is sustained by
divine grace and the sacramental paraphernalia of the Christian
Church. Although nature is held to possess a *potentia oboedientialis*
for grace and the supernatural, this consists of little more than
a lack of antagonism towards it, and the two orders are thought
of rather as if they were two apartments on adjacent floors, with
a layer of soundproof packing between the natural ceiling below
and the supernatural floor above. The Thomist maxim 'Grace
does not destroy nature but perfects it'[2] has been interpreted as
if it means simply that it is better for man to enjoy grace in
addition to nature, although nature would be perfectly complete without it. Now it must be recognised that the purpose, or
one of the purposes, of this rigidly separatist view has been to
preserve the sheer gratuitousness of the grace of God; it is a free
gift from God, and man can have no right, either physical or
moral, to demand it. Protestant theology, no less than Catholic,

[1] *The Future of Roman Catholic Theology*, p. 22.
[2] *S. Th.* I, i, 8 *ad* 2; *De Ver.* xxvii, 6 *ad* 1; *et al.*

and for much the same reason, has frequently made the same hard-and-fast barrier between nature and grace, though, having made it, it has tended then to discard or ignore nature altogether, while Catholic theology has tried to hold on to both of them in spite of their virtual isolation from each other. Such a statement as this is inevitably over-simplified and cannot do justice to the best thought in either Catholicism or Protestantism, but it is, I think, substantially accurate and it pinpoints the problem. The nature of the problem is impressively shown by the difficulty, which has exercised generations of Thomist scholars, of reconciling St Thomas's repeated assertions that the end of man—the purpose for which he is made—is the supernatural vision of God with his no less emphatic insistence that man has neither the right to grace and the supernatural nor any powers of his own to attain them.[1] This is not the place to discuss the fine work which has been done by Fr Henri de Lubac, in his attempt to get behind the late medieval and post-medieval scholastics in order to disentangle the theological issues at stake,[2] or to expound the way in which Fr Karl Rahner, writing in the idiom of German existentialism, has made use of the notion of man's endowment with a 'supernatural existential'.[3] To follow up this question and to see the way in which it involves not only the post-Reformation confrontations between Catholics and Protestants in the West but also the much earlier confrontation between Eastern Orthodoxy and Western Catholicism—confrontations which have taken on a new significance in the more inclusive setting of the modern Ecumenical Movement—would lead us beyond the limits that are proper to Gifford Lectures; I have, however, discussed the matter at some length in an appendix to my printed text.[4] Here I will simply point out that if the relation between God and man is of the kind that I have defended in these lectures, we can at least see the main contours of a solution to the problem. For my two chief contentions have been, first, that man, as a creature, is

[1] Cf., e.g., James E. O'Mahoney, *The Desire of God in the Philosophy of St Thomas Aquinas* (1929); Patrick K. Bastable, *Desire for God* (1947).

[2] *Surnaturel: Etudes historiques* (1946); *The Mystery of the Supernatural* (1967, French original 1965); *Augustinianism and Modern Theology* (1969, French original 1965).

[3] *Theological Investigations*, I, pp. 297ff; II, pp. 235ff; IV, pp. 165ff.

[4] Appendix III, *infra*.

fundamentally open to God and capable of receiving fresh and unpredictable influxes of God's creative activity; secondly, that God and man are personal beings and therefore can enter into that intimacy of self-communication and mutual possession that is proper to persons. That God is not only personal but transcendent and self-existent adds indeed to the wonder of this mutual intercourse of God and man, but does nothing to contradict or impede it. And here the scholastic tags, which can seem so dry and dull as mere formulas, take on an unexampled lucidity and warmth. 'Grace does not destroy nature but perfects it',[1] because nature always lies open to God. 'Grace presupposes nature',[2] not in the sense that grace is a mere superstructure erected on top of nature and needing nature only to prevent it from falling through the floor, but that nature is the very material in which grace works and for whose ultimate perfection grace itself exists. As I have written elsewhere:

It is quite wrong to suppose that grace is a kind of supernatural substance and that nature exists for the sake of it. On the contrary, grace apart from nature is a pure abstraction; and it is for the sake of nature that grace exists. Supernature simply means nature supernaturalised by grace, and the possibility of this supernaturalisation lies in the openness of nature to God. For a nature which was closed in the Greek sense, supernaturalisation would be identical with destruction, for it could only mean the replacement of one nature by another. For a nature which is open in the Christian sense, supernaturalisation means expansion, development, perfection, a realisation of hitherto unsuspected potentialities, a new infusion of the creative activity of God; and when this supernaturalisation has taken place unlimited possibilities of further supernaturalisation lie ahead. In each stage of the process God takes the initiative; the creature can neither envisage what the next stage will be, nor demand its fulfilment as a right, nor initiate its achievement. Nevertheless, as the process goes on the creature finds its own activity not by-passed or suppressed, but on the contrary liberated and enhanced. The more it is supernaturalised, the more truly natural it becomes. And all this because openness to God is of its very essence; dependence upon him is part of its definition.[3]

[1] *S. Th.*, I, i. 8 *ad* 2.
[2] *S. Th.*, I, ii, 2 *ad* 1.
[3] *The Importance of Being Human*, pp. 61f.

The third point which I said that I intended to argue in this lecture is that man's capacity to be elevated above the purely natural level includes an ability to recognise and apprehend God's word if and when God speaks to him. If I have carried my hearers with me until now, I do not think there will be any special difficulty here. It must however be said that more is involved than the mere reception of information about God; if God is able to give himself to man by fresh influxes of creative power, man will *know God* and not merely *have knowledge about him*. And knowing God is sharing God's life. This is the truth that was concealed, however imperfectly it was expressed, in the saying that revelation is given in acts and not in words. That God can reveal himself in words if he so wishes should be obvious; whether he has done so and what means, human or other, he has used to do it is the business of the positive religions and not of natural theology, though natural theology might have something to say about the ways by which revelation could be recognised. We may recall that the second volume of A. E. Taylor's Gifford Lectures, *The Faith of a Moralist*, bore the subtitle 'Natural Theology and the Positive Religions'. I shall not myself embark upon that enterprise, but I would underline the contention of all the great theoreticians and practicians of the spiritual life that God's revelation of himself to human beings, whether it comes in sacred scriptures, ecclesiastical pronouncements, theological formulas or in personal experience, is of necessity baffling and obscure. I have in an earlier lecture said something about the inevitable limitations of human language, limitations which are at the maximum when the object of the language is not the finite world but its transcendent ground. As regards personal experience, it is perhaps sufficient to remind ourselves of the phenomenon of the dark night of the soul, a phenomenon which has recently come to be recognised as a common feature not only of advanced states of mystical union but of any attempt to know God and to live in accordance with his will. It is not surprising that our knowledge of God should be limited and obscure; what is surprising is that it is as extensive as it is, when we remember the disparity between its human subject and its divine object. But, whether we are considering the heights of mysticism, man's knowledge of God by revelation and grace, or the simple recognition of God as the transcendent ground of natural objects, in every case what makes this possible is the fact that God incessantly energises every finite being and in so doing gives it an openness for further influxes of his creative activity.

But this is not the end of the story, at least as far as one of the great world-religions is concerned. It is the central affirmation of Christianity that the Creator has entered into an even more intimate union with his creation than any we have as yet considered, that, as the Christian formularies put it, 'for us men and for our salvation he came down from heaven' and that this took place 'not by the conversion of godhead into flesh but by the assumption of manhood into God'. This is not the place for an exposition of Christological doctrine or for a discussion of the various views that have been held in Christendom about the Incarnation and its implications. It is, however, relevant to observe that if we enquire about the *possibility* of an incarnation we are raising issues that fall within the scope of natural theology. Few indeed, if any, Christian thinkers have tried to prove on purely rational grounds that God was bound to become incarnate, though St Anselm, in his treatise *Cur Deus Homo?*, perhaps came closest to doing this. Christians have in fact always seen the Incarnation as an entirely unexpected and unforeseeable act of divine grace and goodness. Even the great Old Testament prophecies of a future redemptive act on the part of God were obscure and mysterious, and it was only after the coming of Christ that their true content was identified. The revelation in Jesus Christ was, in the words of the Apostle Paul, 'the revelation of the mystery which was kept secret for long ages, but is now disclosed and through the prophetic writings is made known to all nations'.[1] Nevertheless, if God became man, man must be the kind of being it was possible for God to become.[2] *Ab esse ad posse valet consecutio.* It may therefore be proper for us briefly to consider what the possibility of an incarnation of God in manhood would imply about human nature itself.

It is, I think, only on the hypothesis of a strictly orthodox view of the Incarnation that there is really anything special to discuss.

[1] Rom. xvi. 26.
[2] Cf. J. A. Baker: 'When God enters our space and time, a man is what he becomes. There must therefore be something appropriate about manhood which makes it a possible way of life for God' (*The Foolishness of God*, p. 408).

If we held, for example, some form of adoptionist view, such as is quite common today, that is to say, if we held that the union of God with man in Christ differed only in degree from his union with any other good man, there would be nothing to say that we have not said already. When, for example, Dr John Knox writes: 'We can have the humanity without the pre-existence and we can have the pre-existence without the humanity. There is absolutely no way of having both',[1] he is in fact begging the question of the possibility of an incarnation at the start, and begging it in a negative sense. I find it more interesting and less dogmatic to ask the question: If we *can* have the humanity and the pre-existence together, what does this imply about humanity and its relation to God?[2] Now the Incarnation means that in the case of one particular individual human nature—that of Jesus —God is not only the creator who incessantly preserves it in existence but is also the subject of all its activities and experiences, physical and mental alike. If we think of God and man in purely static and spatial terms this will indeed be incredible; how can you cram the quart—and much more than a quart—of divinity into the pint-pot of humanity? But thinking in static and spatial terms is one of the things that we are always told we must not do, and all through this discussion I have tried to avoid doing it. God, let us again remind ourselves, is rational, willing and personal, *eminentissime*; man, of all the beings on this earth, is rational, willing and personal too. Is it perhaps possible for the rational, willing and personal Creator, who sustains all rational, willing and personal creatures as objects of his love and pours into them grace upon grace, so to embrace rational, willing and personal finitude as to become not only its sustainer but its subject, and in doing this to meet them on their own level, share their own life and raise them to even greater heights of union with him? No, says Dr Knox, 'we can have the humanity, etc. . . . . There is absolutely no way of having both.' I am not so sure; perhaps it is in his ability to assume a created nature that the Creator's omnipotence is most fully shown. It is not the business of natural theology to enquire how many Persons there

[1] *The Humanity and Divinity of Christ*, p. 106.
[2] Cf. K. Rahner: 'Only someone who forgets that the essence of man . . . is to be unbounded . . . can suppose that it is impossible for there to be a man, who, precisely by being man in the fullest sense (which we never attain), is God's Existence into the world' (*Theological Investigations*, I, p. 184).

are in the Godhead, whether God might have assumed some
other created nature than that of man, and whether some other
Person than that of the Son might have become incarnate.
Nevertheless——

'Of all the works of God', wrote St Thomas Aquinas, 'the
mystery of the Incarnation most greatly surpasses our reason;
for nothing more wonderful could be thought of that God could
do than that very God, the Son of God, should become very
man.'[1]

'Most greatly surpasses our reason', indeed, but does it therefore contradict it?

[1] *S.c.G.*, IV, xxvii.

CHAPTER TEN

GOD AND TIME

In the place of the omnipotence there is neither before nor after, there is only act.
—Charles Williams, *Descent into Hell*, ch. vi.

IN A DISCUSSION of natural theology one can hardly avoid enquiring how God is related to time, that mysterious and tragic feature of the world concerning which St Augustine remarked in a famous epigram that he knew what it was as long as nobody asked him but as soon as anybody asked him he did not know.[1] On the problems connected with time itself I should like to commend in the warmest terms Dr G. J. Whitrow's book *The Natural Philosophy of Time*, in which the author has brought together, with a quite astonishing versatility, a vast amount of relevant material from the realms of philosophy, psychology, biology and experimental and mathematical physics and has handled it with uniform understanding and sympathy. On the strictly theological issues I would specially mention Dr Nelson Pike's recent book *God and Timelessness*, which is remarkable both for the minuteness and skill of the argument and for the modesty and restraint of its conclusions; if it suffers, as I think it does, from one rather serious oversight, this does not diminish my sense of the very great help that I have received from it.[2]

The matter of the relation of God to time involves in fact two distinct but connected questions: (1) Is God timeless? (2) Is God changeless? That they are connected is shown by the fact that if the former is answered in the affirmative the latter must

---

[1] *Confessions*, XI, xiv, 2.

[2] I would also draw attention to the very interesting article on 'The Timelessness of God' by Mr R. G. Swinburne in the *Church Quarterly Review*, CLXVI (1965), pp. 323ff, 472ff.

receive an affirmative answer as well, for change can be predicated only of subjects that exist in time. (It may, however, be well to add that the changelessness that is predicated of a timeless being is very different from the changelessness that would be predicated of a being that existed in time but did not undergo any change.) We cannot consistently assert both that God is timeless and that he is subject to change, but we could consistently assert that he is immune from change without being timeless.

The main tradition of Christian theology has asserted both the timelessness and the changelessness of God, while admitting that this raises a number of very difficult problems. Popular religion, not surprisingly, has been more concerned with God's changelessness than with his timelessness and has tended to understand it in a moral rather than in a metaphysical sense. Biblical scholars tell us that in the Scriptures the emphasis falls upon God's faithfulness to his own moral nature and to his promises rather than upon sheer immobility, and indeed God is represented as manifesting love, anger, patience, impatience, sorrow, joy and a variety of other emotions and also as intervening in often very decisive ways in the events of individual lives and of world history. Philosophical theologians, too, have been anxious to assert that God is concerned with the changing events of the universe without himself being dominated by them, and they have admitted that there is a genuine problem of reconciling God's compassion with his impassibility.[1] They have, however, for the most part interpreted such apparent changes in God as arising rather from the changing perspectives under which he appears from a standpoint within the historical process than from any real alterations of God himself; thus they have asserted that the wrath of God is nothing else than the love of God as it appears to and impinges upon creatures whose wills are set against him in obstinacy or rebellion. Only by philosophers whose basic metaphysic is pantheistic or at least immanentist has it been held that God is himself the subject of vicissitudes or developments. Two such notable cases must, however, receive our attention; namely those of the late A. N. Whitehead and of Dr Charles Hartshorne.

Whitehead's Gifford Lectures, delivered at Edinburgh in

[1] Cf. my *Existence and Analogy*, pp. 134ff.

1927–8, were published in 1929 under the title *Process and Reality: An Essay in Cosmology*; they contain, in a highly systematic presentation, the fully worked out statement of his metaphysics.[1] I have discussed them at length in my book *He Who Is*. Whitehead's ambition was to bring into a synthesis the insights of all the chief philosophies and religions of mankind. In particular he was concerned to give due weight to both the stable and the dynamic aspect of the universe, represented, to use his technical terminology, by 'eternal objects' on the one hand and 'actual entities' or 'actual occasions' on the other.[2] The latter, he held, are the only *reasons*;[3] in this he is fundamentally an empiricist. The actual occasions, while distinct and substantial, are not isolated; each of them mirrors all the others, either in positive prehensions as being relevant to the prehending entity or in negative prehensions as being discarded. And they are constantly passing away and entering into new complexes of entities. And out of this perpetual self-relinquishment and self-creation of actual entities the history of the physical universe is built up. Each of them is an embodiment of 'creativity', which Whitehead describes as 'the principle of *novelty*',[4] and it must be noted that it is this creativity, and not either God or being, that is his ultimate metaphysical principle. This would suggest that Whitehead's philosophy is essentially immanentist, and in the last resort I am convinced that it is. The matter is, however, complicated by his introduction of an entity which he names 'God'; though this God is very far from the God of classical theism. The function of Whitehead's God is to be the locus of eternal objects; actual entities prehend one another and the eternal objects, and thus bring about their own creation, in accordance with the valuation of the eternal objects by God. This valuation occurs in God's 'primordial nature', but this primordial nature of God is entirely abstract, for only actual occasions have concrete actuality. It is only by his interaction with the world of actual occasions that God acquires a 'consequent nature' and thus becomes concrete and conscious. Thus

---

[1] Cf. William A. Christian, *An Interpretation of Whitehead's Metaphysics*; D. M. Emmet, *Whitehead's Philosophy of Organism*.

[2] The difference between actual entities and actual occasions is that the former may include God, the latter do not; cf. *Process and Reality*, p. 122.

[3] *Process and Reality*, p. 33.

[4] ibid., p. 28.

for Whitehead there is no question of God having an ultimate status in reality; that status belongs not to God but to Creativity.

> God and the World are the contrasted opposites in terms of which Creativity achieves its supreme task of transforming disjoined multiplicity, with its diversities in opposition, into concrescent unity, with its diversities in contrast. . . . For God the conceptual is prior to the physical, for the World the physical poles are prior to the conceptual poles. . . . God and the World stand over against each other, expressing the final metaphysical truth that appetitive vision and physical enjoyment have equal claim to priority in creation.[1]

It is difficult to do justice in a few words to a system as elaborate and, in some places, as obscure as Whitehead's but it will, I think, be clear from this brief summary that the God of Whitehead is not the God of classical theism. So independent a thinker as the late L. Susan Stebbing asserted that 'Professor Whitehead's indefensible use of language becomes nothing short of scandalous when he speaks of "God".'[2] As I have already said, the ultimate principle of existence in Whitehead's system is what he calls 'Creativity', not what he calls 'God'. However, we cannot identify his Creativity with the God of classical theism, even if we understand the term 'God' in the minimal sense in which I have defined it, as denoting the transcendent cause of extramental material beings. For in Whitehead's system these beings have no transcendent cause at all; as embodiments of creativity they are self-creating. A. E. Taylor was, I believe, right when he accused Whitehead of 'unconscious tampering with his own sound principle that all possibility is founded on actuality' and asserted that 'the attempt to get back somehow behind the concreteness of God to an *élan vital* of which the concreteness is to be a product really amounts to a surrender of the principle itself.'[3] As an analysis of the structure and development of finite beings Whitehead's doctrine of eternal objects and actual entities is, I think, ingenious and suggestive, though it is open to criticisms which other philosophers have not been slow in making; in particular his account of the emergence of con-

[1] ibid., pp. 492, 493.
[2] Review of *Process and Reality* in *Mind*, XXXIX (1930), p. 475.
[3] 'Some Thoughts on Process and Reality', in *Theology*, XXXIII (1930), p. 79.

sciousness has been accused of question-begging *légerdemain* with such metaphors as 'prehension' and 'feeling'. More seriously from our standpoint, it is difficult to see Whitehead's justification for investing his 'God' with personal attributes and for describing him in his consequent nature as 'the great companion —the fellow-sufferer who understands'.[1] It is, nevertheless, hardly surprising that Whitehead's final attitude to his God is not one of adoration so much as of sympathy. It is instructive to note that, when Lionel Thornton, who had a great admiration for Whitehead, adopted Whitehead's philosophy of organism as the medium for a modern reformulation of the Christian doctrine of the Incarnation, he found it necessary to part company with Whitehead at the precise point where the relation of finite being to ultimate reality is involved. (It should be remembered that, although Thornton's work *The Incarnate Lord* appeared only when Whitehead's Gifford Lectures were in course of delivery, Whitehead's thought had been maturing and finding expression in a series of books during the previous decade.)

My reason for referring at such length to a system which saw the light over forty years ago and has been ignored by most professional philosophers ever since is that quite recently there has been, first in the United States and now to a lesser degree in Britain, a revival of process thinking which seems to have obliterated the short-lived death-of-God theology and to have become the latest fashion in the theological world. This has largely been due to the other philosopher whom I mentioned at the beginning of this lecture, Dr Charles Hartshorne. One of Hartshorne's chief interests is, as we saw in an earlier lecture, the ontological argument of St Anselm of Canterbury.[2] I summed up Hartshone's judgment on Anselm by saying that, according to Hartshorne, while almost everyone since Anselm has radically misunderstood Anselm, Anselm himself radically misunderstood the nature of God. More explicitly, while Anselm was right in holding that God—that than which nothing greater can be thought—is, in fact and in principle, unsurpassable by any other being, he was wrong in not recognising that God is perpetually and without limit surpassing himself. The best-known exponents of the movement in Britain are Dr W.

---

[1] *Process and Reality*, p. 497.
[2] Cf. pp. 48ff *supra*.

Norman Pittenger, Mr John B. Cobb and Mr Peter Hamilton;[1] it is typical of Pittenger's whole-hearted commitment to process metaphysics that he takes Lionel Thornton to task for thinking it necessary, as a Christian thinker, to make certain modifications in Whitehead's doctrine.[2]

It would take me too far from our present concern if I were at this point to attempt a full critique of process-theology, but it is important to distinguish between two senses in which it might be alleged that God was personally involved with time. The first is the sense maintained by the process-theologians, for whom God himself is subject to temporal process and undergoes vicissitudes and developments. This sense is altogether alien to the line of argument which I have followed in these lectures, for which temporality is a characteristic of the finite world and for which God's transcendence of the finite world necessarily includes transcendence of temporality and of becoming. God is the 'strength and stay upholding all creation, who ever doth himself unmoved abide'—

> *rerum Deus tenax vigor,*
> *immotus in te permanens.*

There is, however, another sense in which God may seem to be involved with time and which arises out of God's transcendence itself. God is the perpetual creator and sustainer of the finite temporal world and is in the most intimate relation, as creator, with every one of its constituents and with every phase of their history. Admitted that in his own ontological depth he is entirely timeless and changeless, must not his creative relation to the whole web of temporal events and his knowledge of them constitute a genuine experience of change and development on the level of his activity and consciousness? Classical theism has, of course, not been oblivious of this problem. St Thomas tells us that the relation of God to creatures, while it is 'real' as regards the world, is only 'logical' (*secundum rationem*) as regards God,[3] and he warns us that our mind 'is unable to conceive one thing as related to another without on the other hand conceiving the

---

[1] W. N. Pittenger, *Process Thought and Christian Faith*; P. Hamilton, *The Living God and the Modern World*; J. B. Cobb, *A Christian Natural Theology*.

[2] W. N. Pittenger, *The Word Incarnate*, pp. 107ff; *Christology Reconsidered*, pp. 19f, 101f.

[3] *S. Th.*, I, xiii, 7 *ad* 4; xlv, 3 *ad* 1. *S.c.G.*, II, xiii.

relation as reciprocal'.[1] Such an answer may well appear inadequate and it will no doubt seem to many to be a clever but
unqualified evasion; it should in any case be remembered that
St Thomas amplifies it considerably and makes many statements about God which imply that God has a genuine, if not
in the technical sense a 'real', concern for his creatures. However, I do not intend here to embark upon a vindication of the
Angelic Doctor, but to enquire how we are to think about the
transcendent God and his relation to a temporal and changing
world in the light of our previous discussions.

   First it must be emphasised that temporality is an essential
characteristic of the created world or at any rate of the material
part of it. (St Thomas, we might remember, ascribes to pure
spirits a mode of existence of their own, termed *aevum* or 'eviter-
nity', which, though differing in many ways from time, is quite
distinct from God's eternity and does not involve absolute
changelessness.) I would further hold that time is a derivative
from, or an aspect of, the existence of finite beings and is not an
antecedently existing medium into which they are launched.
In this I am in the line of Christian tradition going back at least
to the time of St Augustine, with his famous assertion that God
created the world not *in time* but *with time*.[2] I am also in line with
the outlook of modern physical science, which conceives the
spatio-temporal continuum as a systematic structure of relations
between concrete physical point-events; the Newtonian view of
time as a river which 'of itself, and from its own nature, flows
equably without relation to anything external',[3] though it is
associated with the great triumphs of the modern scientific
revolution, has only an episodic status in the history of scientific
thought.[4] Again, if we turn from the time of physics to that of
biology and psychology, the *temps vécu* of Bergson, it is even more
evident that each sentient individual has its own process of time,
which is intimately involved with its own vital rhythms in spite
of its complicated interrelation with the time-processes of others.
It is at this point that I find the weakness, to which I have

---

[1] *De Pot.*, I, i, 1 *ad* 10. Cf. my *Existence and Analogy*, pp. 130ff.
[2] *De Civ.*, XI, vi.
[3] *Principia*, trans. A. Motte, ed. F. Cajori, p. 6.
[4] Professor T. F. Torrance, in his book *Space, Time and Incarnation*, has
shown the harm that has been done to theology by the adoption of a recep-
tacle view of space and time.

previously referred, in the very lucid and impressive book of Dr Nelson Pike; for, though he is quite explicit that, for orthodox theism, God is not merely changeless but is also timeless, he apparently assumes, though admittedly without clearly stating this, that there is one time-process common to all finite beings and that it is, at least logically (though obviously not temporally), antecedent to them. They are in time, time is not in them. A good deal of Pike's argument is unaffected by this, or it is at least easy to make the necessary adjustments; it is, however, of some importance when we enquire how we are to understand the apparently time-referring statements which we are accustomed to make about the confessedly timeless God.

Many of the statements which philosophers and theologians make about God are, of course, intended to be understood as describing one or other aspect of his timeless existence. Thus, when it is said that God is wise or good, the verb 'is' is taken as relating not to a temporal present, sandwiched between a past and a future, but to a 'timeless present' before which the time-processes of all finite existents and the successive moments of each are uniformly and indifferently displayed and which would belong to God even if he had not created a world and was himself the only being in existence. This does of course raise questions about the possibility for time-conditioned beings such as ourselves of conceiving a timeless mode of existence and of talking about it intelligibly. Clearly, the relation between our temporal present and God's timeless present, and between the ways in which we use the same word 'is' in connection with both, is a highly analogical one. It may be helpful, though it is not altogether sufficient, to point to the contrast between the 'is' of the mathematical proposition 'The square of three is nine' and the 'is' of the empirical proposition 'There is a wart-hog in the garden'; for, without entering on the much disputed question of the logical status of mathematical entities,[1] we may say that, for anyone except an extreme Platonist, the mathematical 'is' is omnitemporal rather than strictly timeless; the square of three always was, is now, and ever will be nine, but there was not always a wart-hog in the garden. Now the 'is' of 'God is good' may also be taken in a temporal or omnitemporal sense; when I

[1] Cf. e.g., S. Körner, *The Philosophy of Mathematics*, or any other of the many text-books on the subject.

say 'God is good' at a particular moment, I certainly mean that
God is good at that moment and very probably mean that he
always was, is now and ever will be good. However, when I
remember that God is in fact timeless, I recognise that the implied reference to time in this sentence arises from the fact that
I am speaking of God from within my own temporal order of
existence and does not, or should not, suggest that God is himself in time. We might draw a rough parallel with the fact that,
if I say 'God is good', I am making an assertion in English, but
this does not imply that God himself is English. Exactly the
same assertion could be made by a Frenchman by saying 'Dieu
est bon'. What is being ascribed to God is neither the English
word 'good' nor the French word 'bon', but that which both
these words denote. Similarly, when several human beings in
talking about God use the superficially temporal verb 'is', the
implied temporality belongs to the mode of existence of the
speaker, not to the object denoted by the subject of the sentence,
'God'. We may add that the different speakers do not even share
a common time-scale; each has his own, though they are systematically connected, much as the Englishman and the Frenchman have each his own language, though the two are connected
in the ways described in grammar-books and dictionaries.

   There is not, I think, any substantial difference if we consider
not timeless statements about God but statements which ascribe
to God actions within the temporal process: 'God spoke to
Abraham', 'God saved the Israelites at the Red Sea', 'God raised
Jesus from the dead', and so on. The difference here is that the
element of temporality arises not from the fact that the sentence
is spoken or written in time, but from the fact that it describes
an action taking place in time. The temporality is, so to speak,
inside the sentence and not outside it. Nevertheless, the action
is, at its subjective pole (at God's end, if we may use the phrase),
timeless, even though at its objective pole (at the creature's end)
it is temporal. God timelessly exerts a creative activity towards
and upon the whole spatio-temporal fabric of the created universe. This will be experienced as temporal by each creature
who observes it and describes it from his own spatio-temporal
standpoint; but it no more implies that God is in time (even his
own special grade-one time) than the fact that I describe God
in English means that God is English. English may be the only

language that I know; temporal language certainly is. And since temporal existence is the only existence that creatures have, God's activity towards them is necessarily experienced by them in terms of time. But the fact that we can experience and speak of God only in temporal terms does not mean that we cannot speak of him accurately; it means that even when we speak of him accurately we have to speak of him in temporal terms. It does of course mean that there is a great deal about God that we cannot know or about which we cannot speak, except perhaps in the most distant and obscure way, but that is a different matter. God is supremely mysterious and transcendent. As Dr Cahil Daly has said, the final alternative is not between mystery and clarity but between mystery and absurdity.[1] And it is not absurd, though it may sound paradoxical, to say that it is only in temporal language that we can talk about God's timelessness.

But, it may be asked, are we not making unnecessary difficulties for ourselves in describing God as timeless or even as changeless? Has not Dr Hartshorne argued that God is perpetually surpassing himself, while remaining unsurpassable by any of his creatures? Has not Whitehead maintained that God and the world are in ceaseless interaction and come to the conclusion that God is 'the great companion—the fellow-sufferer who understands?' Has not Dr W. R. Matthews asserted that the '*Deus philosophorum* is not the God and Father of our Lord Jesus Christ'[2] and said that 'the conception of the self-sufficiency of God in and for himself is an abstract idea which cannot be allowed to dominate our theology without disastrous results'?[3] Does not, in fact, the notion of a transcendent and timeless God take all the warmth and consolation out of religion?

I do not believe that it does, especially if one believes in the doctrines of the Trinity and the Incarnation, that is to say, if one believes that God's eternal being is a life of infinite love and self-giving and that God the Son has made himself the subject of a created human nature so that, as has been finely said, the central point of Christian belief is that the maker of the universe is now a man.[4] The assertions of revealed religion must, however, not

[1] *Prospect for Metaphysics*, ed. I. T. Ramsey, p. 204.
[2] *God in Christian Thought and Experience*, p. 104.
[3] *The Purpose of God*, p. 173.
[4] Kenelm Foster, O.P., Introduction to Vol. IX of the Blackfriars edition of the *Summa Theologiae*, p. xxi.

be expounded here. It is, nevertheless, proper to point out that even strictly natural theology should not admit that its God is remote and callous or that, like the first unmoved mover of Aristotle, he is entirely unconcerned with the world and is interested only in himself and his own perfection. For, as I have emphasised many times, the timeless God and his temporal creatures are in the closest possible relation. Their radical difference from him consists in their dependence upon him; not for one instant is he absent from them at the ontological root of their existence. And, although they can experience his timeless relation to them only under the forms of their own temporal existence and although they have only their temporal concepts and speech in which to envisage and describe his timelessness, the relation which they so describe is more intimate than any that can hold between two or more temporal beings. Once again, there is mystery but not absurdity. Nevertheless, it may still be asked, why, in ascribing transcendence to God, do you find it necessary to include timelessness in that transcendence?

The simple answer to this is that temporality is precisely one of the characteristics of finite beings which, when we pass from finite beings to God, needs to be transcended. I have stressed the fact that time is neither a kind of *Ungrund* or *Urgrund*, antecedent to God himself, nor a medium created by God in which, having created it, he then finds himself to be immersed and into which he subsequently launches his creatures. The whole outlook of modern science, both physical and biological, supports us in holding that temporal process is inherent in creaturely existence and, indeed, that each individual physical or mental subject has its own individual spatio-temporal frame of reference, which is distinct from, although systematically related to, the spatio-temporal frames of others. Thus, the act in which God both preserves and knows the finite universe must necessarily be timeless and spaceless, since its object is the totality of spatio-temporal existence. If it is asserted that, in spite of this, there must be in God's own mode of existence something analogous to time, we can only reply that this must in fact be God's eternity and that what differentiates it from time is the absence of change and succession. And I do not think that we shall find a better description in our time-bound mode of speech than is given by Boethius's famous definition of eternity as 'the total, simultaneous and perfect possession of interminable life' (*in-terminabilis vitae tota simul et perfecta possessio*).[1] It may, however, be worth while to enquire how it is that Whitehead, who was thoroughly versed in the outlook of modern science and who moreover formulated a theory of relativity that was for some time a quite serious rival to the better-known theory of Einstein and Eddington,[2] should have propounded a doctrine according to which God is inherently mutable and temporal.

The explanation is, I suggest, to be found in the fact, on which I have already remarked, that the entity to which White-head gives the name 'God' is a very different being from that which is called 'God' in classical theism and has quite a different metaphysical status and function in relation to the world. It has indeed been suggested by some critics that Whitehead's God is an *ex post facto* principle of interpretation, introduced into his metaphysical system after it had been constructed and owing its introduction to Whitehead's religious cast of mind; one of Whitehead's most recent and careful students, Mr William Christian, has however come to the conclusion that this is not so and that the conception of God is 'a part of the *structure* of the system'.[3] Whatever is the truth about this—and I think Mr Christian makes his case—it is clear that for Whitehead God is not the ultimate metaphysical reality but that this position is reserved for what Whitehead calls 'creativity', a principle which is manifested in all actual entities, God not excepted. God differs from the others in that he is 'primordial'. 'Every other actual entity originates at some time and emerges into being from some definite past actual world. God originates at no time. . . . His conceptual experience is unlimited. . . . He does not perish, as all other actual entities do. For primordial means "not *before* all creation, but *with* all creation" (*Process and Reality*, p. 521). In his "consequent" nature he prehends every other actual entity throughout the course of nature.'[4] Christian adds that 'there is not explicit reference to God in [Whitehead's] categoreal scheme. . . . Categoreally speaking, the conception of God like the conception of the extensive continuum is a

[1] *De Consolatione*, V; cit. Aquinas, *S. Th.*, I, x, 1.
[2] A. N. Whitehead, *The Principle of Relativity with Applications to Physical Science* (1922).
[3] Christian, op. cit., pp. 335f.
[4] ibid., p. 288.

"derivative notion". The existence of a primordial and ever-lasting actual entity follows not from the categoreal scheme but from the nature of the world.'[1] And, in spite of the extreme elaboration of his system, Whitehead never seriously asks the basic metaphysical question, what is the explanation of the existence of contingent being? In this sense, he is not really concerned with *explanation* at all but rather with logical arrangement. 'Speculative Philosophy', he writes, at the beginning of his exposition, 'is the endeavour to frame a coherent, logical, necessary system of general ideas in terms of which every element of our experience can be interpreted', and he adds 'By this notion of "interpretation" I mean that everything of which we are conscious, as enjoyed, perceived, willed or thought, shall have the character of a particular instance of the general scheme.'[2] Here, it seems to me, Whitehead makes his purpose quite clear. In spite of his frequently expressed concern with empirical reality and with process, his final ambition is to make everything fit into a niche that he has provided for it. 'The philosophical scheme', he writes, 'should be coherent, logical, and, in respect to its interpretation, applicable and adequate',[3] and he significantly adds, not that an 'adequate' scheme will be one which gives a satisfactory answer to all reasonable questions, but simply that it will be one in which no items are incapable of the interpretation which it provides for them. And, as we have already seen, God, while unique, is in no sense ultimate; he is an accident of creativity.

> In all philosophical theory there is an ultimate which is actual in virtue of its accidents. It is only then capable of characterisation through its accidental embodiments, and apart from these accidents is devoid of actuality. In the philosophy of organism this ultimate is termed 'creativity'; and God is its primordial, non-temporal accident.[4]

We may be surprised to find God here described as 'non-temporal', in view of what we find later on in the book about the development which God undergoes in the course of his dialogue with the world, but the key is to be found in the juxta-

[1] ibid., pp. 288, 289.
[2] *Process and Reality*, p. 3.
[3] ibid.
[4] ibid., p. 9.

position here of 'non-temporal' with 'primordial'. It is only in his primordial nature that God is non-temporal, and his primordial nature is purely abstract. He attains actuality in his consequent nature and, although he has presumably his own time-scale which is different from the time-scales of other actual entities, in his consequent nature he is anything but timeless.

Two points, then, emerge from our examination of Whitehead: first, that his God has a totally different nature from that of the God of theism and plays a quite different cosmological role; secondly, that Whitehead fails to pose the basic cosmological and metaphysical question but addresses himself to a quite distinct task. It is therefore not surprising that he arrives at the notion of a changing and developing God. He writes: 'God is not to be treated as an exception to all metaphysical principles to save their collapse. He is their chief exemplification.'[1] There is an important sense in which this is true, but it needs to be supplemented by Dr H. D. Lewis's reminder: 'The infinite is not an extension of the finite but its condition.'[2] Whitehead's process-philosophy may or may not give an adequate account of the nature and development of the finite world —I think that it is in fact very largely successful—but his introduction of the actual entity which he calls 'God' seems to me to confuse rather than to clarify the situation, and his application to it of the name 'God' increases rather than lessens the confusion. I would add that, although it is common to look upon Dr Hartshorne as a disciple and expositor of Whitehead, his fundamental position is really very different. For the basis of his theism is Anselm's ontological argument, while Whitehead, with his background in Cambridge mathematical physics, was above all else an empiricist.

Process-philosophy, then, has performed a valuable task in stressing the essentially time-involved and developing character of the finite world and in exorcising a tendency, which is persistently recurrent in European thought, to identify the real with the static and to dismiss what is changing as mere appearance. But, just because time and change are genuinely inherent in the finite world and are not just an ocean in which it floats or a backcloth against which it casts its shadows, its transcendent

[1] *Process and Reality*, p. 486.
[2] *Freedom and History*, p. 282.

Creator must transcend its temporality as he transcends all its other limitations. A God to whom, in his timelessness, the whole spatio-temporal fabric of the world is eternally present is not less but more concerned with the world and its affairs than would be a God who was entangled in it. For the latter kind of deity would be limited in his experience at each moment to the particular stage in its development that the world had reached at that moment, while the former, in his extra-temporal and extra-spatial vision and activity, embraces in one timeless act every one of his creatures whatever its time and place may be. Difficult, and indeed impossible, as it is for us to imagine and feel what timeless existence is like, we can, I think, understand that a God to whom every instant is present at once has a vastly greater scope for his compassion and his power than one would have who could attend to only one moment at a time. Thus, in emphasising the timelessness of God, we are not conceiving him as remote but quite the opposite. And we can all the more whole-heartedly endorse that concern with history and finality which marks the thought of such outstanding contemporary writers as Karl Rahner and Johannes Metz and which provides one of the most hopeful starting-points for dialogue between Christians and Marxists.[1] It is equally characteristic of the writings of the great Jesuit priest Pierre Teilhard de Chardin, who, in spite of the many points at which he laid himself open to criticism, has done more than any other thinker to synthetise the religious and the scientific outlook upon the universe. Indeed it might well be maintained that it is only in the light of the timelessness of God that the temporality of the created world can be made fully intelligible.

If, then, we hold fast to God's timelessness, all those problems about foreknowledge, predestination and the like, which can only be formulated in sentences that, explicitly or by assumption, speak of God as being subject to time, simply do not arise. Neither the act of creation nor anything that happens within creation involves any change in God or in his relation to the world, true as it is that when we describe that relation from our temporal standpoint we inevitably make use of temporal language. There is, however, one point to which, in concluding this lecture, I must briefly refer, although I have discussed it at

[1] Cf. my *Theology and the Future*, pp. 81ff.

greater length elsewhere.[1] Even when we have conceded that in
God's relations with the changing world the change is all at the
world's end of the relations and not at God's end, the fact
remains that for the world to exist as well as God is more than
for God to exist without a world, and that therefore the presence of the world to God appears to add something to God,
even if it adds it to him timelessly. Even when we have said that
the creation of the world is a timeless act of unconditioned will
on the part of God, does not the existence of the world add
something to God's own existence and therefore, however timelessly, make God different from what he would be without that
timeless act? The answer to this problem lies, I believe, not, as
in the former case, in the contrast between God's timelessness
and the world's temporality, but in the contrast between God's
infinity and the world's finitude. God's presence to the world
makes all the difference conceivable to the world—the difference between existence and non-existence—but, in the strict
sense, the presence of the world to God makes no difference in
God; and this, not because the world is any less in God's sight
than it is in its own, but because God himself is infinitely more.
Finitude and infinity simply do not add together; or, if this is
too mathematical a manner of expression, let us say that
dependent and self-existent being do not add together; and this,
not because there is no link between them but for the precisely
opposite reason that it is from its dependence on self-existent
being that dependent being derives its character as dependent.
That there is mystery here we gladly affirm, but it is not
absurdity, for we can see that in the mystery the answer lies
hidden. But let us be quite sure of this: that if we mitigate the
mystery in the least degree in the hope of making understanding
easier, we shall defeat our own purpose, and absurdity will be
the penalty. Admit the tiniest element of time into God's timelessness, admit the tiniest element of finitude into God's infinity,
admit the tiniest element of dependence into God's self-
existence, and the very existence of the temporal, finite and
dependent world becomes altogether inexplicable and unintelligible.[2] That self-existent being should create a world is indeed

[1] *He Who Is*, ch. viii; *Existence and Analogy*, ch. vi.
[2] Here I must part company with Professor A. Boyce Gibson, in his
Theism and Empiricism (1970), pp. 98f *et al*, in spite of the many points in his
most interesting book with which I agree. Cf. Appendix I *infra*.

mysterious. It is, we say—and rightly—an act of supreme love, but this is another way of saying that it is unnecessary. For is it not of the essence of love that it does what it need not do?

Here I must end, very much *in mediam rem*. Mr J. A. Baker, in his astonishing book *The Foolishness of God* has said many things with which I wholeheartedly agree and some about which I am less confident. In the former class are the two assertions that 'the present contempt for natural theology must be exorcised' and that 'the supposed conflict between reason and revelation is a phantasm.'[1] If these lectures have done anything to assist the said exorcism and to evaporate the said phantasm, I shall feel that they have been worth while.

[1] op. cit., pp. 367, 368.

THE EMPIRICAL THEISM OF PROFESSOR BOYCE GIBSON

THOSE OF US who are convinced of the basic validity of the cosmological approach to theism and who believe in addition that it may rightly be called empirical will feel encouraged by Professor Boyce Gibson's recent work,[1] which represents in a reasoned argument the results of a lifetime's thought on the matter by a professional philosopher of the highest reputation.

> On the one hand [Professor Boyce Gibson writes], I believe in God, not merely on authority, but because I think there are good reasons for believing in God: . . . On the other hand, my belief in God is based not on inference but on experience: and my background is one which has not been much represented in recent controversy on the philosophy of religion: that of a Christian independency which rests on the assembled testimony of believers and not on the authority of church or academy [p. 1].

Recognising that both traditional theists and traditional empiricists will declare that his hope of showing that there is no contradiction between the theistic and the empirical outlook is doomed to disillusionment, he begins his argument with a trenchant exposition of what he describes as 'the Misadventures of Empiricism'. The first of these is the 'epistemological misadventure', which consisted in equating empiricism with sensationalism. Hume is the great offender here:

> Hume took the only way out, by resolving the mind into constituent sensations, and thereby depriving his conclusions of any

---

[1] *Theism and Empiricism*, by A. Boyce Gibson (1970) New York: Schooken Books, London: S.C.M. Press.

claim to truth. It is notable, however, that he found them impossible to live with. .... His philosophy is not a response to
environment, but the pursuit of an unempirical thesis unempiri-
cally to its logical outcome. He does not listen for contexts or
overtones. He is just a Scots dominie who has got the better of
the minister in argument. . . .

Now [Boyce Gibson continues] it is the linking of empiricism
with sensationalism which, more than anything else, has made
it implausible to talk about the empirical approach to God. If it
is possible experientially to be aware of one's self and other
people and Platonic 'kinds', distinguished from sensation by
activity on the one hand and permanence on the other, one of
the *a priori* objections to an alliance between theism and empiricism is removed [pp. 19f].

The second 'misadventure' is that of 'Subject–object Parallel-
ism', the 'standard view that ways of knowing stand in a defined
one-one relation to ways of being' (pp. 20f). The third 'misadventure' consists of the assumption that any claim to direct
insight or intuition must lay claim to incorrigibility. On the
contrary, 'the next phase of the argument is to show that religious assertions and practices are corrigible and that if they
were not they would not be properly religious' (p. 26). For the
avoidance of these and further misadventures five suggestions
are made: awareness (1) is of things-in-relation, (2) is of the
continuous, (3) is not a fact in its own right but is 'intentional'
and directed to objects, (4) has to discover the objects to which
it is directed and (5) is inseparable from valuations. 'It is only if
all of them are accepted that the road is clear for the empiricist
approach to God' (p. 27). In a vigorous criticism of Professor
R. B. Braithwaite's famous Eddington Lecture, the assertion is
made that 'there is today a greater ignorance about religion
than at any time in our history, and it is the sense of its irrele-
vance among the uninstructed (including graduates) which
gives power to the elegant and technical attempts to discredit
it' (p. 32).

Starting, as an avowed empiricist must, with experience,
Boyce Gibson insists that this must be 'ordinary experience'.
However, he asserts,

unfortunately, ordinary experience is frequently interpreted
either as the experience of ordinary men (the appeal to 'com-

mon sense', determined by numbers), or, much more misleadingly, as the experience of a fashionable cultured clique,
parading as a popular mouthpiece (*e.g.* Western intellectuals
alienated from their religious background). Neither of these
senses is here intended. In ordinary experience is included everything, however uncommon, which belongs to the scheme of
nature: *e.g.* mystical states are not to be ruled out because most
people do not have them, or are determined not to have them;
nor are the normal uncorrupted expectations of the outback
chapel or the suburban household, however, repugnant they
may be to 'advanced' or 'liberated' persons. We use the word to
denote whatever can be cited in evidence without appealing to
special revelation [p. 40].

The author then proceeds to examine what he describes as 'the
most pressing candidate', namely religious experience. 'As a
matter of phenomenological description', he writes, 'what is
given in "religious experience" is given as unqualified reality'
(p. 40). It will not do, however, to take this without argument
as an experience of God or even as experience of what we believe
to be God. 'Experience is conditioned by the worshipper's
interests and convictions. . . . The ordinary Presbyterian in
Inverness or the ordinary Catholic in Salamanca translates
anything beyond his compass into the familiar religious language, just like the ordinary Moslem in Mecca or the ordinary
Buddhist in Mandalay' (p. 42). Furthermore, 'there is experience not improperly called religious which is not directed to
God at all' (ibid.). The answer to this difficulty, Boyce Gibson
replies, 'will be that religious experience is not a separate com-
partment of life, but includes, amongst other things, an intellectual component' (p. 43).

Space is now devoted to the consideration of this intellectual
element. The force of the word 'component' is emphasised.
Religion is not a purely intellectual matter; nevertheless, the
place of the intellect is not to be minimised and, even when it is
recognised how much religious knowledge makes use of images,
'it is impossible to estimate the value of the images except inside
a conceptual scheme' (p. 47). Religion manifests wide variety,
but, 'in order to discuss the variations of religious discourse, we
must presume that there *is* an intellectual component. Otherwise religion is undiscussible, that is to say, irrational' (p. 51).

The intellectual component is closely bound up with personal religion and faith, but this does not impair its scientific character. 'Religious knowledge is empirical knowledge (imperfect, but growing) of something which is. It is an empirical knowledge of the non-empirical' (p. 56).

So much for the prolegomena to an empirical theology. The investigation proper begins with 'an enquiry into those general structures of the world with which belief in God has most commonly been associated, in the hope that there, if anywhere, the overlap, and the distance, may be brought to light' (p. 62), and it is maintained that in this the empirical enterprise is not being abandoned. 'We are looking for those features of the world that have the greatest persistence and constancy. We are *looking*; we are not inventing, or asking what *we* are contributing to the interpretation of things. . . . If this is our approach, the knowledge of God will on the one hand be as immediate as realists claim knowledge of the external world to be, and on the other opaque and discontinuous' (p. 63). 'The traditional way of recording these impressions', Boyce Gibson continues, 'is to say that we know God through his effects', but 'that is to sacrifice the factor of immediacy, and requires us to envisage God, not as presence, but as cause.' Later on, he promises, the attempt to recover the cause from the effect will be studied in detail; if such recovery is possible, cause and effect must in some sense *overlap*. Hence he prefers to speak of a 'presence' rather than of a 'cause'. More precisely, he 'propose[s] to describe it as, from the Godward side, a prolongation, and our approach to it, from the worldward side, as a grasping for fringes' (p. 64). And the most striking instances of this 'presence' or 'prolongation' which he finds in the world are those of order and creativity; these he sees as mutually correlated, but they are not simply opposites.

> Order . . . is the concrete expression of the drift to unity. It cannot be similarly said that creativity is the concrete expression of the drift to multiplicity. Multiplicity is just presented to us, and in itself is not creative at all. It is, in fact, the raw material of order. It is not, however, the opposite of order, which is chaos. Creativity is not chaos; it only looks like it to minds accustomed to traditional kinds of order. It is invention, initiative, an excursion into the unforeseen. So far from being resistant

to order, it depends doubly upon order. Order is the springboard from which it leaps, and order is what (in a new pattern) it creates. The relation between order and creativity is therefore asymmetrical [pp. 70f].

But why, is the obvious question, need we look to God to account for two features which already pervade the world?

To establish our case, we have to show that the constitutive structures of the world are neither mere effects on the one hand, nor wholly autonomous on the other. If they are considered as mere effects, we should have to argue (dubiously) from effect to cause. If they are understood as autonomous, the reference to God is unnecessary. If they are discerned as unfinished but demanding fulfilment, we can best make sense of them if we see in them the continuation (not simply the effect) of a divine presence, the approach to which will be more like the extension of a view than a transference of the mind from one thing to another [pp. 74f].

This notion of prolongation, continuation or extension of God into the world is quite fundamental to Boyce Gibson's argument, and we must stress that it is in no way pantheistic, any more than is St Thomas's doctrine that God is present in all things by 'essence, presence and power'.[1] For its justification it must be shown that order and creativity are in this world exhibited incompletely and that they demand a supplement. 'Is there anything about them, at any time, in respect of which they are less than what they have to be?' (p. 75).

Boyce Gibson rejects 'one answer, common in many religious traditions, . . . that they must be less than what they have to be if they operate in time at all', for he is going to argue later on 'that non-temporal order and creativity are inconceivable':

Order is of temporal things, and creativity requires time to move in. What is unsatisfying about order and creativity as they stand is not their temporality or even their particularity . . ., but that order and creativity are *not quite* what their deployment in the world nevertheless requires them to be. What we are in search of is an order and a creativity which shall be wholly what they are, and deny nothing of what they are: for example, their involvement in time [pp. 75f].

[1] *S. Th.*, I, viii, 3.

G

Thus, to anticipate, Boyce Gibson's God will not be timeless, or 'above' (or 'outside') time; and everything depends on his being able to argue that the 'not-quiteness' of order and creativity as we know them is due neither to their mutual interference nor to the alleged limitations of time, but to a 'prolongation' of God into the finite realm. He reasserts the primacy of creativity over order and their mutual asymmetry:

> Order does not produce creativity; creativity does produce order. If we press order alone back towards its own perfection, all we shall find is more and better order. If we similarly press creativity, we shall find more creativity, and order besides. So it is at least a possible speculation that at the far end, where each merges with the other in its own perfectness, creativity brings about the order of the world, as well as giving rise to its own image in the world. In that case, creativity assumes a certain precedence, and the world would issue from the tension between its product, order, and its own continuance [p. 78].

'Thus,' Boyce Gibson continues,

> in general terms, we have prepared the way for the view that there is an overlap of God into the world; that from the side of the world there is a grasping of fringes of God in the world; that from the side of God the overlap is a prolongation: and that there is something about the prolongation which requires to be traced back to its divine hinterland. Starting from scratch, and without religious assumptions, this is the direction in which the analysis of structures seems to call us. But that is only a beginning. It needs to be supplemented by reference to specific situations and especially the human situation; structures may pass over into *attributes* of God, but only situations can reveal his *presence* [ibid.].

Before taking this further step, however, Boyce Gibson utters two reservations. The first is that the imperfections in the world's structures need no less attention than the structures themselves. The second is that all that philosophy can provide is an increasing probability; at this point faith will take over and many things which were hitherto merely reasonable anticipations will become clearer. Faith and empiricism will then join hands.

'We have tried to show in general terms', writes Boyce Gibson, summing up the stage which he claims now to have reached in his argument, 'the perfections of the world are continuous with a beyond to which they are pointers, and at the same time and for that reason not complete in themselves' (p. 80). This might suggest something like what the Transcendental Thomists[1] have to tell us about the horizon of being, which Fr J. Donceel has briefly stated as follows:

> Man [is] the being which possesses an infinite horizon. The horizon which we see with our eyes is finite, we share it with animals. The horizon which we see with our intellect is infinite. It is the horizon of being.[2]

However it is not with the intentionality of human knowledge that we are now to be confronted, but with the structure of human values, and the chapter which deals with them is headed 'Values as Fringes'. Furthermore, 'because it exhibits the problems most clearly, we shall', our author tells us, 'concentrate on the evidence from ethics' (ibid.). 'In human behaviour,' he continues, 'structure and defect are accessible to consciousness. There is a gap between performance and possibility which the best man never quite closes. . . .'

> From one point of view, the transition from this-worldly structures to their continuation in God is easier in the case of values: easier, because it is forced upon us. . . . From another point of view, the transition is more complicated. Through experience of obstruction, the moral agent acquires a self-standingness which is often in tension . . . with the specifically religious mood of adoration. . . .
>
> Thus only if we are conscious of the gap are we sufficiently disturbed to explore new shapes of God beyond our knowledge; but in endeavouring to cope with the gap we keep ourselves so consciously erect that we sometimes do not think about God at all [pp. 80f].

In developing his argument Boyce Gibson states as a general principle that '*when any morality reaches its own peak, it moves forward into another dimension*' (p. 84), and he applies it specially to agapaistic morality. 'One way, agapaistic morality leads up to God; the other, agapaistic morality is stranded without God.

---

[1] Cf., e.g., Karl Rahner, *Spirit in the World*; Emerich Coreth, *Metaphysics*, Also chh. IV and V *supra*.

[2] Preface to E. Coreth, *Metaphysics*, p. 11.

In neither case is it independent of God' (p. 88). He denies that the excellence of morality consists of obedience to the will of God, but he also denies that morality is complete without reference to God or that it can be secured by depersonalising God. This leads him on to 'the next open frontier: the frontier of personality' and he tries to show 'that at its highest point human experience reveals an incompleteness which points on to something of the same order but relieved of the limitations' (p. 90). Divine omnipotence, he argues convincingly, is not only compatible with human freedom but positively requires and establishes it, though in this matter he is, I think, less than fair to St Thomas. 'If men are engaged on [God's] business, even unknowingly, the more they have, the more he has' (p. 93). Might we not also add: the more he has, the more they have too? Persons, it is insisted, are essentially incomplete: 'If any finite existent ever called for completion in its own idiom, it is personality.' But this involves participating in a personal existence which is more than human.

> But participation is not merely a reference back to another world. It involves an overlap; God reaching down to be a constituent of the world, and the world rising to incorporate it. As Whitehead observed, alluding to one of the said constituents, 'creativity is not separable from its creatures'. This is the picture which will be elaborated later: at present we merely reaffirm, concerning personality, the open-endedness of the finite creature, and his testimony that, if he is to be what he is, there must be somewhere something which is in greater measure what he is, with which he is somehow continuous [pp. 94f].

At this point, Boyce Gibson tells us, the drift of his argument is sufficiently clear to provoke objections. The first is that he has stressed continuity between God and man at the expense of their distance from each other. He replies that he has no intention of eliminating distance but only of putting it in its proper place. It is, however, disturbing to find that he estimates this distance purely in moral terms; some people are less distant than others and no one scores 100 per cent; furthermore humility counts for more than achievement. Little, if any, attention is paid to the *metaphysical* distance between the creator and the creature, a distance which is, of course, the other side of a most intimate propinquity, since the creature's existence from

moment to moment is entirely due to the never failing presence
within it of the creative activity of God. This defect in Boyce
Gibson's exposition is not perhaps surprising since he has conducted his argument in moral, rather than metaphysical terms;
that is to say, he has explored man's ethical relation to the
'beyond' rather than man's sheer lack of existential necessity.
More than this, even when all allowance has been made for the
fact that analogies are only analogies, it seems to me that there
is a lack of subtlety in his handling of the concepts of prolongation and of 'fringes'. For, in his exposition, both of these seem
to me to stand for some almost spatially conceived self-insertion
of God into the finite realm, rather than for his existential
energising of it. This suspicion is confirmed when one looks at
Boyce Gibson's answer to the second objection which he antici-
pates, namely that through his prolongations God will be involved in time, for he replies 'The statement is undoubtedly
true: but is it an objection?' (p. 98). 'If God is not in time', he
continues, 'he cannot love, heal, listen to prayer, make differences in the world, engage in encounter, stir, soothe, create; in
fact he cannot *do* anything whatever. The timeless God is a
legacy from the Alexandrian Neo-Platonists, for whom *doing*
anything was far too vulgar' (ibid.). The full force of the reference to Whitehead in the passage quoted above from p. 94 is
now evident, for it is notorious that Whitehead conceived God
and the world as engaged in a perpetual process of mutual
improvement.[1] What is astonishing is Boyce Gibson's complete
indifference to the way in which traditional Christian theism,
as exemplified by Aquinas among many others, replaced the
self-absorbed Aristotelian first unmoved mover, who was ignorant of the world's very existence, by the living and loving
Creator, whose sheer goodness pours itself out in giving being to
his creatures and who is the Lord of time precisely because he is
not involved in time himself. The reconciliation of God's immutability with his compassion does indeed posit a problem for
theology, but the consistent tradition classically expressed by
St Augustine in the statement that God created the world not
in tempore but *cum tempore*[2] deserves more serious attention than

---

[1] Cf. A. N. Whitehead, *Process and Reality*, pp. 492f, discussed in my *He
Who Is*, ch. xi.
[2] *De Civitate Dei*, XI, vi.

Boyce Gibson gives it. He himself sees the chief challenge to his theme as voiced by the existence of evil. His provisional answer is that God has to permit evil if he is committed to freedom: 'We have re-interpreted omnipotence as the leading of free men; the test for power is not the absence of limits, but the extent to which freedom issues from it.'

> When the time comes [the author continues] this contention will be all-important: it provides some kind of answer to the question, why should God permit any evil at all? But the fact remains that he does, and we cannot accept it uncomplainingly unless he provides some way of getting rid of it. That is something for which the Christian tradition is equipped, and the Christian tradition alone [p. 105].

At this point Boyce Gibson makes a provisional summary of his argument:

> We have groped for fringes, and we have found them. . . . Nevertheless, we can hardly be satisfied. The power of the counter-evidence is still with us; we have kept the issue open, but it is far from settled. What we have to understand is that, groping for fringes, we can expect no more. We are lucky to have the intimations that we do [ibid.].

Anticipating later discussion, he lays stress on the element of faith, which he describes as 'a trust displayed in the absence of certainty, a personal commitment filling the gap between reasonable evidence and unfaltering action'. Nevertheless, he adds, 'the demand for certainty (as opposed to necessity) is not wholly unjustified. . . . The demand for certainty comes from the side of action. How it combines with intellectual empiricism will appear later in this essay' (p. 106).

Having now established at least a provisional statement of his thesis, Boyce Gibson goes on to make an assessment of the traditional approaches to theism. He begins this by considering two positions, one philosophical and the other religious, according to which all proofs of God's existence are *a priori* self-contradictory. The *philosophical* position is the famous one of Kant. Boyce Gibson's judgment on it is that Kant's objection is valid, provided it is taken as a protest against claims to produce rigid demonstrations of theism, since demonstration involves extending to the world as a whole the ways of thinking suitable to natural objects. He holds, however, that 'there are traces in [Kant] of an empirical approach to metaphysics which he rejects as inadequate, but on which others may work with profit' (p. 113). The *religious* position considered is that of Kierkegaard, according to which 'there can be no proof of the existence of God, because proof is objective and God is not an object' (p. 114). To the first part of this objection Boyce Gibson replies: 'To admit the importance of an objectively true conception of God is not to say that God can be clearly and distinctly known, or that his existence can be proved. But to deny the importance of an objectively true conception of God is to lend ourselves to any imposture which can stir our depths' (p. 117). To the second part he replies: 'If objective truth has no standing, this statement ["God is not an object"], which is objectively intended, has no standing either. If it is to register, it must rest on an *objective* distinction between subject and object, each of them with discernible characteristics' (p. 118). The attitude in which he approaches the traditional 'proofs' is expressed thus:

> We shall expect to find that they fall short of demonstration, but contain pointers and indicators which, taken together, considerably enlarge our understanding. Kant and Kierkegaard between them have established the first point, but, thanks to their all-or-nothing frame of reference, have underestimated the second. It is to this mast that a religious empiricist must nail his colours (pp. 120f).

Passing on, then, from the general to the particular, Boyce Gibson first examines the ontological argument, first as students of Anselm and Descartes have commonly understood it and then in the interpretation recently given it by Charles Hartshorne and Norman Malcolm, according to whom what it really shows is that if God is possible he is also necessary: he cannot, so to speak, merely 'happen' to exist. Boyce Gibson's chief objection (he has others) is that to validate the argument it would need to be shown that the concept of God is not self-contradictory. On the cosmological argument, as stated for example by St Thomas in the first three of the Five Ways, he writes:

> As part of the Thomist vista, it fits perfectly. But it depends on assumptions which in the eighteenth century were becoming increasingly insecure. Its flank was no longer covered by the

Aristotelian philosophy of motion. It is clearly incompatible with the revised notion of cause, either in its Humian form, which subjectivises necessity, or in its Kantian form, which restricts objective necessity to the connexion of phenomena. . . .

Nevertheless, no matter what scientific or confessional props are withdrawn, necessary being is something that philosophical theists are not disposed to abandon. That is why an increasing proportion of the decreasing number of philosophers concerned for religion look to Thomism for a life-line. What, it is asked, could be made of a God who might not have been, or merely happened to be? It is this question, along with less enduring matter, with which the cosmological argument is so properly concerned [p. 134].

Boyce Gibson concludes 'that the facts justify hope but not complete assurance' (p. 136). 'St Thomas thought the existence of God could be proved; Kant denied it. Neither of them saw that the business of philosophers in the matter was not to prove but to provide indications' (p. 140).

Whether the two characters (necessity and perfection) can coalesce is one of the main problems of natural theology. Suffice it to say at this stage that arguments pointing to an *ens necessarium* or an *ens realissimum* do not show that they can. The cosmological argument has therefore either to be supplemented by a moral argument or to fall back on the ontological argument. But as a constructive brain-stretcher, as a destroyer of premature absolutes, and as an insistent pointer to what it does not quite establish, the argument provides a tightly reasoned prelude to that maturer conviction which is fed by other arguments and is vindicated in practice [p. 141].

A similar judgment is passed on Descartes' arguments from the existence of the idea of God in his own mind and from the fact of his own imperfect existence. More space is given to the argument from design, but with the same result. It is interesting to note that Boyce Gibson remarks: 'In my considered view, the neglect of [F. R. Tennant's] great work *Philosophical Theology* (1929), by philosophers interested in religion figures with the neglect of Whitehead by philosophers interested in science as one of the most unfortunate and gratuitous refusals of a heritage in the history of British thought' (p. 152). The general result of his extended review of the classical proofs is summed up by Boyce Gibson in the following words:

We conclude:

1. that they do not achieve demonstration;
2. that many arguments used against them do not hold water;
3. that they provide good reasons for believing;
4. that they are confronted with counter-evidence which must be faced without evasion [p. 158].

'At this point', Boyce Gibson writes, 'we pass from the shadow of the syllogism to the analysis of faith' (ibid.).

It may help us to avoid confusion if we say at once that Boyce Gibson's use of the word 'faith' is not to be identified with either its use in traditional Catholic theology or its use in traditional Protestantism, though it has affinities with both. He admits the distinction between having good reasons (which is all that the philosopher can supply) and the finality of religious conviction: 'good reasons facilitate, but do not constrain' (p. 160). He makes the important assertion: 'In analysing further the nature of religious assurance, we shall suggest that it belongs to an open-ended human situation, and its triumph is not that it limits open-endedness, but that it is completely at home in it' (pp. 159f). 'That being so', he asks, 'what are we to make of the assurance which leaps to a personal certainty and leaves even the good reasons trailing behind it? The answer is that this is what is meant by faith, and that the sphere of its operations is in the first instance in practice' (p. 160).

He begins his analysis of faith with what he calls 'faith, full stop' or 'first faith' and which he sees as antecedent to both 'faith in' and 'faith that', though he insists that in a matured faith both these have their place. Its basic feature is 'refusal to accept "the impossible"' (p. 161). It is forward-looking; unlike fear, which keeps us behind our defences, faith takes us out from behind them. In the normal cases it is not specifically religious; 'it is the more difficult cases which drive us to religion. But both alike spring from a *natural resilience* transmitted by the creator to the creature for continuing the work of creation" (p. 163). (This last statement is presumably a reflective judgment made from the later standpoint of a matured faith.)

It is clear [Boyce Gibson continues] that faith arises in the first instance in the context of *action*. All the classical instances relate to something being *done*. This is the foundation on which the more sophisticated elaborations are created and which, in expounding them, we must never be tempted to forget. Faith as a whole relates to life as a whole, and life as a whole is a doing —even if the particular kind of doing is, in a few selected cases, thinking. . . .

We have set forth the simple faith which is continuous with the vitality and elasticity of nature on the one hand, and is the first movement towards God on the other. We have now to trace its development into its more complete manifestations [pp. 163–5].

Passing on from 'first faith' to faith in God, Boyce Gibson emphasises that ' "faith in" a friend or a spouse is a specification of "first faith" to a particular person' (p. 165). He condemns the tendency to think of faith as one-sided, as if we could have faith in God but God could not have faith in us; the Bible, he reminds us, shows God having 'faith in some very bad risks indeed' (p. 166). This is, I think, a valid point, but it emphasises the fact that 'faith' designates something different from what it designates in the scholastic tradition. There is an impressive argument, which it would be difficult and unjust to summarise, supporting the assertion that 'first faith' can legitimately become 'faith in', and not merely faith in *something* but faith in *God*. This leads to a discussion of the relation between 'faith in' and 'faith that':

There is room both for *assensus* and for *fiducia*. . . . The view here put forward is that the 'articles of faith 'are empirically elaborated from the structure of faith itself, and that faith itself is not a matter of assenting to articles. The traditional view is that they are delivered to us as articles, or at any rate as a system of articles, by an authority which we absolutely trust. The intellectual component, in the first case, is a corrigible transcript of faith; in the second, it is an infallible dictate of faith. In the first case, the problem is to find an appropriate set of conceptual symbols for a total response. In the second case, the problem is how a conceptual assent shall (as Calvin put it) 'penetrate to the heart, so as to have a fixed seat there'. The distinction is crucial for those exploring the empirical approach to religion [pp. 173f].

The piquant remark is added that, 'paradoxically, it was the father of British empiricism, John Locke, who most unequivocally identified faith with assent to propositions' (p. 174).

Clearly, Boyce Gibson is here raising a question of the utmost importance, not only for natural theology but for any religion which includes a genuinely institutional element. What is the relation between dogmatic truth and the socially and culturally conditioned conceptual and verbal forms in which it expresses itself? How are we to be sure of retaining the former if and when we find it necessary to change or modify the latter? It is no criticism of Boyce Gibson to point out that he does not deal with this problem, for it lies outside the scope of his discussion; it is nevertheless well to recognise it. And Boyce Gibson does in fact avoid any facile anti-intellectualism. In an able discussion of Newman's work on the notion of 'assent', he writes:

> We are driven to the conclusion that, 'faith in' being anchored to an object, 'faith that' is already implicit in it. Therefore, to retreat from the intellectual complexities of 'that' to the religious simplicities of 'in' is a mistake, both religious and philosophical. It is a religious mistake because all retreating is a religious mistake; it displays a failure of original faith. It is a philosophical mistake, because what is denied reappears in what is affirmed. What has rendered it plausible is that 'faith that' may exist without 'faith in' [p. 177].

The telling point is made that 'the objection to "faith that" as prejudicial to "faith in" stems from a view about thinking which would be misleading in contexts other than of religion: and this is an opportunity for considering it in general terms' (p. 178).

Boyce Gibson admits the contention that the inner preserves of the spirit must not be subjected to an over-simplifying intellectualism, but he replies that 'in thinking about our experiencing, we do not eliminate the experience: we find for it proper symbolic forms which communicate it to others and make it available for them', and he adds that 'herein lies the peculiar value of Newman's distinction between notional and real assent'. He denies 'that "faith that", which retrieves the implications, is false to "faith in", which exhibits but does not explore them.' Nevertheless, 'it remains true that "faith that" disengages them and does not justify them.' In line with his basic empiricism he asserts that 'faith does not need to be justified by anything other than practice, or, if practice already embodies it, it does not need to be justified at all' (pp. 179f). The proper

task of theology, in the narrow sense of the word, is to disengage
and set in order the presuppositions of our profoundest experiences, with their concealed intellectual content. The difficulty
of the task is emphasised, and not least the extent to which
the theological expressions will vary both with the degree of
faith and with the secular assumptions and personal idiosyn-
crasies of the theologian. Furthermore the acceptance of any
infallible authority is disowned as cramping and curtailing the
free development of faith: 'a *continuous* revelation finds room, as
a fixed revelation does not, for the exploratory genius of faith'
(p. 182). Once again we are on the fringe of the problem of the
relation between the revelation and its developing expressions
and, indeed, of the problem of the sense in which revelation can
be said to be complete in Christ and of the distinction, if there
is one, between revealed and natural knowledge of God and his
acts. I shall not attempt to deal with them here. It is, however,
important to notice that Boyce Gibson distinguishes between
'faith that' and general philosophy: 'They move in the same
area: they deal with the general characters of things; and both
are concerned with problems about God. But they are directed
to them at different levels of a spiritual dialectic' (pp. 182f).
'Without philosophy faith would lack rational antecedents.
Without theology it would lack rational formulation' (p. 183).
Nevertheless, we are told that both faith and philosophy 'are
exhibitions of empirical reasoning and neither can lay claim to
necessity' (p. 182), and this might cause us to qualify the statement 'We shall find ourselves nearer to the Thomist model than
at first appeared: the distinction between natural and revealed
theology will be retained, together with the hierarchical relation between them. But faith will not be identified with any
assent to propositions, however supernatural; it is the initial and
sustaining activity which carries the propositions on its shoulders'
(p. 183). It is in accordance with this point of view that Boyce
Gibson goes on to draw a firm distinction between 'faith' and
'belief'.

What, we might wonder, is the point of this analysis of faith?
It is to enable us to have a rational answer to the counter-
affirmations, the obstacles to theism, which philosophical enquiry
alone cannot rebut; and of these the most serious is, of course,
posed by the problem of evil, in the forms both of suffering and

of wickedness. And here the specifically Christian answer is given. In a discussion to which a summary could hardly do justice it is argued that, if God is what Christ is, the promise of faith—the promise that evil can be overcome and dissipated—not only *can*, but *will*, be fulfilled. It is not easy to see what kind of Christology is implied in this discussion. We are told that

> the doctrine of Incarnation [not, we observe, *the* Incarnation] changes the whole face of the problem of evil. But the failure to press the point home lies with those of its exponents who do not actualise it in psychological terms, who do not relate it to the human dealings of Jesus Christ. To reverse the normal order: he did not do what he did because he was God: he was God because he did what he did [p. 201].

It is difficult to know what is the precise force of the words 'because' in the last sentence. Does it mean that 'doing what he did' is the *meaning* of 'being God', or that doing what he did is *evidence* for his being God?[1] Boyce Gibson is too proficient a philosopher to fall easily into a logical confusion, but he does seem here to come close to doing so and to saying 'Jesus must have been God, because what I mean by God is Jesus'. Thus he continues:

> It is useful to over-simplify in this sense, because it brings out a fundamental ambiguity. If it is part of the definition of God to be up-there and *not* down-here, then of course Incarnation is impossible, a *priori*. But that definition of God, like all definitions, has to run the gauntlet of experience, and the time came when it wore out. That was when people found out that God was amongst them and could not make God real to themselves in any other way: those 'who through him do believe in God, who raised him up from the dead and gave him glory' (I Peter 1.21). The concept of God, at that moment, turned a sharp corner.

Nevertheless, Boyce Gibson immediately adds: 'And once it was turned, it was realised that what had been revealed had always been there. "Before Abraham was, I am."'(p. 201). I think therefore that he is in fact innocent of reducing the divinity of Jesus to a mere tautology, though, as I shall assert later on, I

---

[1] The use of quotation marks in this sentence is deliberate. In the first alternative we are concerned with concepts, in the latter with events.

think he has, on philosophical as well as theological grounds, an inadequate understanding of God.

Summarising this very crucial stage in his argument, Boyce Gibson writes:

> We have spoken of faith as if its function were to break down a theoretical objection. So it is, amongst others: but faith is not primarily a theoretical activity. It is, in the widest sense of the word, a practical activity: in the sense, that is, in which practice includes theory but surpasses it [p. 202].

'All through,' he writes, 'the reference is to a practice which outruns theory. And therefore, he continues 'with this is combined a demand for verification' (ibid.). And his complaint about the 'verificationist' school is that their notion of verification is too narrow.

> The trouble about the so-called verification principle, like the trouble about empiricism in general, lies in its limitation to the area of sense-perception. In itself, it is not only unobjectionable, but, as a sequel to empirical philosophy and religious faith, indispensable. It is in the moment of practice that the philosophy is vindicated and the faith receives embodiment. . . . What is now required of us is a re-interpretation of the verification principle which its usual exponents would energetically repudiate [pp. 202f].

Boyce Gibson thus passes on from his Analysis of Faith to a consideration of Faith and Practice. In spite of his emphasis upon experience and verification, he refuses to accept without qualification the comparison which is sometimes made between religious dogmas and experience on the one hand and scientific theories and experiments on the other; and this for two reasons. In the first place, in the case of religion it is extremely difficult, and indeed undesirable, to exclude 'complicating factors'; in the second, in the case of religion it is impossible to send an action back for modification and the agent has had to commit *himself* with his experiment. Nevertheless, 'the risks being so much greater, verification is not less, but more, indispensable' (p. 212). But what kind of verification?

> Verification can only take the form of a gradually widening conviction, spread over the years from the hopes of youth to the meditations of age, and over situations swinging between crisis

and routine, that the way of faith is the sufficient way, and one in which each of its phases promotes its own perpetuation. The verification of faith is not, like the verifications of science, particular verification, though it is shown forth in particulars, even in 'minute particulars', but an overall verification, broadening as it goes along, starting as an unforgettable firing of the imagination, and validating itself in every actual situation, both through its own successes and through the manifest failure of the recognised alternatives. This does not make it any the less a verification. It means that verification in science, which is often taken as a universal model, is only one kind of verification [p. 213].

This contention is developed at considerable length and it takes the author into the field of ethics:

The principle that there is a carry-over from God to practice does not settle the matter, for there are many ideas of God and many more or less consequential kinds of practice. Admitting that faith in God completes itself in practice, which God and what practice? [p. 221].

The principle which Boyce Gibson invokes is (1) that there must be no collision between religion and other excellences and (2) that there must be no limit to the field in which religion operates. These, it is recognised, while they are necessary, are not sufficient to exclude all religions but one; they embrace most of the major religions. It is, however, argued that the specifically Christian ethic of charity provides a strong case for Christianity, and R. B. Braithwaite's attempt to detach an agapaistic way of life from factual belief is dismissed as ineffectual:

[The ethic of charity] certainly finds a response in human experience, but it needs a great deal of sustaining, and it is noteworthy that Braithwaite finds it necessary to keep nourishing the imagination with ritual and stories. Would ritual and stories serve the purpose if the ritual were merely an artistic performance and the stories merely untrue? [p. 230].

Finally, Kant's doctrine that God is a postulate of morality and not an object of contemplation is alleged to be insufficient: 'Because we have accepted provisionally metaphysical theses which Kant thought inadmissible, and have been verifying faith rather than erecting postulates, we can appeal directly to practice for our sanction, instead of finding, indirectly, a sanction for our practice' (p. 236).

At this point Boyce Gibson's argument is substantially complete, but he adds a further chapter entitled 'Return to Metaphysics', in which he raises the question: 'Assuming that a faith verified in practice can take care of the counter-evidence, how can we elaborate the concept of God?' (p. 238). He adds two cautions: first, we can make no more than a penultimate approach to an ultimate mystery, and, secondly, we must not read the assurance of faith back into the tentative recognitions of empirical metaphysics. 'In the renewal of metaphysics, faith must remain faith: otherwise there would be no renewal of metaphysics; and metaphysics must remain empirical, otherwise there would be no room for faith' (p. 239).

In this renewal our author first considers the notion of God as necessary being, *ens necessarium*. While admitting that it is repugnant to suppose that God just *happens*, he holds that the application of 'necessary' and 'contingent' to God is a category mistake; these words belong only to the world. We might note in passing that Fr W. Norris Clarke has pointed out that St Thomas himself never uses 'necessary' as an attribute proper to God:

> This came in only through the Augustinian tradition stemming from Anselm. It became fixed as a primary attribute of God only in modern scholasticism through which it spread to other modern philosophers in the rationalist tradition which tended to deduce or at least explain the existence of God as somehow flowing from his essence. Duns Scotus is a prime example of this procedure, even though he stays clear of the ontological argument in its pure form.[1]

Boyce Gibson repeats his previous assertion that God is himself subject to time and change; this he holds to follow from the fact that God is the principle not only of order but also of creativity:

> God, then, is not timeless. He is coeval with all possible time and he is expressed in the world in some structures admitted to be changeless. But changelessness is not timelessness: it could just as well be indefinite continuance. And as the changeless structures of the world reappear in different contexts in different

[1] 'Analytic Philosophy and Language about God', in *Christian Philosophy and Religious Renewal*, edited by George F. McLean, O.M.I., p. 55.

individual cases, being integral elements in the most variable situations, this would appear to be the more appropriate form of expression. God, then, as shown by his prolongations, has his continuances and his mobilities; in our picture, the latter predominate, and even the former do not suggest timelessness [pp. 242f].

From this Boyce Gibson passes on to a discussion of God and Body. It is not easy to discover the precise sense in which 'body' and 'matter' are understood here, but it is quite clear that God is himself bodily. This leads on to some very original reflections upon the Incarnation: 'If God has no body,' we are told, 'there is an unbreakable dilemma between universal Idealism and universal materialism, under both of which dispensations God disappears. All this follows without any reference to the specific features of Christian revelation' (p. 244). Nevertheless, the Christian revelation is held to throw light upon it.

Boyce Gibson rightly remarks that God has a body in the sense that he became incarnate in Jesus Christ, and he laudably ignores the view implicitly held by many people that, while God was in some sense incarnate in Jesus during the period of his earthly life, he ceased to be incarnate at the end of it. He goes on, however, to assert that, if God *was* incarnate in human nature during the earthly life of Jesus, this can only have been possible if he was, in some sense, incarnate before:

> How can what is wholly immaterial become body *at any time*?...
> It is better [presumably this also means 'truer'] to say that incarnation is perpetual, and what is unique about the Incarnation of God in Christ is its definitive form and direction: it perfects a long-standing process, and provides for its perpetuation in the perfected form. ... The divine body pre-dates the Incarnation, though it is only in the Incarnation that it achieved perfection and was backed into a point of time [pp. 245f].

It must, I think, be recognised at this point that there is a very close connection between this highly idiosyncratic view of the Incarnation and the special type of empiricism that Boyce Gibson has adopted from the start. It is, I think, implicit in his view of the 'prolongations' of God in the world and our apprehension in it of his 'fringes' that, for him, God, however much he may differ from us in certain respects, is essentially *finite* and therefore mutable. It is not surprising therefore to find Boyce Gibson speaking so sympathetically about Whitehead and Hartshorne. It is very significant that, although there are five references to 'analogy' in the Index, there is no serious discussion of the principle of analogy itself. In consequence, such words as 'prolongation' and 'fringes' are applied to God in a purely univocal way; there is no adequate discussion of the unique relation of the Creator to his creatures. Nor, in spite of the author's obvious desire to be in line with contemporary thought, is there any attention to the view that time is not a medium in which God and creatures are alike immersed but is an inherent property of creatures, arising from their fundamental finitude and their mutual relations. I think there is real force in Karl Rahner's insistence, in his recent book *The Trinity*, that there is an essential conformity of human nature to the Second Person of the Godhead, that the Son is the only one of the Persons that could become incarnate, and that human nature is the only nature that God, if he was to become incarnate, could hypostatically assume. But this is very different from Boyce Gibson's view that, if the Incarnation in Jesus was to be possible, God must have been, in some diffused way, incarnate all the time: Boyce Gibson does indeed assert that the Incarnation, while it is not 'rationally incredible', does, 'rationally speaking, eclipse all possible expectations' (p. 248), but he does not seem to me to have reached that point of wondering awe which led St Thomas to write:

> We must now speak of the mystery of the Incarnation, which of all the works of God most greatly surpasses our reason; for nothing more wonderful could be thought of that God could do than that very God, the Son of God, should become very man.[1]

There is, I would suggest, behind Boyce Gibson's unreflectively unanalogical use of the notions of 'prolongation' and 'fringes', a slightly but significantly mistaken understanding of the nature of the datum of a satisfactorily empirical theology. 'Prolongations' and 'fringes' suggest that God, as it were, extends himself or lowers himself into the world, so that we apprehend immediately the periphery of his own substance. (If it

[1] *S.c.G.*, IV, xxvii.

is retorted that one need not understand the notions in question is so ham-fisted a way, my reply is that Boyce Gibson fails to make the necessary qualifications.) It is not surprising, therefore, that God does not appear to differ qualitatively from finite beings, since we can apprehend *him* as directly as we apprehend *them*. This is very far removed from that apprehension of creatures as dependent upon their transcendent ground—that apprehension of 'God-and-the-creature-in-the-cosmological-relation'—which is the starting-point of the natural theology of such scholars as the late Austin Farrer, Dom Mark Pontifex, Dom Illtyd Trethowan and the present writer. This is, I think, a serious criticism and it seems to me to be borne out by Boyce Gibson's subsequent remarks on Transcendence, Tension, Goodness and the Divine Concern. I do not wish in any way to minimise the problem that there is on the traditional view in reconciling the divine compassion with the divine immutability, though I am sure that the heart of the solution lies in the divine infinity and the relation of infinite to finite being. And it is because the God of Whitehead, Hartshorne and Boyce Gibson is not strictly infinite that their solutions are, as I believe, unsatisfactory. Boyce Gibson tells us that in 1968 an article by Arthur Koestler imaginatively depicting the human feelings of Christ on the cross was 'denounced as blasphemous by several sincerely Christian correspondents who forgot . . . that he would not have gone through with the humanly speaking (and divinely speaking) ghastly business if he had not had to be man to the last limit of suffering and humiliation' (p. 253). I am led to comment that in the very animated discussions that took place some years ago about the authenticity of the Holy Shroud of Turin it was taken for granted without reservation by all concerned (many of whom were certainly 'traditional' in their theology) that, until the moment of his resurrection, the body of Jesus was, in all its reactions, physiological, physical and chemical, exactly the same as any other human body would have been. No doubt there have always been adherents of a docetic Christology, but they are not specially to be found among traditional theologians. I am reminded, too, of a remark made by a tourist after contemplating for some time the mosaic of the Pantocrator in the dome of the church at Delphi, a representation which many have criticised as barbaric, severe and even menacing, 'My word', he said, 'what he had been through before he rose from the dead!'

This has been a long discussion, but Boyce Gibson's book is so carefully constructed and so closely knit together that only a long discussion could do it justice; this must be my excuse for the very extensive quotations from it which I have found it necessary to make in the course of my critique. If I have felt obliged to express disagreement on several points, and in particular on one that is fundamental to its approach, this does not mean that I am blind to its merits or unappreciative of the combination of religious concern and philosophical integrity which characterises its author. It is, I venture to say, one of the most interesting and instructive works on natural theology that we have seen in recent years.

A SOCIOLOGICAL APPROACH
TO THEISM

I T WAS NOT until the text of the present work was completed that there came into my hands the short but original and, in my judgment, very significant book of Dr Peter L. Berger *A Rumour of Angels*, written in 1968, published in the United States of America in 1969 and in England in 1970. His approach is very different from that which I have adopted, but I have more than once emphasised that mine is not the only valid approach and the two, though different, are quite consistent with each other. Its special importance arises from the fact that Dr Berger is professionally not a theologian or a philosopher but a sociologist with a special interest in religion. Furthermore, unlike most sociologists who have studied religion, he is not merely interested in religion as a social phenomenon but as something of vital concern in itself. 'I think', he writes, 'that religion is of very great importance at any time and of particular importance in our own time. If theologising means simply any systematic reflection about religion, then it would seem plausible to regard it as too important to leave to the theological experts. Ergo, one must stick out one's neck. This implies impertinence as well as modesty. To try at all may well be impertinent. This should make it all the clearer that the effort is tentative and the result unfinished' (pp. 10f).

Berger thus belongs to that honourable body of persons, of whom C. S. Lewis, Dorothy Sayers, Mr Sherwin White and Mr Harry Blamires are notable examples, who, while highly distinguished in their own expertise, have devoted a great deal of thought to matters of religion. And, like those I have just mentioned, he comes, in spite of his modest disclaimer, to conclusions much more positive than those of many of the professional theologians. This does not mean that his arguments are any less convincing than theirs.

His opening chapter is entitled 'The Alleged Demise of the Supernatural' and it opens with the assertion that 'if commentators on the contemporary situation of religion agree about anything, it is that the supernatural has departed from the modern world. This departure', he continues, 'may be stated in such dramatic formulations as "God is dead" or "the post-Christian era".' (p. 13). He instances the pronouncement of Dr Thomas Altizer that 'we must realise that the death of God is an historical event, that God has died in our cosmos, in our history, in our *Existenz*'; and he remarks that 'the departure of the supernatural has been received in a variety of moods—with prophetic anger, in deep sorrow, with gleeful triumph, or simply as an emotionally unprovocative fact' (ibid.). Unlike many writers, however, Berger immediately enquires how much evidence there is for this alleged demise of the supernatural and he points out that the answer hinges on what may be called the secularisation theory of modern culture, the term 'secularisation' referring not to what has happened to social institutions but to processes within the human mind, that is, a secularisation of *consciousness*. And here, he tells us, 'the empirical evidence is not very satisfactory' (p. 16), since sociologists, even those professing the 'sociology of religion', have regarded religion almost exclusively in terms of the traditional religious *institutions*. In this realm he admits that there has been a progressive decline, in Europe at least, while in America the increase in church-membership figures has been accompanied by very much altered motives for participation. (Had he written two years later he might have sensed an impending numerical decline in America as well.) And, while stressing the need for more plentiful and precise evidence, he concedes that, 'whatever the situation may have been in the past, *today* the supernatural as a meaningful reality is absent or remote from the horizons of everyday life of large numbers, very probably of the majority, of people in modern societies, who seem to manage to get along without it quite well' (p. 18). Thus, those to whom the supernatural is a meaningful reality form a *cognitive minority*, a group whose view of the world differs significantly from that of society in general; a group formed around a body of deviant 'knowledge'. ('Knowledge', we are warned, is here used in the sociologists' sense of what is taken to be true or believed to be true, regardless of whether it is true in fact.) Such a cognitive minority, it is pointed out, will always find itself under very considerable social and psychological pressures; it is thus not surprising that a profound theological crisis exists today. 'The theologian like every other human being exists in a social milieu. . . . The theologian more and more resembles a witch doctor stranded among logical positivists—or, of course, a logical positivist stranded among witch doctors. Willy nilly he is exposed to the exorcisms of his cognitive antagonists' (p. 21). Berger very perceptively describes the way in which, since the First World War, this impact of secularisation has affected Protestant, Catholic and also Jewish communities and goes on to say that one's predictions of the future will depend on one's understanding of the process in the past. He admits that we must always be ready for surprises but judges that a reversal of the secularising movement is unlikely. Thus for the 'cognitive minority' there is the choice between hanging on to or sur-rendering its 'cognitive deviance'.

Berger develops a very interesting discussion of the options that are open to religious groups in this situation. 'Cognitive deviance', he shows, runs into considerable difficulties of 'social engineering' and is complicated, in the case of the major Christian groups, by a profound aversion to sectarian forms and to the mentality of the ghetto. The opposite attitude—that of 'cognitive surrender'—involves an almost unreserved con-cession to the '*Weltanschauung* of modern man'. 'Modernity is swallowed hook, line and sinker, and the repast is accom-panied by a sense of awe worthy of holy communion' (p. 34). And Berger adds that at the moment 'the feast lacketh not in attendance'. The intellectual task involved in this is that of *trans-lation* of traditional religious terms into those appropriate to the frame of reference that conforms to the modern *Weltanschauung*, and it is remarked that there is striking disagreement about the grammar that is to be employed. Existentialism, Jungian psy-chology, linguistic philosophy and popular sociology have all been brought into service. Nevertheless, 'whatever the differ-ences in method, the result is very similar in all these cases: the supernatural elements of the religious traditions are more or less completely liquidated, and the traditional language is transferred from other worldly to this worldly referents' (p. 35).

Berger mildly remarks that 'these procedures require a good deal of intellectual contortionism', but, he adds, 'the major sociological difficulty, however, lies elsewhere'. Many benefits are offered:

> The lay recipient of these blessings will be either a happier person (his existential anxieties assuaged or his archetypal needs fulfilled) or a more effective citizen (usually this means a bigger and better political liberal), or perhaps both. The trouble is that these benefits are also available under strictly secular labels. . . . Why should one buy psychotherapy or racial liberalism in a 'Christian' package, when the same commodities are available under purely secular and for that very reason even more modernistic labels? . . . In other words, the theological surrender to the alleged demise of the supernatural defeats itself in precisely the measure of its success [ibid.].

Berger goes on realistically to point out that neither of these extreme solutions is likely as regards the larger religious groups. Rather there will take place some kind of compromise, 'a bargaining process with modern thought, a surrender of some traditional (which here equals supernatural) items while others are kept' (p. 36). And he sees this as the classical pattern of Protestant theological liberalism; it has the unfortunate result that, once the cognitive antagonist has been admitted within the theological gates, it is hard to see where the process will stop. There is the added disadvantage that, in the modern world, adaptations can very quickly become out of date. Dr Harvey Cox's celebration of the advent of modern urbanisation in 1965 in his book *The Secular City* is instanced as having lost some of its glamour in the present American urban predicament. Berger sees little hope for theological compromise at the present day.

The obvious alternatives of the avowedly unreligious systems are not, however, seen as much more hopeful. 'They fail . . . in interpreting and thus in making bearable the extremes of human suffering. . . .

> The Marxist case is instructive. The Marxist theory of history does, indeed, provide a kind of theodicy: all things will be made

whole in the post-revolutionary utopia. This can be quite comforting to an individual facing death on the barricades. Such a death is meaningful in terms of the theory. But the wisdom of Marxism is unlikely to afford much comfort to an individual facing a cancer operation. The death he faces is strictly meaningless within this (and, indeed, any) frame of reference of theodicy slanted toward this world [p. 41].

Berger adds that 'these remarks are not, at this point, intended as an argument for the truth of religion. Perhaps the truth is comfortless and without ultimate meaning for human hope.' He is still speaking simply as a sociologist. But, as a sociologist, he feels constrained to stress that 'sociologically speaking, . . . the stoicism that can embrace this kind of truth is rare. Most people, it seems, want a greater comfort, and so far it has been religious theodicies that have provided it' (ibid.). His conclusion therefore is that

There are therefore some grounds for thinking that, at the very least, pockets of supernaturalist religion are likely to survive in the larger society. As far as the religious communities are concerned, we may expect a revulsion against the more grotesque extremes of self-liquidation of the supernaturalist traditions. It is a fairly reasonable prognosis that in a 'surprise-free' world the global trend of secularisation will continue. An impressive rediscovery of the supernatural, in the dimensions of a mass phenomenon, is not in the books. At the same time, significant enclaves of supernaturalism within the secularised culture will also continue. . . . The large religious bodies are likely to continue their tenuous quest for a middle ground between traditionalism and *aggiornamento*, with both sectarianism and secularising dissolution nibbling away at the edges [pp. 41f].

'This is not a dramatic picture', Berger adds, 'but it is more likely than the prophetic visions of either the end of religion or a coming age of resurrected Gods' (ibid.).

It is important to remember that this is a purely rational judgment, made from the detached standpoint of a sociologist, and it prescinds altogether from questions of the truth or falsehood of religious beliefs. Nevertheless it is instructive to contrast it with the very different judgments of the secularising theologians, who, it must be recalled, profess to base their conclusions on an equally detached and unsupernaturalistic foundation. A theist may perhaps envisage the possibility of a more widely religious future, for he will be prepared for God to do unexpected things, and he will remember that the sociologist very properly made his prophecies on the presupposition of a 'surprise-free world', that is 'a world in which present trends continue to unfold without the intrusion of totally new and unexpected factors' (p. 30).

So much, then, for Berger's assessment of the religious situation. In his second chapter, entitled 'The Perspective of Sociology: Relativising the Relativisers', he begins to get to grips with the real problem. He maintains that at the present day it is from the side of sociology that the authenticity of religious belief is challenged.

> Sociology is simply the most recent in a series of scientific disciplines that have profoundly challenged theology. The physical sciences were probably first in the line of attack, and it is they that first occur to most people when a scientific challenge to theology is mentioned. . . . The revolution in biology during the nineteenth century further aggravated the challenge. If Copernicus dethroned man cosmologically, Darwin dethroned him even more painfully biologically. . . . Contrary to the popular assumptions, I would, however, argue that the physical sciences' challenge to the theology have been *relatively* mild. . . . The challenges of the human sciences, on the other hand, have been more critical, more dangerous to the essence of the theological enterprise. . . . Put simply, historical scholarship led to a perspective in which even the most sacrosanct elements of religious traditions came to be seen as *human* products. Psychology deepened this challenge, because it suggested that the production could be not only seen but explained . . .
>
> I, for one, take the claims of history more seriously than those of psychology. Be this as it may, the challenge of sociology can be seen as a further intensification of the crisis [pp. 45–7].

As instances of this Berger gives the studies by Gabriel LeBras of Catholic practice in France and of studies of the outlook and beliefs of religious congregations in the United States. The latter have often led to the discovery that 'what many in [the minister's] congregation mean by religion has very little relationship to what he means or to the denominational tradition to which the congregation claims allegiance' and that 'his own role is understood by members of the congregation in a way that is diametrically opposed to his self-understanding' (p. 49). A more profound dimension in the sociological challenge is, however, asserted to come from that department of sociology called 'the sociology of knowledge', which began in the 1920s and was made accessible to English-reading people in the writings of Karl Mannheim. One of its basic theses is that we derive our views of reality from other persons and that their continued plausibility depends upon others continuing to affirm them. 'When we get to the more sophisticated of these conceptions, there are likely to be organised practices designed to still doubts and prevent lapses of conviction. These practices are called therapies. There are also likely to be more or less systematised explanations, justifications, and theories in support of the conceptions in question. These, sociologists have called legitimations' (pp. 50f). The inference is then drawn that the beliefs which a man has about the nature of reality (and this, of course, includes his religious beliefs) depend almost entirely on the plausibility structures with which he is surrounded. What, then, is the consequence once this is recognised?

> The mystery of faith now becomes scientifically graspable, practically repeatable, and generally applicable. The magic disappears as the mechanisms of plausibility generation and plausibility maintenance become transparent. The community of faith is now understandable as a *constructed entity*—it has been constructed in a specific human history, by human beings. Conversely, it can be dismantled or reconstructed by use of the same mechanisms. . . . In other words, the theologian's world has become *one world among many*—a generalisation of the problem of relativity that goes considerably beyond the dimensions of the problem as previously posed by historical scholarship. To put it simply: history posits the problem of relativity as *a fact*, the sociology of knowledge as *a necessity of our condition* [pp. 54f].

Sociology, Berger tells us, is thus the debunking discipline *par excellence*, but as far as theology is concerned he claims that there are unexpected redeeming features. 'One cannot throw a sop to the dragon of relativity and then go about one's business as usual, although Max Scheler, the founder of sociology of knowledge, tried to do just that' (p. 55). In the theological realm he discerns a similar tendency in those theologians who have drawn a distinction between 'religion', which is vulnerable to all the attacks of relativism, and 'Christian faith', which is somehow immune from them. This gambit, exemplified both by Karl Barth and by the Bultmannite school with the distinction between *Historie* and *Geschichte* or between 'profane' and 'salvation history', Berger sees as quite inadequate: 'it curiously repeats the old Calvinist doctrine of election—you don't get there unless you start from there' (p. 56). His own reply to the relativisers is very different. It is that, if you adopt the relativising principle, you must see it through to the end, and that when you do this 'the question of truth reasserts itself in almost pristine simplicity. Once we know that all human affirmations are subject to scientifically graspable socio-historical processes, *which affirmations are true and which are false?* We cannot avoid the question any more than we can return to the innocence of its pre-relativising asking' (p. 57).

Berger illustrates the point by reference to recent 'radical' or 'secular' theology, which translates the Christian tradition into terms supposedly consonant with the alleged modern consciousness. He instances Bultmann's programme of demythologising, 'which begins with the premise that no one who uses electricity and listens to the radio can any longer believe in the miracle world of the New Testament, and ends by translating key elements of the Christian tradition into the categories of existentialism' (ibid.); other theologians, he remarks, prefer linguistic philosophy or Jungian psychology to existentialism. What they are doing in fact, though they do not recognise its illegitimacy, is to apply the socio-historical weapon to the beliefs of the *past* while keeping the beliefs of the *present* (their own beliefs) immune from it. This, says Berger, is really rather funny but it will not do, since the beliefs of the present-day radical theologians are just as much socially conditioned as those of the New Testament writers.

It may be conceded that there is in the modern world a certain type of consciousness that has difficulties with the supernatural. The statement remains, however, on the level of socio-historical diagnosis. The diagnosed condition is *not* thereupon elevated to the status of an absolute criterion; the contemporary situation is not immune to relativising analysis. . . . We may agree, say, that contemporary consciousness is incapable of conceiving of either angels or demons. We are still left with the question of whether, possibly, both angels and demons go on existing despite this incapacity of our contemporaries to conceive of them [p. 59].

Berger, thus, does not deny the socially conditioned character of all beliefs and indeed he goes on to emphasise the problems that it raises in a pluralistic society such as our own, in which the individual man or woman may find his life divided between two or more communities which have different criteria of plausibility. Nevertheless, he alleges,

the perspective of sociology, particularly of the sociology of knowledge, can have a definitely liberating effect. While other analytic disciplines free us from the dead weight of the past, sociology frees us from the dead weight of the present. Once we grasp our own situation in sociological terms, it ceases to impress us as an inexorable fate. .... The perspective of sociology increases our ability to investigate whatever truth each age may have discovered in its particular 'immediacy to God' [pp. 62f].

Berger passes on from this to suggest that 'what could be in the making here is a gigantic joke on Feuerbach', with his view of religion as a gigantic projection of man's own being and his programme of reducing theology to anthropology. Berger holds in fact that a case could be made out for the view that the whole historical–psychological–sociological analysis of religious phenomena, including the procedures of Marx and Freud, is a vast elaboration of this procedure. He does not contemplate abandoning his sociological approach; quite the opposite. But he holds that both the human and the divine perspective can coexist, each in its own frame of reference. 'What appears as a human projection in one may appear as a reflection of divine realities in another' (p. 64). But he insists that 'the theological decision will have to be that, "in, with, and under" the immense array of human projections, there are indicators of a reality that is truly "other" and that the religious imagination of man ultimately reflects' (p. 65). It is with this conviction that, in the third chapter of his book, he develops his theme that, 'if the religious projections of man correspond to a reality that is superhuman and supernatural, then it seems logical to look

for traces of this reality in the projector himself' (p. 65). However, before examining his application of this principle, I would
raise a further consideration of importance which he appears to
have entirely overlooked.

Berger has very convincingly argued that, if the secularisers
and relativisers claim the right to apply the criterion of the
sociology of knowledge to the beliefs of traditional supernaturalist believers, they cannot, if they are consistent, refuse to allow
those criteria to be applied to their own desupernaturalised
views: what is sauce for the goose is sauce for the gander. And
he holds furthermore that this leaves the question of truth and
falsehood unaffected and indeed sets it in a clearer light, since
it is one thing to ask how a belief originated and is maintained,
and another thing to ask whether it is true. I am, however, surprised to see that he never raises the question whether the diag-
nostic method of the sociology of knowledge ought not to be
applied to the sociology of knowledge itself and what would be
the consequences if it were. I do not think they would necessarily be destructive, provided it were firmly kept in mind that
the question of origin and the question of truth are distinct; if
the question of origin were held to supersede or to invalidate the
question of truth it would have that same suicidal and self-
destructive character which infects all types of scepticism. But
it is, as I have said, surprising that in relativising the relativisers
he has overlooked the fact that sociologists can be relativisers
too. What is sauce for the goose is not only sauce for the gander;
it is also sauce for the cook.

All that has been said up to the present has been in the nature
of prolegomena. Berger's own statement of what one might
describe as anthropological arguments for theism comes in his
third chapter, which has as its title 'Theological Possibilities:
Starting with Man'. If anthropology is understood in the broad-
est sense, he tells us, any kind of theology will have to include an
anthropological dimension, as indeed has always been the case.
'The real question, then, is not so much whether theology relates to anthropology—it can hardly help doing so—but what
kind of relation there will be' (p. 66). Berger recognises that the
neo-orthodoxy of the Barthian school, in its violent reaction
from the shallow and utopian optimism of bourgeois liberal
theology, denied that there were any inductive possibilities

from anthropology to theology and held that any valid anthropology must be theologically deduced, but points out that, within the neo-orthodox movement itself, such dissidents as Emil Brunner tried to find some *Anknüpsfungspunkt*—some point of contact—between God's revelation and the human situation. It was, however, the 'lostness' and misery of the human condition that, logically enough, received the main stress. In Berger's own words: 'The worse the picture of man, the greater the chance to make credible (*anknüpfen*) the claims of revelation. The gloomy anthropology of existentialism was amply suited to this purpose' (p. 68).

> Later, particularly in America, the more pessimistic versions of Freudian anthropology were added. Thus concepts such as despair, *Angst*, 'thrown-ness' became stock-in-trade terms of neo-orthodox theologians. For a while it seemed that the necessary counterpoint of the Christian proclamation was an anthropology of desperation—man, the object of the proclamation, was a murderous, incestuous figure, sunk in utter misery, without any hope except the hope of grace offered by God's revelation [p. 68].

The reaction to this reaction came with the celebration of secularity in such books as John Robinson's *Honest to God* and Harvey Cox's *The Secular City*. 'Logically enough, notions such as "autonomy", "man come of age", and even "democratic humanism" came to be substituted for the earlier expressions of existential anguish' (p. 69). Berger himself suggests that his own sociological approach, outlined in the earlier chapters of his book, may provide a way out from this oscillatory sequence of what he aptly describes as 'mood theologies'. He repudiates the notion of relevance and up-dating and holds that an anthropological approach may provide something rather more permanent. His programme is the seeking within the empirically given human situation for *signals of transcendence* which may be constituted by certain *prototypical human gestures*. Thus his approach has at least this in common with classical natural theology that it looks within the natural order for characteristics that indicate the dependence of the natural order upon a transcendent reality. It differs from it, however, in looking for these characteristics not in the finite realm as a whole but in one particular member, man. Berger tells us that he is not using 'transcendence' in a technical philosophical sense (I take it that he means the sense which it has, for example, in Kantian and similar systems) but 'literally, as the transcending of the normal, everyday world that [he] earlier identified with the notion of the "supernatural"' (p. 70). He explicitly excludes the Jungian 'archetypes', whose locus is the unconscious, and insists that his own concern is with what belongs to ordinary everyday awareness. And within this ordinary awareness he claims to discern five characteristics which have a transcendent reference. He bases on each a separate argument.

The first of these is the *argument from order*. Throughout human history, Berger points out, men have believed that the human ordering of society corresponds to an underlying order of the universe. Man's propensity for order is grounded in a faith that ultimately reality is 'in order', 'all right', 'as it should be'. He takes as typical the way in which a mother will comfort her startled child with the assurance that 'everything is all right', and he puts the blunt question: *is the mother lying to the child*? If the answer is 'no', there is at least some truth in the religious interpretation of human existence. 'The world that the child is being told to trust is the same world in which he will eventually die. If there is no other world, then the ultimate truth about this one is that eventually it will kill the child as it will kill his mother' (p. 74). It is, of course, possible to analyse religion on Freudian lines as a projection of the experience of parental love, but, Berger argues, 'what is projected is . . . itself a reflection, an imitation of ultimate reality' (p. 75).

The second argument is the *argument from play*. Play, Berger tells us, constructs a joyful enclave within the 'serious' world of everyday life and within the chronology of the latter: 'in joyful play it appears as if one were stepping not only from one chronology into another, but from time into eternity' (p. 77). It can be justified only if there is an 'eternal', a 'supernatural' realm, to which it points.

Thirdly, there is the *argument from hope*. Berger remarks that a number of theologians, influenced by the Marxist Ernst Bloch, have taken up the theme of hope in their dialogue with Marxism; he mentions Karl Rahner among Catholics and Jürgen Moltmann and Wolfhart Pannenberg among Protestants. For Marxists, man's unconquerable propensity to hope for the future is related to their hope of transforming this world for human betterment; for Berger the most significant aspect of hope is its exercise in the face of death. 'The profoundest manifestations of hope are to be found in gestures of courage undertaken in defiance of death. . . . These phenomena are signals of transcendence, pointers towards a religious interpretation of the human situation' (pp. 8of).

> Psychologists tell us (correctly no doubt) that, though we may fear our own death, we cannot really imagine it. . . . Yet it is precisely in the face of the death of others, and especially of others that we love, that our rejection of death asserts itself most loudly. . . . It would seem, then, that both psychologically (in the failure to imagine his own death) and morally (in his violent denial of the death of others) a 'no!' to death is profoundly rooted in the very being of man [p. 81].

In all these three arguments Berger is at pains to stress that nothing like an unanswerable demonstration is involved; he sees the affirmation of a transcendent order as exemplifying what he describes as 'inductive faith', which he explains as follows:

> Since the term 'inductive faith' will appear a number of times, its meaning should be classified. I use induction to mean any process of thought that begins with experience. Deduction is the reverse process; it begins with ideas that precede experience. By 'inductive faith', then, I mean a religious process of thought that begins with facts of human experience; conversely 'deductive faith' begins with certain assumptions (notably assumptions about divine revelation) that cannot be tested by experience. Put simply, inductive faith moves from human experience to statements about God, deductive faith from statements about God to interpretations of human experience [pp. 75f].

Inductive faith, then, is the affirmation that these acts and experiences in which man, from within the finite empirical realm, instinctively reaches out to something beyond and above that transcends it are not devoid of a genuine object. Thus, Berger writes, in relation to hope, that 'the argument from hope follows the logical direction of induction from what is empirically given. It starts from experience but takes seriously those implications or intentions within experience that transcend it—

H

and takes them, once again, as signals of transcendent reality' (p. 83). He sums up as follows:

> This reinterpretation of our experience encompasses rather than contradicts the various explanations of empirical reason (be they psychological, sociological or what-have-you). Religion in justifying this reinterpretation, is the ultimate vindication of hope and courage, just as it is the ultimate vindication of childhood and joy. By the same token, religion vindicates the gestures in which hope and courage are embodied in human action—including, given certain conditions, the gestures of revolutionary hope and, in the ultimate irony of redemption, the courage of stoic resignation [p. 84].

Here we would seem to have a particular application, related as closely as possible to our most deeply felt experiences, of the Thomist principle that it is impossible for a natural desire to remain unfulfilled.[1]

Berger's fourth argument is named by him the *argument from damnation*. 'This refers to experiences in which our sense of what is humanly permissible is so fundamentally outraged that the only adequate response to the offence as well as to the offender seems to be a curse of supernatural dimensions' (p. 84). He takes as examples the cases of Nazi war criminals such as Eichmann and he alleges that, whatever may be said about the conditioning of our moral judgments by our cultural and social background, it seems impossible for us to admit that in cases of this kind our sense of disgust is purely relative and has no transcendental significance. 'These are deeds that demand not only condemnation, but *damnation* in the full religious meaning of the word—that is, the doer not only puts himself outside the community of men; he also separates himself in a final way from a moral order that transcends the human community, and thus invokes a retribution that is more than human' (p. 87). This is seen as a counterpart to the argument from hope. 'Just as religion vindicates the gesture of protective reassurance, even when it is performed in the face of death, so it also vindicates the ultimate condemnation of the countergesture of inhumanity, precisely because religion provides a context for damnation' (p. 88). Nothing is said as to

1 *S.c.G.*, III, li; *Comp. Theol.*, I, civ; cf. *S. Th.*, I, xxi, 1c.

whether forgiveness is possible for even the most atrocious sins, but I think the answer would have to be given that forgiveness could come from no merely human source. If it is not merely human decencies that have been violated but the transcendent superhuman order, it is only from that transcendent order that forgiveness could be granted. Berger does not, however, discuss the possibility of atonement; he is, however, quite clear about the necessity of hell.

> We give the condemnation [he writes] the status of a necessary and universal truth. But, as sociological analysis shows more clearly than any other, this truth, while empirically given in our situation as men, cannot be empirically demonstrated to be either necessary or universal. We are, then, faced with a quite simple alternative: either we deny that there is here anything that can be called truth—a choice that would make us deny what we experience most profoundly as our own being; or we must look beyond the realm of our 'natural' experience for a validation of our certainty [pp. 86f].

In other words, sociology is not enough; not enough, that is, to account for the deepest convictions of our experience.

Berger's final argument is of a very different kind; it is the *argument from humour*. He remarks that 'a good deal has been written about the phenomenon of humour, much of it in a very humourless vein' (p. 89). He admits the common assertion of Freud and Bergson that the comic is fundamentally discrepancy, incongruity, incommensurability. But he goes on to ask what is the nature of the incongruous objects, and he replies that it is only human situations that can be comic. 'The biological as such is not comic. Animals become comic only when we view them anthropomorphically. . . . Within the human sphere, just about any discrepancy can strike us as funny' (ibid.). However, he goes on beyond this to assert that 'there is one fundamental discrepancy from which other comic discrepancies are derived —the discrepancy between man and universe. . . . *The comic reflects the imprisonment of the human spirit in the world*' (p. 90). And this accounts for the very close relation between comedy and tragedy. Thus, 'the comic is an objective dimension of man's reality, not just a subjective or psychological reaction to that reality' (ibid.). Furthermore the fact that man can laugh at a comic situation even in the most tragic conditions—Berger

H2

cites an example from a Nazi concentration camp—indicates an ingrained assumption that the tragedy is not final and can be overcome. This provides yet another signal of transcendence, in this case in the form of an intimation of redemption.

Thus, like St Thomas Aquinas, Berger has constructed five ways to belief in the transcendent, though they are very different from those of the Angelic Doctor. He adds that the list is by no means exhaustive. He excuses his omission of any consideration of specifically religious experience on the ground that, without any depreciation of efforts to study it and understand it, his own method has been to examine the projector rather than the projections and to give his attention to empirical data about man; indeed to data that can be found within the experiences of everybody in his ordinary daily life. Finally, Berger makes two emphatic disclaimers. 'My procedure', he writes, 'does *not* presuppose a static "human nature", somehow outside history. Neither does it presuppose a theory of historical "evolution" or "progress"' (p. 93). He speaks drastically about the way in which secularisation has ignored what he calls the 'night-side' of human existence. 'The treatment of death in modern society, especially in America, is the sharpest manifestation of this. Much more generally, modern society has not only sealed up the old metaphysical questions in practice, but (especially in the Anglo-Saxon countries) has generated philosophical positions that deny the meaningfulness of these questions' (p. 95). 'The denial of metaphysics', he concludes, 'may here be identified with the triumph of triviality. . . . A philosophical anthropology worthy of the name will have to regain . . . a metaphysical dimension' (p. 96).

At this point Berger's argument is virtually complete. I am very conscious that, in spite of the ample quotations which I have made from his text, I have given a somewhat bald impression of his exposition. This is inevitable, since his book is short and compressed and it needs to be read in full if one is to get a really adequate understanding of his thesis. His last two chapters (IV: 'Theological Possibilities: Confronting the Traditions'; V: 'Concluding Remarks—A Rumour of Angels') are devoted to setting his position in its proper location in the contemporary theological scene. Here I find myself for the first time definitely parting company with him. While repeating his repudiation of the 'trivialities' of recent 'radical' theology, he claims that he is not proposing a theological programme of conservative restoration and that the natural affinities of his outlook are with theological liberalism, especially with that movement of Protestant liberal theology that began with Schleiermacher. The reason he gives for this is that conservative theology tends to *deduce* from the tradition, while liberal theology tends to *induce* from generally accessible experience. This seems to me to be an oversimplification, for it is perfectly possible for a theological system to be deductive in some of its parts and aspects and to be inductive in others; indeed, the traditional distinction between revealed and natural theology assumes just such a duality. It seems clear that Berger understands conservative theology simply on the model of Barthian neo-orthodoxy and altogether overlooks the existence of a third position, which is characteristic of Thomism in particular but of other schools of both Catholic and Protestant theology as well. Thus, while he recognises that a genuine experience of God is to be found outside the formal boundaries of the Christian community, he feels bound to deny the uniqueness of the person and work of Jesus of Nazareth. Some attention to the writings of such Catholic thinkers as Dr R. C. Zaehner and Dom Bede Griffiths and to the documents of the Second Vatican Council, especially the Declaration on the Non-Christian Religions, shows that no incompatibility need be assumed. Nevertheless, Berger's main argument is of real importance, since he shows that an examination of human existence from the standpoint of such a very down-to-earth and empirical discipline as sociology shows that human life as such contains indications of a transcendent order and aspirations towards it which need to be taken very seriously. From one point of view Berger's argument contrasts significantly with the equally empirically based argument of Dr A. Boyce Gibson in his book *Theism and Empiricism*.[1] For Boyce Gibson discerns 'fringes' of the supernatural extending into the natural order, while Berger sees the natural order, in its highest representative, man, as extending itself towards the supernatural. There is, however, no ultimate contradiction. It is perhaps a limitation in Berger's argument that he devotes little attention to the character of the supernatural itself, though the implications

[1] Cf. Appendix I *supra*.

would seem to be that it is personal and benevolent. From the standpoint which I have adopted this does not much matter. As I see it, the function of natural theology is to locate precisely the point or points at which the natural empirical order impinges upon the transcendent and supernatural and opens towards it. In the text of the present work I have located that point in the dual character of reality and contingency inherent in the finite as such. Dr Berger has located it in certain intuitions of, and aspirations towards, the supernatural which are characteristic of the empirical existence of human beings. Once the point has been located (Berger might not agree with me here), once the crack has been discerned, the work of natural theology is in principle performed; we can insert the knife and open up the passage later. What is really important is to understand that the natural order is not just closed in upon itself.

GRACE AND NATURE IN EAST AND WEST

I SUGGESTED IN Chapter Nine above that both the post-Reformation confrontations between Catholics and Protestants in the West and also the earlier confrontation between Eastern Orthodoxy and Western Catholicism may, as regards their theological aspects, involve very basic questions about the nature of the relation between God and man, the doctrine of creation and, arising out of that, the doctrine of grace and the supernatural. I also suggested that if the relation between God and man is of the kind that I have represented it as being, if man, as a creature, is not a rounded off and finished essence but is, by his very dependence on God, inherently open to fresh and unpredictable influxes of the Creator's activity, the way may be open for a new and hopeful reopening of the matter in the ecumenical field. With this in view I propose to consider in some detail two short discussions of very different types, both of which appeared on the Continent as long ago as 1954, in French and German respectively, and in this country in English translations in 1961.

I

The first of these, published under the title of *The Theology of Grace and the Oecumenical Movement*, was compiled by two Professors of the University of Louvain, Canon C. Moeller[1] and Mgr G. Philips, from the proceedings of a conference held at the monastery of Chevetogne in 1953, in which the chief participants were two Roman Catholics (Mgr Philips and Fr Walty,

[1] Canon Moeller has since become Sub-Secretary of the Sacred Congregation of the Doctrine of the Faith in Rome.

O.P.), two Eastern Orthodox (Dr J. Meyendorff and M. A. de Ivanka) and two Protestants (Pastor Bruston and Pastor P. Y. Emery). Apart from the intrinsic interest of their contributions, the presence of the two Orthodox scholars was of special value as immensely widening the theological range of the discussion; for, on the one hand, the objections which Protestants have traditionally felt against the Catholic doctrine of grace (namely, that it postulates a change in man which is inconsistent with his creaturely character) apply far more strongly against the Orthodox doctrine, while to the Orthodox the Catholic teaching about created grace seems not to provide for a real transformation at all and to be merely a slightly less extreme version of Protestantism. The stage was therefore set for a very searching and vigorous argument, but, as far as one can tell from the Report, it seems to have been both good-tempered and constructive.

The Report begins by taking the three terms 'deification', 'created grace' and 'extrinsic grace' as characteristic of the respective viewpoints of Orthodoxy, Catholicism and the Reformation. Catholics, it remarks, 'usually get no further than the over-simplified picture of justification in Protestantism which hides the sinner under the cloak of Christ, but leaves him in his sin'. Protestants, on the other hand, condemn the Catholic doctrine that grace is an infused *habitus*, a created reality, for turning grace into 'a "thing" that is at man's disposal, like a kind of accumulator of a divine energy with the human will operating the switchboard'.[1] The Orthodox, in their turn, reject the whole notion that something can be both supernatural and created, 'affirming that only God can give God, and that no created reality, whatever it may be, can be commensurate with him';[2] it is added that the Orthodox theology of grace as 'deification' interprets this whole process as affecting the whole being, body no less than soul, and that the most characteristic version of this theology is Palamism.[3] This

[1] op. cit., p. 1.
[2] ibid., p. 2.
[3] For a brief account of Palamism, cf. my *Via Media*, pp. 157ff; for longer discussions, V. Lossky, *The Mystical Theology of the Eastern Church*, ch. iv; P. Sherrard, *The Greek East and the Latin West*, pp. 36ff; though this last writer has been accused of exaggerating the extent to which the Palamite doctrines occur in earlier writers than Palamas. However, in support of the view criticised, cf. G. Habra, 'The Sources of the Doctrine of St Gregory Palamas', *Eastern Churches Quarterly*, XII (1958).

approach, it is remarked, is particularly bound up with Christology and ecclesiology, while Western theology has thought of grace much more in terms of pneumatology, starting from the gift of the Spirit; Peter Lombard seems in fact to identify grace with the Holy Spirit *tout court*. 'While, therefore, Eastern theology is chiefly preoccupied with finding out what, *in God*, makes him able to give himself, that of the West is concerned particularly with what it is, *in man*, which allows him to receive God.'[1] So the scholastics worked out a view of created grace as a *habitus* in the very substance of the soul; and this emphasis on the soul, so sharply contrasted with the Eastern notion of the transfiguration not only of soul but also of body, is carried further by the Reformers, whose theology 'brings into prominence all the wickedness of our nature, and arrives at a theology of imputation and of a grace which is extrinsic and whose realisation is deferred until the last days.'[2] 'Any theology of grace must insist both upon the *primacy of God* who justifies and sanctifies man, and at the same time on the *reality of regeneration*.'[3] It is suggested that here the argument is mainly between Catholics and Orthodox on one side and Protestants on the other, though attention is also drawn to Père Bouyer's argument that 'the Reformation principles, *sola fide*, *sola gratia*, *soli Deo gloria*, are, in the positive sense in which the first Reformers advocated them, profoundly biblical and catholic.'[4]

After this introductory display of the field to be covered, the first main chapter is devoted to an account of the Orthodox approach. 'The starting point for the theology of deification is the *real and deifying presence of Christ in the world and in the Church*.'[5] Salvation is the assimilation of human nature to God, and this is a work that only God can do. Palamism is thus, in one aspect, a theological reaction against neo-Platonism. The whole point of the Palamite distinction between the divine essence and the divine energies is that it makes for a real deification of the creature; no creature can receive the divine *essence*, but to receive the divine *energies* is nevertheless to receive God. With reference to the famous controversy between Palamas and the

[1] ibid., p. 3.
[2] ibid., p. 4.
[3] ibid.
[4] ibid., p. 5 (L. Bouyer, *The Spirit and Forms of Protestantism*).
[5] ibid., p. 6.

Calabrian monk Barlaam, we are told that 'Palamas wants to reconcile the impossibility of knowing God, who is beyond all being, *hyperousios*, with the fact that he is communicated in the "divine energies"; and this conception he opposes to that of Barlaam, whom he considers too "humanist", too preoccupied with the "discovery of the divinity present in every spiritual soul", in the neo-Platonic fashion.'[1] So, with regard to the 'hesychast' spirituality, which is the counterpart in prayer of the Palamite theology, we are told that 'the hesychast is not contemplating his own image but the glory of God about his soul and also about his body; the hesychast is not seeking a spiritual state, but Christ living in him.'[2] If only our Niebuhrs, Brunners and Auléns had recognised this how much less ready they might have been to condemn all forms of Christian mysticism as essentially pagan![3] The Report goes on to say that the Orthodox consider that this doctrine of the uncreated energies rules out the Western notion of created grace as a *habitus*, which is both supernatural and created; but it goes on to suggest that what that doctrine maintains is expressed by the Western distinction between the natural and the supernatural and it repeats the point that East and West are really concerned with different questions, the East with the question what it is in God that enables him to give himself, the West with the question what it is in man that enables him to receive God. Later it will be shown how the Western doctrine was evolved in a particular philosophical and theological situation which explains its peculiar character, but the Report concludes its discussion of Orthodoxy by expressing the opinion that, while the Palamite doctrine, in spite of its neglect of the notions of *fides obscura* and of the basing of faith upon authority, is fundamentally reconcilable with Catholic orthodoxy, it provides a much more obstinate nut for Protestants to crack. While granting that the doctrine preserves the absolute primacy of God and appreciating its likeness to the thought of Peter Lombard, with whom Luther himself expressed sympathy, they will be unhappy about the idea that man can 'participate' in the divine life and even less

[1] ibid., p. 7.
[2] ibid.
[3] Cf. E. Brunner, *Man in Revolt*, ch. v (c) and App. I; R. Niebuhr, *The Nature and Destiny of Man*, I, ch. x; G. Aulén, *The Faith of the Christian Church*, p. 280.

attracted by the part which the Sacraments are alleged to play
in the process of deification. But the final point is made that
opposition to neo-Platonism has played much the same part in
the East as opposition to Pelagianism in the West, namely in
stressing the absolute primacy of God.

At this point I will interrupt my discussion of the Report to
remark that the thought of Gregory Palamas may turn out to be
very much more important in the ecumenical sphere than has
yet been recognised. We are fortunate in having two admirable
books about him from the pen of Dr John Meyendorff, the long
and authoritative scholarly *Study of Gregory Palamas* and the
exquisitely produced and illustrated little book *St Grégoire
Palamas et la Mystique orthodoxe*, which is none the less reliable
and is in fact a comprehensive guide to the whole Orthodox
tradition of spirituality. The impression which one derives is,
surprisingly enough, that, whatever may be true as regards
verbal idiom and the strictly philosophical setting, there is a
fundamental *dogmatic* and *religious* agreement between St
Gregory Palamas and St Thomas Aquinas. This impression
may be justified by some specific examples.

First, the famous controversy between Palamas and Barlaam
about the uncreated light. Whether Barlaam knew the works
of his contemporary William of Ockham is doubtful, and there
appears to be a difference of opinion about his knowledge of
'Thomism'; Meyendorff tells us that Barlaam's first theological
essays were directed against 'the Latin theology which for him
was identified with that of "Thomism"',[1] while the Report says
that he 'had no knowledge of Thomism, whatever has been
alleged'[2] (the two statements are perhaps not irreconcilable).
What seems to be clear is that he was a professed nominalist:
'Barlaam, who fled in the West from the intellectual realism of
the Thomist scholasticism, threw himself in the East against the
mystical realism of the monks.'[3] In fact, Meyendorff tells us, his
two great tenets were nominalism and essentialism; and these
are the two great *bêtes noires* of Thomism, as M. Maritain and
M. Gilson have taken such pains to make clear to us. If the
Eastern Church, under the leadership of Palamas, had not

[1] *St Grégoire Palamas et la Mystique orthodoxe*, p. 90.
[2] op. cit., p. 6.
[3] op. cit., p. 91.

firmly suppressed this nominalist movement, Meyendorff somewhat pointedly maintains, it would have been led into 'a crisis
like that which the Christian West has undergone, namely the
neo-paganism of the Renaissance and the Reformation of the
Church in conformity with the new nominalist philosophy.'[1]

Viewed from this aspect, the doctrine of the divine energies
can appear even to a Western in a less baffling light. Recent
commentators have seen the heart of St Thomas's thought to
lie in its firm hold upon the principle of existence (*esse*) in contrast to the primacy given to the principle of essence by both
his opponents and his more pedestrian disciples.[2] Now, according to Meyendorff, it was precisely to counteract the essentialist
trend that Palamas developed his distinction between the
divine essence and the divine energies; and it is noteworthy
that, just as many modern Thomists have hailed St Thomas as
the true existentialist, Meyendorff gives this honourable title to
St Gregory. It would, of course, be rash in the extreme to identify the divine existence in Thomism with the divine energy in
Palamism; nevertheless it would be a fascinating and really
important question for investigation whether Thomas and
Gregory were not ultimately concerned with the same theological and religious question, even if they expounded it in
terms of divergent metaphysical systems. Admittedly, the Palamite insistence upon the basic unknowability of God seems at
first sight to be contrary to the Thomist doctrine that God is
supremely intelligible. Nevertheless, some Thomists, such as Fr
Victor White, O.P.,[3] have discerned in Aquinas an agnosticism
that has scandalised some of their less intrepid colleagues, while,
on the other hand, M. Vladimir Lossky has argued that the
Palamite doctrine, while ascribing to God in his essence an unknowability exceeding that asserted by Plotinus, holds him to
be wholly communicated in the energies by which he deifies us.
And, even if we cannot simply equate *existence* with *energy*, perhaps we can see a difference between *essence* as it is understood
by Aquinas and by Palamas, and the reconciliation may lie
along this line.

[1] ibid., p. 103.
[2] Père B. Montagnes, O.P., has even brought this charge against the great
commentator Cajetan (*La Doctrine de l'Analogie de l'Etre d'après Saint Thomas
d'Aquin* (1963)).
[3] Cf. *God the Unknown*, chh. i–iii.

Again, this *apophaticism*, this stress on the negative way in our approach to God, which is so characteristic of Palamas and of Eastern theology and spirituality generally, is it so very different from what we find in St John of the Cross? And if M. Maritain is able to allay our fears in the case of the great Spanish Carmelite by a skilful application of Thomist epistemology and a discreet distinction between the language of theoretical and of practical theology,[1] may not the Palamites be performing the same task when they assure us that God, though inaccessible in his essence, imparts himself fully in his energies? Would St John of the Cross in fact have found the hesychasts uncongenial, even if they might have found his own brand of apophaticism somewhat violent? Is not the revival of hesychasm in modern Orthodoxy strikingly paralleled by the revival of contemplative prayer in the West, and may not both be different species of the same generic response to a situation which is common to Christians of both East and West today? And may it not be significant that both of these are accompanied by a recovery of the sense of the Liturgy and a movement for more frequent communion? I am not sure that the answers to these questions are as simple as one would like them to be, but they seem to me to be the kind of questions that theologians ought to be investigating.

One final aspect of the importance of Palamas in the present ecumenical setting must be stressed. Dr Meyendorff shows how clearly and radically *Christian* Palamas's theology and spirituality are, in spite of the neo-Platonist mould in which they are cast. (Perhaps he is not altogether fair in contrasting Palamas as sharply as he does with Evagrius. The suggestion has been made that Palamas is supremely successful in reconciling the Evagrian and Macarian traditions, and if this is so he is all the greater.) Thus, he insists that progress in the Christian life is the fruit of the sacrament of baptism and that it takes place within the sacramental life of the Church; that the whole man, body and soul together, is deified by grace through his union with Christ, in contrast to any Plotinian flight of the alone to the alone. Even the Palamite doctrine that the light that streamed from Christ on the mount of Transfiguration was no created radiance but the uncreated energy of God—a doctrine which will seem to many Westerners to be somewhat remote and

[1] Cf. *The Degrees of Knowledge*, ch. viii.

speculative—was concerned to emphasise that the whole of Christ's human nature, and not only his soul, was united to the Person of the Divine Word, so that his body itself was the instrument of the Divine Person. And there is a fundamentally biblical emphasis in Gregory which was to stand Orthodoxy in good stead in the face of the Platonic revival associated specially with the name of Gemistos Plethon. Such emphases as these in Palamism are surely in tune with the most vigorous insights of religious thought in the West today, and it may well be that Eastern Orthodox spirituality had remembered them when the West had largely forgotten them.

We must return from this digression to the Report of the Chevetogne conference. The chapter on Eastern Orthodoxy is followed by a long and detailed historical exposition of the development of the Western concept of 'created grace'. This is not altogether easy reading, but it is significant as manifesting a growing recognition by many Roman Catholic theologians that a great many difficulties may be removed if theological formulations are carefully located and assessed in the context in which they took their rise and are not simply interpreted in the light of later and sometimes unsatisfactory developments. As comparable examples we might mention Fr Tavard's careful consideration of the relation between Scripture and Tradition as discussed by the Council of Trent,[1] Fr M. Bévenot's discussion '"Faith and Morals" in the Councils of Trent and Vatican I',[2] and Dr Gustave Thils's study of the relation between the Papacy and the Episcopate as conceived at the First Vatican Council.[3] (On this last issue it is interesting to notice the usefulness which has been discovered in the Declaration of the German Episcopate of 1875[4] and which may well have influenced the teaching on collegiality in the Constitution *De Ecclesia* of Vatican II.) On the general question, Fr P. Fransen, S.J., has condemned the flippancy with which conciliar and other official texts are sometimes used as material with which to bombard the enemy, with little attention to their original context and

---

[1] *Holy Writ or Holy Church*, ch. xii.

[2] *Heythrop Journal*, III (1962), pp. 15ff.

[3] *Primauté pontificale et Prérogatives épiscopales: 'Potestas ordinaria' au Concile du Vatican* (Louvain, 1961). Cf. also his *L'Infaillibilité Pontificale* (Gembloux, 1969).

[4] Commented on, e.g., by H. Küng, *The Council and Reunion*, App. I.

purpose,[1] while Dr Hans Küng has stressed the complementary point that even the most solemn dogmatic statements, just because they are made in a particular context to deal with particular problems, have necessarily a certain limited and historically conditioned character, so that 'it is the serious duty of theologians to see all theological formulae and dogmas *against the background and in the context of revelation in its entirety, in both Old and New Testaments.*'[2]

So the Chevetogne Report points out that the notion of grace as a *habitus* became explicit in connection with the development of the theology of infant baptism, when the question was raised as to what can be the 'grace' which is given to an infant who is incapable of performing an act. However, the phrase 'created grace' does not appear until about 1245, in the *Summa* of Alexander of Hales, although the idea of it seems to occur in Alan of Lille in the latter half of the previous century. Earlier thinkers, such as Augustine, speak only of the contact of the Creator with the creature, with no mention of any created intermediary, and Peter Lombard's identification of charity with the Holy Spirit looks like a throw-back to Augustine. However, the Report penetratingly remarks, what Peter failed to see was that a *habitus* of love could be at the same time a direct participation of the Spirit; but at any rate he knew of no created *habitus*.

It is with the great scholastics such as St Bonaventura and St Thomas that the doctrine of created grace becomes prominent, and it is pointed out that Bonaventura had two reasons for promoting it. First, he was concerned to rule out any Pelagian doctrine of the righteousness of human works: 'If there were no created grace, one might think that man by his own works gives himself grace.'[3] And, secondly, 'the love of God, giving itself, is effective, producing a change in man. Consequently, the disposition, the created *habitus*, is the *result of the presence of the God of love.*' And Bonaventura is quoted as asserting: '*Habere est haberi*, to possess (a *habitus*) is to be possessed by God.'[4] Side by side with these two admirable reasons, it is remarked that two others, less fortunate, can be discerned in the scholastics

---

[1] 'The Authority of the Councils' in *Problems of Authority*, ed. J. M. Todd.
[2] *The Council and Reunion*, pp. 163f, 165.
[3] op. cit., p. 17.
[4] ibid., pp. 17f.

and can be traced back to St Albertus Magnus. First, 'for an act to be meritorious, a man must in some sense be master of it; for an act to be his own, a man must be able to act as he wants.'[1] Secondly, there is the highly misleading image of God and creation as separated by a kind of gulf, which needs to be bridged by an intermediary, and created grace claims to perform this function.[2] However, the Report replies, the created *habitus* must not be thought of as an *ens completum*, inserted between man and the Spirit; it is an *ens dynamicum*, that is to say, a dynamic entity which exists only through the direct and continuous action of God who is present in the soul and disposes it to receive him. The risk of 'turning grace into a thing' is thus not to be dismissed as a myth, but the risk can be avoided, and St Thomas does in fact avoid it.

For St Thomas, we are told, grace is a reality but it is not an object. If the Spirit dwells in a man, the man is changed and the *habitus* results from this. No antecedent *habitus* is needed: the *habitus* has no cause but God himself, in the very moment in which he gives himself. And it is 'an active tension set up by God at work in man . . . nothing less than the will of God expressing itself unceasingly within the complex reality of the being of man.'[3]

Why, then, it is asked in conclusion, did Luther go back to Peter Lombard and accept only uncreated grace? As in other sixteenth-century issues, nominalism was the villain. For the late scholastics, such as Biel and Ockham, the *habitus* 'could not but be something separated from God, shut off inside the closed system of humanity, with God removed to an arbitrary and inaccessible transcendence. Because nominalism could conceive of no real contact between the creature and the Creator, it presented the *habitus* as an intermediate being, a separate entity in itself, possessed by man apart from the influence of grace.'[4] The consequence was that, in order to rule out Pelagianism, Luther rejected the very notion which had been originally

[1] ibid., p. 18.
[2] The idea of the 'gulf' has also misled a good deal of thought about the natural as distinct from the supernatural order, and it has been conceived as bridged by 'creation'. Cf. A. Sertillanges, *L'Idée de Création*, p. 46; E. L. Mascall, *Christian Theology and Natural Science*, p. 134.
[3] op. cit., p. 20.
[4] ibid., p. 21.

introduced for that precise purpose. But he would not have rejected Bonaventura's *Habere est haberi* and, in spite of his repudiation of the doctrine that grace produces a habitual transformation in us, he did recover from elsewhere the idea of a real transformation of man by grace.

The final episodes of the story are related very briefly. Trent made no use of the terms *habitus* or *gratia creata*, so the field is left clear. Later theology concentrated more and more on *gratia creata*, and indeed on actual rather than on habitual grace. However, the idea of *gratia increata*, the indwelling of the Spirit, began to come back and now everything is ready for a synthesis.[1]

The synthesis (described accurately as 'brief') is outlined in the following chapter. The dualism between created grace and indwelling is emphatically excluded, as is the notion of the infinite 'gulf'. Five positive points are made. (1) God's love is *effective*, therefore grace makes a change in man; he becomes a 'new creature'. (2) The change *lasts*; grace increases simply because the union with God grows closer and deeper. (3) God acts *directly* in the *habitus*; there is no 'object' between the man and God. (4) The *vitalism* of the *habitus*: God is present in an exchange which leaves our free will unimpaired: 'He makes us act . . . without its being possible to say that God alone acts.'[2] (5) *Merit* must be properly understood, and three things need to be stressed: (i) it is an *ontological* quality, 'not a "cheque" presented in exchange for *something else*';[3] (ii) it is *personal*, 'one's "merits" are not rewarded because one is in credit on a sort of moral bank account, but because of what one *is*';[4] and (iii), as Trent taught, when God crowns our merits, he crowns his own gifts.

---

[1] Cf. P. Fransen: 'History bears out the contention that the notion of created grace is not entitled to the central place which it has usurped in the treatise of grace. Prior to the eleventh century, generations of orthodox theologians thought and wrote without ever so much as mentioning created grace. . . . Undeniably "created grace" has meaning, though it is *not* an independent entity, *and still less* something that becomes our possession, that we can dispose of at will or glory in before God as the fruit of our own strength and endeavour. Created grace, seen in its inner nature, belongs to a *higher unity*. It is to be thought of only *within* and *not next to* or *apart from* the mystery of the trinitarian indwelling in us' (*The New Life of Grace*, p. 98).

[2] ibid., p. 27.
[3] ibid.
[4] ibid.

Two final points are made. The first is that the *personal* character of the relations between man and God needs to be emphasised much more than in the past. I heartily agree; it has always seemed to me that most of the discussions since the Reformation about divine premotion and human freedom, and about predestination and merit, have been vitiated from the start by an image of divine and human activity as two quasi-mechanical forces, to be compounded by something like the parallelogram-law, rather than as the activities of a personal Creator and a personal creature; the unhappy history of the Congregation *De Auxiliis* is perhaps the most glaring example of this. Secondly, it is suggested that more attention needs to be given to the idea of *participation*, a union which is not to be thought of merely in terms of either efficient or exemplary causality but rather of active presence. And finally, the term 'created grace', for all its venerable past, is called in question as having acquired a number of secondary and unfortunate meanings, and strong recommendation is given to a phrase which Fr de la Taille used in a slightly different connection, *actuation créée par acte incréé*. This is extremely difficult to render succinctly in English, as the English order of words separates the adjectival and participial functions of *créée*, which are combined in the French, but what it is intended to state is that there is a real created actuation, not a mythical one, and that it is created by the uncreated act which is God himself.

After this long and detailed statement and reinterpretation of Catholic doctrine the Report passes on to consider Justification in Protestant theology. It does this very briefly, giving as its excuse that Père Bouyer has already shown, in his book *The Spirit and Forms of Protestantism*, that the view of Protestant doctrine held by most Catholics is a sheer caricature. For Reformation theology, it says, grace cannot be thought of as a thing; it is inseparable from the person, God, who gives himself. Grace has three aspects, justification, sanctification and redemption. Justification and sanctification are inseparable, for we receive them together, but they must not be confused, for justification is absolute, perfect and extrinsic, while sanctification is relative, imperfect and intrinsic. A footnote calls attention to the danger of separating the two stages, making justification God's part and sanctification man's part. Trent did not consider sanctification, and much of what it attributed to justification the Reformers attributed to sanctification instead. Calvin's stress on the external and imputed character of justification was intended to make it clear that God's act is a free gift and eschatological in nature; the realisation of redemption is still to come. Reformed theology is ill at ease with 'theology of glory'. For Calvin, the foundation of the Christian's life is the union of God with man and its direct result is sanctification by the Spirit. Reformed theologians dislike terms like 'merit', but they would accept the term 'created grace' as equivalent to the statement of Phil ii. 13 that God works in us both to will and to work. The conclusion is that 'sanctification is *real* and internal. And justification and sanctification are in fact inseparable, as *complementary* aspects (not parallel), one external and one internal, of the same act.'[1] We may note that there is not any explicit reference to the doctrine of Lutheranism, or any suggestion that on the matter in question it might in any way differ from that of the Reformed tradition. It was perhaps both a strength and a weakness of the Conference that its Protestant membership was apparently purely Calvinist.

There follows a very short chapter stressing that both Orthodoxy and Protestantism have insisted on the fundamentally *trinitarian* nature of grace. This is asserted as being no less true of Catholicism, and a fine passage is quoted from Trent in support, but the post-Tridentine manualists are trounced for neglecting it. The final chapter of the Report realistically opens by remarking that, while the discussion has shown there to be a much greater basic agreement than a superficial or polemical approach would reveal, nevertheless 'infinitely deeper divisions appear' at the same time.[2] These are then investigated with frankness and sympathy. They fall under the three heads of Philosophical Systematisations, Original Sin and Christology.

The section on Philosophical Systematisations is extremely stimulating, rather complicated and no doubt in some respects controversial. The different traditions describe the change that justification brings about in man in different ways: for the Orthodox it is a divine life, for Catholics a holy life, for Protestants a battle against sin and the devil. For Orthodoxy the

[1] ibid., p. 33.
[2] ibid., p. 37.

encounter between God and man is 'synergism', for Protestants an 'enduring creation', for Catholics *actuation créée par acte incréé*. But there is no contradiction in this, only a difference of emphasis. What is more serious is that Catholicism thinks in terms of the *nature of man*, Protestantism in terms of grace given to *the sinner*. Catholicism contrasts natural and supernatural, Protestantism sin and grace. The Orthodox are alleged to incline to the Protestant view; this seems to me to be highly questionable, true as it is that the Palamite doctrine of the energies leads them to a different view of the relation of grace to nature from that of the Catholic West and to a dislike of the word 'supernatural'.

The dispute between East and West is now seen in terms of Platonism and Aristotelianism. Aristotelian anthropology, we are told, sees man as a self-sufficient unity enclosed in himself; his elevation to a supernatural state would be elevation to a condition which he cannot attain in his natural state and so would imply the production of a supernatural, but created, quality to give him the ability to perform supernatural acts. Platonist anthropology, in contrast, sees man as capable by nature of reaching the highest degree of spiritual life. The Orthodox tend to think in terms of Platonism; Catholics, in their bad periods, in terms of Aristotelianism, though the main scholastic tradition has made use of both. This somewhat loaded statement is redressed by the assertion that it is better to use only Platonism than, as in the case of the decadent scholastics, to use only Aristotelianism. It seems to me that the characterisation given of Aristotelian anthropology needs very considerable qualification. No doubt Aristotelianism can be Christianised to do what is alleged, but I should have thought that the authentic Aristotelian doctrine would make it impossible for man to be supernaturalised in any way whatever. For Aristotle, just because every nature, including man's, is a self-sufficient unity, whatever it can become is given in it from the start; for it, to be supernaturalised would be to be destroyed. If, however, we hold the Christian doctrine of creation—and I have argued in this book that this is in fact the doctrine to which we are led by reflection upon the contingent character of finite beings—we hold that man's nature is *not* a self-sufficient unity, for it depends for its very existence upon the creative activity of God and, in virtue of this very dependence, is open to fresh influxes of this creative activity which, without contradicting the nature it already has, can elevate it to a higher order of existence.[1] St Thomas, I think, says this, at least implicitly, but I think his power to say what Aristotle did not say came not from Plato but from Christianity .

But to return to the Report. The Reformers adopted Platonism, with their exclusive emphasis on the uncreated source of justification and sanctification. But why did they not go the whole way and accept the whole process of deification, which begins in faith but will be manifested in glory? Whatever they may say, it is not because of their loyalty to the Bible, for the Bible stresses the present reality of the risen life of the Christian and does not simply defer it to the last day. Two reasons are given in the Report. The first is that they received their Platonism—and their biblicism—from Augustine, but from that side of Augustine which was narrow and distorted—the Augustine who was concerned with Pelagianism, original sin and concupiscence. Faced with scholasticism in decay, the Reformers accepted this outlook as more biblical and Christian, but in so doing they left out all that the Greek fathers had and that Augustine, as they saw him, had not. The second reason is that the 'Augustinian Platonism' of the Reformers is fettered by a system of philosophy that was neither Platonist nor Aristotelian, namely the agnostic nominalism of Ockham. For nominalism, any participation in the divine life is impossible, all being is reduced to what is perceived.[2] However this may be (the Report concludes) the points which fundamentally separate Protestantism on the one hand from Catholicism and on the other from Orthodoxy are a too pessimistic view of man's sin (deriving from St Augustine) and a exaggerated fear of the biblical idea of the participation of the sanctified creature in the very life of God.

So the Report passes on to Original Sin, and here it suggests that Protestantism has been satisfied with a far too negative opposition to Pelagianism and that this has led to a purely futurist eschatology, for which, instead of man enjoying here

[1] Cf. ch. ix *supra*. I have shown the implications of this fact in some detail in chapter iv of my book *The Importance of Being Human*.
[2] Cf. my *Recovery of Unity*, pp. 23ff.

and now the beginning of his deification, he is merely waiting in the certainty of faith for an event wholly in the future. (It is added that the 'realised eschatology' of such Protestant scholars as Dr C. H. Dodd has done a good deal to counteract this.) And finally it is suggested that there is a deep cleavage in the matter of Christology. Here, I believe, there is something of real importance, which we in Britain have tended to ignore, mainly no doubt because Protestant Christology here has tended to be of a rather special type and to owe little to the Reformers. Briefly, the point made is that, for all its awe-inspiring insistence upon the work of the Father, the Son and the Spirit in salvation, there is a tendency to ignore the part played in our present salvation by the manhood of Jesus. The manhood seems in its exaltation to have 'become Spirit'; 'we wonder whether the glorified manhood of Jesus has not been unconsciously allowed to evaporate into a kind of mysterious and irresistible force exerted by God alone',[1] the 'Spirit of Yahweh' which 'breatheth where he will'. In fact, it is suggested, there is found in Protestantism an oscillation between two kinds of *kenosis*, a 'Nestorian' kenosis during our Lord's earthly life, in which his deity is absorbed by his humanity, and a 'monophysite' kenosis after the Ascension, in which his manhood is absorbed by his divinity and the divinity acts on the justified sinner without any intermediary.[2] Hence the fear on the part of Protestants of the place which is held in both Catholicism and Orthodoxy by the Church and the sacraments, as the means by which man is given a present union with the manhood of Christ and of his real transformation in Christ by that union.

I have given this fairly full account of the Report of the Chevetogne conference because, in spite of the rather heavily Catholic bias of the concluding section, it provides an admirable example of the sort of thing an ecumenical conference ought to be and also to have achieved a great measure of success in the task which it set itself to perform. There was clearly a real determination on the part of all the participants not simply to repeat the battle-cries of the past, to score debating points against their opponents or to whitewash their own traditions, but to face

[1] op. cit., p. 48.
[2] This criticism might seem to apply more accurately to Luther than to Calvin.

honestly all the historical facts, whether comforting or embar-
rassing, to understand accurately and sympathetically the real
theological and religious positions lying beneath the various
verbal formulations, and to assess them in the light of their relevant contexts. It was perhaps a pity that neither Lutheranism
nor Zwinglianism was adequately represented and that the
Protestant position was stated almost entirely in Calvinist terms.
I think also that Anglican representatives, had any been present,
might have had something of value to contribute. I have at
various places indicated points where I think the Report is
probably wrong in its judgments. But it does go further in bringing into the open the basic issues in divided Christendom than
anything else that I have seen. And although it was published
more than seventeen years ago I think it might, both for its form
and its content, well be made compulsory reading for all persons taking part in ecumenical discussions.

II

I shall now turn to another discussion of a very different type,
but, in my view, of equal importance, namely the two essays on
Grace in Fr Karl Rahner's *Theological Investigations*, volume I.

   Karl Rahner, is, of course, one of the best known of German
Roman Catholic theologians today. He combines an intense
reverence for the living *magisterium* of the Church with an unsparingly critical attitude towards much of its recent and current theology; he is the bitter enemy of the textbook mind. There
is something ironical in the fact that he was until recently the
editor of Denzinger's *Enchiridion Symbolorum*, for no one could be
more opposed than he to what has sometimes been called 'Denzinger theology', that is, the attitude which settles all theological
questions by looking up the passages from official utterances
that someone else has assembled and repeating them without
reference to their original context or to the Church's tradition
as a whole.[1] He writes, as will be clear from the discussion of his
'transcendental Thomism' in Chapter Four above, in a difficult

---

[1] Cf. the remarks of Fr P. Fransen, S.J., in his essay on 'The Authority of
the Councils' in *Problems of Authority*, ed. J. M. Todd, p. 69, and especially
the excursus on 'The need for the study of the historical sense of conciliar
texts' (ibid., pp. 72ff). Cf. pp. 25f *supra*.

idiom largely derived from the existentialist thinker Martin Heidegger. Nevertheless the issues with which he is concerned (and one is sometimes tempted to wonder whether there are any with which he is not!) are fundamental both to the Christian religion as such and to our present ecumenical situation. Seven volumes of his most important essays are in course of publication under the title *Theological Investigations*. Here I shall consider at length the two essays in the first volume entitled 'Concerning the Relationship between Nature and Grace' and 'Some Implications of the Scholastic Concept of Uncreated Grace'. These were both written with direct reference to matters of current theological controversy within the Roman communion, but their implications are extremely wide and a consideration of them will usefully supplement the previous discussion of the Chevetogne conference. They are highly technical in their thought and terminology, and neither the author nor the translator makes any concessions to the untrained reader; the latter may prefer to derive the essence of Rahner's position from the first essay in his small volume *Nature and Grace*.

The first of the two essays begins from a question which has much exercised the minds of Roman Catholic theologians in the present century, namely, how it is possible to reconcile two apparently equally firmly grounded doctrines: (1) that man has a natural desire for the vision of God and it is impossible that a natural desire should be ultimately unachievable;[1] (2) that man's elevation to the supernatural order, which culminates in the vision of God, is entirely gratuitous and beyond the reach of man's natural powers. A very full survey of the solutions that have been offered appeared in English in 1947 in Dr P. K. Bastable's book *Desire for God*. Beginning with an analysis of St Thomas's texts and the interpretations of his commentators Cajetan, Sylvester of Ferrara and John of St Thomas, Bastable then gave a historical account of the problem from its adumbration in the thirteenth century to the present day, with specially detailed attention to the views of Scotus and Suarez. The final chapter, on the present century, after mentioning the work of P. Rousselot, G. de Broglie, J. Maréchal and G. Laporta, discussed the very interesting book by Fr James O'Mahoney, O.S.F.C., *The Desire of God in the Philosophy of St Thomas*. It was

[1] Cf. *S.c.G.* III, li.

not possible for Bastable to turn his attention to the important
work by Père H. de Lubac, *Surnaturel: Etudes historiques*, which
was published in France in 1946. The third part of this book is
on the origins of the word 'supernatural' and, although Fr de
Lubac carefully limited himself to a strictly historical account,
his results were taken by certain *avant-gardistes*, especially those
whose outlook became known as the *'nouvelle théologie'*, as implying that the whole of the traditional teaching of Western
Catholic theology about nature and supernature was mistaken;
they received, though not by name, a firm rebuke in the en-
cyclical *Humani Generis* in August 1950.[1]

As Rahner points out, the *nouvelle théologie* reproached the
teaching about nature and grace in the average textbook for its
'extrinsecism', that is, for viewing grace and the supernatural
order as a mere super-structure, imposed upon nature by God's
free decree, so that the *potentia oboedientialis* of nature for grace
implied a simple freedom from contradiction which excluded
any organic relation between the two orders. Rahner, while
dissociating himself from the *nouvelle théologie*, which was taken
as holding that God could not have created rational creatures
without designing them for the beatific vision, endorses its
criticism of the textbooks and of 'the average teaching on grace
in the last few centuries'. He condemns this last for a number of
reasons. First, it assumes that human nature is sharply circum-
scribed and that we can know *precisely* what it is like. Secondly,
it makes man's supernatural vocation and the gift of grace a
kind of *disturbance* of man's nature, an attempt 'to force something upon him (however elevated this may be in itself) for
which he is not [already] made'.[2] And Rahner very pertinently
asks, how can I know that everything I encounter in my existential experience of myself does simply belong to 'nature' and
would also exist if I were not called to supernatural communion
with God, seeing that to experience grace is not necessarily to
experience it *as* grace (that is, to know that it is grace that I am
experiencing)? Again, on the ontological plane, if we hold, as
Christian theism does, that what man concretely *is* depends
utterly upon God, how can we be content to say that
God's ordination of man to a supernatural end is simply a

[1] Denz. 2318; Denz.-Schoen. 3891.
[2] *Theological Investigations*, I, p. 300.

juridical decree and does not penetrate to man's ontological depths?

These questions are put by Rahner with the utmost ruthlessness. 'If', he insists, 'God gives creation, and man above all, a supernatural end and this end is first *"in intentione"*, then man (and the world) *is* by that very fact always and everywhere inwardly other in structure than he would be if he did not have this end. . . . We admit the basic contention that there is widely prevalent in the average teaching on grace an extrinsecist view which regards this as being merely a superstructure imposed from without upon a nature in itself indifferent with regard to it. It would seem to be a genuine concern of theology to put an end to the extrinsecism.'[1] Nevertheless, Rahner rejects the view attributed to the *nouvelle théologie*, that this inner reference of man to grace is a constituent of his nature in such a way that his nature cannot be conceived without it. Everyone, he says, agrees that grace is *unexacted*, that is, that nature cannot demand grace as something 'owed' to it. At this point the argument becomes extremely involved and is by no means easy to follow. Play is made with the attractive suggestion that, where *personal* being is concerned, it is of the very *nature* of personal being that it is ordained to personal communion with God in love and yet must receive this love as a free gift. This view, however, is reluctantly abandoned for reasons which need not be given in detail here.[2] Rahner holds, indeed, that God creates man 'in such a way that he *can* receive this love which is God himself, and that he can and must at the same time accept it for what it is: the ever astounding wonder, the unexpected, unexacted gift.' But, he adds, characteristically and realistically, 'ultimately we only know what "unexacted" means when we know what personal love is, not *vice versa*: we don't understand what love is by knowing the meaning of "unexacted"'.[3] And, secondly, God must create man in such a way that, when man accepts this free gift, he can accept it as a real *partner*, for all its 'unexactedness'. This,

[1] ibid., pp. 302f.

[2] I must confess that in my review of Rahner's book in the *Church Quarterly Review* (CLXIII (1962), p. 129) I quoted Rahner in support of this view. Repeated reading of an extremely obscure paragraph has, however, convinced me that I was mistaken and that his view, while superficially similar, is, as will be seen above, different.

[3] op. cit., p. 310.

says Rahner, is all we need say 'kerygmatically', that is, when we are preaching the Gospel. But, when we talk theology, we need to remember four things:

1. Man must have a real 'potency' for grace, and must have it *always*. He is always being addressed and claimed by the Love which is God himself, and this 'potency' is the most inward and authentic characteristic of man. 'The capacity for the God of self-bestowing personal Love is the central and abiding existential of man as he really is.'[1]

2. Man must be able to receive this love as what it is, namely a free gift. So this 'central, abiding existential' is itself to be characterised as unexacted, as 'supernatural'. Man must therefore be something more than this existential, for if it were simply coextensive with his nature, it would be unconditional in its essence.

3. So we must distinguish what man always is into (i) this unexacted real receptivity, the supernatural existential, and (ii) what is left over when this is subtracted from the substance of his concrete quiddity, his 'nature'. 'Nature' *as contrasted with the supernatural* (not, we must notice, nature in the sense of the content of the concrete contingent entity) is thus a 'remainder-concept', a *Restbegriff*. And, since we know man only as the concrete being who is the object of God's love, we can never state with precision just what the content of his 'nature' in this sense is, even though we may approximate to it by philosophical concepts such as *animal rationale*.

4. Hence, we need not, with de Lubac, scorn the concept of *potentia oboedientialis*. Man's spiritual nature has an openness for the supernatural, which is a real inner ordination and not a mere non-repugnance and yet is conditional. What we must guard against is simply identifying this openness with the inner dynamism of man's nature *as we find it*, for in this the supernatural may be already at work, as Revelation will subsequently reveal to us. It is suggested that the scholastic concept of nature as applied to man has owed too much to the model of what is sub-human. Man has indeed a nature and it has an end assigned to it; but we must not conceive it on the model of a pot in relation to its lid or a biological organism in relation to its

[1] ibid., p. 312.

environment.[1] Nature is, in fact, a highly analogical concept, and to see what it means for man we must look at man as he is and as God deals with him.

These, then, are the main features of Fr Rahner's discussion; he is the first to admit that he has not answered all the questions. And I suggest that, even if we are not particularly attracted by either his scholasticism or his existentialism, we should be ready to welcome his outlook as a whole. He is determined to insist upon the sheer gratuitousness of grace and the supernatural; man's ordination to union with God in the beatific vision is a sheer gift of God which man can neither claim in his own right nor attain by his natural powers. On the other hand, it is not a disturbance but a fulfilment of his natural constitution, and it is something for which God has ordained him and ordains him continually. Furthermore, grace is essentially personal; to be in grace is to be the object of the love of the God who is himself Love, and in any notion of grace as either a quasi-material substance or a quasi-mechanical force is firmly excluded. And, while Rahner is obviously opposed to the extrinsecism which has, rightly or wrongly (the Chevetogne conference would say 'on the whole wrongly'), been attributed to Protestantism, he is even more obviously opposed to the extrinsecism of the Catholic manualists, with their mental image of nature as being passively manipulated by grace. There is much here that theologians of other communions should be ready to welcome. But we shall, I think, see even more clearly the relevance of Rahner's approach to the issues raised at Chevetogne when we go on to consider his second essay, which is concerned with uncreated and created grace.

His purpose here is stated with disarming modesty; it is simply to enquire whether *within* the concepts of scholastic theology it may not be possible to obtain a better definition of uncreated grace than has hitherto been achieved, and any intention of introducing new concepts, such as those of a more personalist metaphysics, is disowned. But where this will lead we shall see.

---

[1] I would again refer to chapter iv of *The Importance of Being Human*, where the implications of this fact are worked out in some detail. It is perhaps a weakness in Rahner's discussion that he does not make more explicit use of the distinctively Christian doctrine of creation.

The starting-point is the doctrine of grace in the New Testament, and particularly in St Paul. For St Paul, we are told, man's justification and renewal is seen as endowment with the *Pneuma hagion*, the Holy Spirit, who is given to us and dwells in us. This, however, does not exclude but rather implies a created effect of the gift of the Spirit. It is pointed out that, while in many Pauline texts, the *pneuma* is the personal Spirit of God, there are others in which 'our' *pneuma* is clearly a supernatural principle in the sanctified man and is not just our *nous* or our *psyche*; and this second sense of *pneuma* is seen as following from the first and not *vice versa*. Thus 'for St Paul, man's inner sanctification is first and foremost a communication of the personal Spirit of God, that is to say, in scholastic terms, a *donum increatum*; and he sees every created grace, every way of being *pneumatikos*, as a consequence and a manifestation of the possession of this uncreated grace.'[1] In contrast, the ordinary scholastic teaching sees God's *pneuma* as being present in us *because* we possess created grace. However, the Fathers, especially the Greek fathers and among these St Irenaeus in particular, quite clearly see 'the created gifts of grace as a *consequence* of God's substantial communication to justified men.'[2]

Rahner makes no attempt to gloss over the apparent contradiction. 'However diverse they may be among themselves,' he writes, 'it is true of all the scholastic theories that they see God's indwelling and his conjunction with the justified man as based exclusively upon created grace. ... Uncreated grace (God's communication of himself to man, the indwelling of the Spirit) implies a new *relation* of God to man. But this can only be conceived of as founded upon an absolute entitative modification of man himself, which modification is the real basis of the new real relation of man to God upon which rests the relation of God to man.'[3] (We must remember that, for scholastic philosophy, *any* relation between God and a creature is real in the creature but only 'logical' in God, that is to say, it involves a change in the creature but no change in God.) Now can the outlook of Scripture and the Fathers on the one hand and that of scholastic theology on the other be reconciled? This is Rahner's problem.

[1] op. cit., p. 322.
[2] ibid.
[3] ibid., p. 324.

He begins by stressing the intimate relation that there is between grace in general and the beatific vision. The life of glory is not a mere reward for the life of grace; it is the definitive flowering and 'disclosure' of the life of divine sonship already possessed. There follows an extremely elaborate exposition of St Thomas's doctrine of knowledge in good German existentialist terms. I am not sure that all Thomists would accept all the elements of Rahner's exposition as faithfully reproducing the teaching of their master or that they would feel that his teaching necessarily gained in clarity and cogency by being expressed in the language of German existentialism. The function of this exposition in regard to the whole movement of the argument is, however, clear. It is to show, first, that the relation between man and God which pertains in virtue of man's knowledge of God in the beatific vision, brings about no 'accidental, real, absolute modification' in either of its terms;[1] secondly, that it must therefore be a relation in the order not of efficient but of formal causality; and, thirdly, that this must be true of the relation of grace in general and not only of the glory of heaven, since, as has already been established, there is an essential homogeneity between grace and glory. Thus Rahner is able to state the final solution of his problem:

> God communicates himself to the man to whom grace has been shown in the mode of *formal* causality, so that this communication is not then merely the consequence of an efficient causation of created grace. Thus it becomes clear that the proposition no longer holds good which maintains that man has uncreated grace because he possesses created grace; on the contrary, with Scripture and the Fathers, the communication of uncreated grace can be conceived of under a certain respect as logically and really prior to created grace: in that mode namely in which a formal cause is prior to the ultimate material disposition.[2]

A number of incidental points are then made. It is stressed that this very formal account says nothing about the *positive* character of either grace here or glory hereafter. Again, we are

---

[1] The reason given (pp. 328ff) is that the only relation between God and a creature which implies an absolute created determination is its relation to God as its creative cause, and that, in the beatific vision, since (on Thomist doctrine) God's essence takes the place of a *species intelligibilis*, there is no *created* effect. Rahner refers in a footnote to his *Spirit in the World*.

[2] op. cit., p. 334.

told that the union of grace as an *ontological* fact is prior to and independent of any actual *awareness* of it. Furthermore, it is pointed out that the position which has been argued is equally consistent with a traditionalist doctrine of the divine indwelling, in the line of St Thomas, Suarez, John of St Thomas or Gardeil (in itself a fairly wide range of choice!), or with a more personalist metaphysics which some contemporaries may prefer. Appeal is then made to texts of some of the great scholastics—Alexander of Hales, Bonaventure and St Thomas, and, of course, Peter Lombard—to show that Rahner's view is not so novel as it might appear to be and that it is at least adumbrated already in the tradition. Even Trent is pressed into service: 'Created grace is seen as *causa materialis (dispositio ultima)* for the formal causality which God exercises by graciously communicating his own Being to the creature. In this way the material and formal causes possess a reciprocal priority: as *dispositio ultima* created grace is in such a way the presupposition of the formal cause that it can itself only exist by way of the actual realisation of this formal causality.'[1] And finally Rahner argues that his introduction of formal causality as the guiding concept makes it possible, without denying the venerable principle that all the acts of God *ad extra* are acts of the one nature and not of the Persons separately, to hold that, in the life of grace, the Persons have dealings with us that are genuinely different for each, and are not different, so to speak, in a merely 'honorary' sense or, to use the technical term, merely by 'appropriation'. A similar case was put forward in 1944 by Père Lucien Chambat, in his book *Présence et Union*, where it was argued that, not only on the level of grace but also on that of nature, the principle of the acts *ad extra* as acts of the one nature applies only in the order of efficient causality and that in the order of exemplary or formal causality creation is an extension into the created order of the processions of the divine Persons. The point may be recommended to the attention of Eastern Orthodox theologians, for it is one of their constant, and perhaps not altogether unjustified, complaints against the West that, from the time of Augustine, it has given the unity of the divine essence priority over the Trinity of the Persons and has in consequence fundamentally 'depersonalised' the Godhead and developed a

[1] ibid., p. 341.

spirituality in which the Trinity comes in only as an after-thought.[1]

It may be interesting, before passing on, to give a brief glance at the discussion of sanctifying grace in M. Jacques Maritain's *magnum opus*, *The Degrees of Knowledge*. Maritain, as is well known, is or believes himself to be a Thomist *pur sang* and for him the commentator *par excellence* is John of St Thomas. The basic problem about grace is nevertheless the same for him as for the writers whom we have already considered. 'How can we thus be made gods by participation, receive a communication of what belongs properly to God alone? How can a finite subject *formally* participate in the nature of the Infinite?' 'Thomists', he replies, 'give this answer: the soul is thus rendered infinite in the order of its *relation to the object*. A formal participation in deity, which would be impossible were it a question of having Deity for its essence . . . is possible if it is a matter of having Deity as object.'[2] No doubt an Eastern Orthodox will be tempted to protest that this is no genuine deification at all; grace means participating in God, not just *knowing* him. We must, however, remember that, for an Aristotelian such as Maritain, to *know* an object is, in a certain mysterious way, to *become* it: 'intentionally', of course, and not 'entitatively', but nevertheless really and not just metaphorically. And Maritain, who is not only an Aristotelian but also a Catholic, presses this principle very far indeed, when, having made use of St Thomas and the Thomists in his investigation of the degrees of rational knowledge, he brings in St John of the Cross as the great doctor of supra-rational knowledge and mystical contemplation. 'By an intuitive vision of the Divine Essence', he writes, 'the beati-fied creature will receive—with no shadow of pantheism—in-finitely more than the most daring pantheism can dream of: the infinitely transcendent God himself, not that wretched idol-God mingled with the being of things and emerging through our efforts, which pantheism and the philosophy of becoming imagine, but the true God who is eternally self-sufficient and eternally blessed in the Trinity of Persons. By vision, the creature becomes the true God himself, not in the order of

[1] Cf. V. Lossky, *The Mystical Theology of the Eastern Church*, pp. 64ff; K. Rahner, *The Trinity, passim*.
[2] op. cit., p. 254.

substance, but in the order of that immaterial union which constitutes the intellectual act.[1]

And this transformation, which is to reach its fulness in heaven, begins here on earth, in the life of grace.

> Sanctifying grace [writes Maritain] is an inherent quality, an 'entitative habit' which is the very rich seed (placed in us, even here below, according to the mode of a nature or *root principle*) of that operation which is the Beatific Vision: . . . It is new spiritual nature grafted on to the very essence of our soul, and demands as its due to see God as he sees himself. Just as our thinking nature has as its proportionate object the being of things material like ourselves; just as the angelic nature has as its proportioned object spiritual essences: so, too, does this supernatural spiritual principle have as its connatural object the subsistent Supernatural and render us proportionate in the depths of our being to an essentially divine object. . . . That is how grace, while leaving us infinitely distant from pure Act [i.e. God] (in the order of being) is still (in the order of spiritual operation and relation to its object) a formal participation in the Divine Nature. A seed of God: *semen Dei.* There is nothing metaphorical in this, nothing merely moral: it is a 'physical' reality, as the theologians say, that is, an ontological reality, all that is most positive and effective, the most solid of all realities.[2]

The transforming character of this supernatural knowledge of God is emphasised when Maritain goes on to point out that it is what the scholastics call 'knowledge by connaturality'; this is exemplified by the very deep knowledge which a man may have of chastity, not by knowing a lot of facts about it, but simply by *being chaste*.[3]

> As we confront God, there is no other way of going beyond knowledge through concepts except by making use, in order to know him, of our very connaturality, our co-nascence, as Claudel would say, or our co-birth with him. What is it that makes us radically connatural with God? It is sanctifying grace whereby we are made *consortes divinae naturae*. And what makes this radical connaturality pass into act; what makes it flower into the actuality of operation? Charity.[4]

[1] ibid., p. 255.
[2] ibid.
[3] *S. Th.*, II, II, xlv 2c. Cf. I, i, 6 *ad* 3, where it is called knowledge *per modum inclinationis*.
[4] op. cit., p. 260.

All this is, of course, a matter of created grace, though Maritain does not adopt the phrase, but it is in the closest possible relation to the uncreated grace, which is God himself.

> The effect of our being elevated to the state of grace is a new mode of God's presence within us, one that theologians call the mission of the Divine Persons and the indwelling of the Trinity in the soul. . . . This special presence . . . of itself, and in virtue of its own proper energies, . . . is a *real* and *physical* (ontological) presence of God in the very depths of our being. How? In what respect? As *object*! Not now as an efficient principle whose primary causality gives being to everything in the soul, but as term towards which the soul is inwardly turned, turned back, converted and ordered as to an object of loving knowledge . . ., not just any knowledge and love; no! but a fruitful, experimental knowledge and love which puts us in possession of God and unites us to him not at a distance, but really.[1]

It must, I think, be admitted that Maritain here follows the traditional scholastic line that uncreated grace is causally subsequent to created grace and not *vice versa*: God's presence in the soul, as we have just seen is described as an *effect* of our elevation into the state of grace. Again, his assertion that we become divine 'intentionally' in virtue of our supernatural knowledge of God is *prima facie* very different from the suggestion of Rahner and Chambat that the divine Persons are present in the soul in the mode of formal causality, though it is not perhaps necessarily contradictory to it. In any case, he is perfectly clear about the theological issue which is at stake, namely the doctrine of a real participation of God by man which does not destroy man's creaturely status. Whether his philosophical account of this is altogether successful is an important issue but a minor one.

To return to Fr Rahner. No doubt to many English readers a discussion such as his will seem to be artificial, over-subtle and speculative in the extreme, but I think they will do him a grave injustice if they fail to appreciate its significance. For it provides an example, which is all the more impressive because its author deliberately writes in the idiom of traditional scholasticism (even if it is a scholasticism liberally spiced with existentialist seasoning), of the fact that many of the most vigorous Roman

[1] ibid., pp. 257f.

Catholic scholars of the present day are anxious to get back behind the frequently restricted and pedestrian formulas of the post-Tridentine manualists into a wider realm in which the special insights of Patristic and later Eastern Christian thought and spirituality can be brought in to correct the distortions and resolve the deadlocks of both Catholic and Protestant thought in the West, without simply writing off as a dead loss either the genuine achievements of Protestantism or the tremendous intellectual triumphs of medieval scholasticism. And this is a truly ecumenical and irenical task.

III

I shall conclude this discussion by emphasising, as I did at the beginning, that behind it there lies, as its necessary presupposition, the doctrine of the essential openness of created being to fresh influxes of the creative activity of God. That doctrine, as I believe, rests on sound rational grounds, and it is on such rational grounds that I have argued for it in the body of this book. Nevertheless, it can, I think, rightly be called a Christian doctrine, for it took its rise in the setting and atmosphere of a Christian culture and emerged from the Judaeo-Christian tradition, and I very much doubt whether it could have appeared, at least with the same clarity, in any other setting. There is nothing incoherent or inconsistent in this; the rational grounds of a doctrine are one thing, its historical and cultural setting another. Upon this distinction rests the validity of the notion of a Christian philosophy or of Christian philosophies for which M. Étienne Gilson has so long and so eloquently argued. And here I shall show, in more detail than was possible in the limits of a lecture, how this Christian doctrine of the character of created being steers a middle course between a Parmenidean view which belittles the essentially changing nature of a finite world and a Heraclitean view which refuses to recognise any element of permanence in it.

Dr Josef Pieper, in his little book *The Silence of St Thomas*, has stressed, against the Sartrian existentialists, the concern of Christian theism to defend the doctrine of 'natures', that is, the view that the beings of which the world is composed (and in particular human beings) are not purely fluid and indeterminate,

but have, for all their striking differences and their mani-
fold potentialities of development, definite ontological and
moral structures, so that we can say that certain modes of behaviour are proper to them and certain others improper. Indeed, Pieper argues that it is only by theism that the concept of
natures can be effectually defended. 'It is superficial, unreasonable and even absurd', he writes 'to maintain that there
is a "nature" of things, anterior to existence, unless one holds
at the same time that things are *creatures*.'[1] I thoroughly sym-
pathise with his defence of natures against the Sartrians, but I
think it must be recognised that there is a doctrine of natures,
and a very 'high' doctrine at that, which is no less atheistic than
Sartrianism; I have referred to it in my ninth lecture.[2] It is the
doctrine which, in various forms, was common in the ancient
pagan world, and it may be briefly characterised as the doctrine of natures as 'closed'. For the pagan Platonist a number of
rabbits looked more or less alike and behaved in much the same
way because they were embodiments (numerically different and
varying in perfection) of the ideal rabbit which was laid up in
heaven while its copies scampered through their burrows or
nourished the frames of their captors. For the pagan Aristotelian there was no ideal rabbit, but there was a form of rabbit-
hood which was variously instantiated in the individuals. But
for both every being had a nicely rounded-off nature which
contained implicitly everything that the being could ever become; if only you could know what the nature really was—if you
could discover its real definition—you could in principle deduce
everything that the being was or ever could be. There were
problems about development and decay—*genesis* and *phthora*—
and about monstrous or deformed specimens, but these could
be solved with a little ingenuity. In this sublunar world forms
were only participated very imperfectly, or else the trouble was
due to matter, which was not only the principle of individua-
tion but was also fundamentally unintelligible and introduced
an element of untidiness wherever it was found. In spite of this,
whatever any being could possibly become was implicitly in it
from the start. If it changed, this could only be either because its
form was being actualised more fully, as when a puppy becomes

[1] op. cit., p. 98.
[2] Cf. p. 145 *supra*.

a dog, or because, in consequence of its material element, the opposite was happening, as when senility sets in, or because one form was being substituted for another and the nature was being changed into a different one, as when a mouse is eaten by a cat. What Greek thought could not have tolerated, because it simply could not have understood it, would have been the idea that a being could become more perfect in its kind by acquiring some characteristic which was not implicit in its nature before. For every being was thought of as ontologically self-contained and incapsulated; it was the master of its fate and captain of its soul, as long as it existed at all.

Now Christian theism, as I have said above, is very much concerned to defend natures, but it has quite a different view from paganism as to what to be a nature is. For paganism, things, unless they are transient condensations in a perpetual flux, have determinate characters because each is incapsulated in itself; for Christian theism they have determinate characters because God has made them that way and because he continually preserves them. For paganism, to be a being is simply to be a being; for Christianity, to be a being is to be the continual recipient of the creative activity of God. As I have written elsewhere:

> Christian metaphysics has a clear grasp of the fact that the ultimate question about finite beings is not why they are the sort of beings that they are but why they exist at all. And the answer which Christian theism gives to that question is that they exist simply because they are being incessantly created, conserved and energised by God, because they are radically dependent upon the creative activity of a Being who is entirely perfect and self-existent.
>
> This does not mean that finite beings are lacking in reality; on the contrary, they have all the reality that finite beings can have. They are real but dependent beings, exercising real but dependent energies; they have nothing that they have not received, but they have not received nothing. Nor does this mean that they have no genuine community of nature with one another. On the contrary, when God creatively thinks of two beings in the same way, this constitutes a common nature for them.[1]

[1] *The Importance of Being Human*, p. 56.

I

From this fundamental fact that finite beings are *creatures* it follows that they are, as I have argued in my text, essentially open to the creative activity of God. Because they are not self-existent they are not ontologically incapsulated; to be a finite being is to be open to the power and love of God, who, without annulling or removing anything that he has given can always, if he sees fit, give more.

Now I do not think it can be denied that many Catholic writers, while of course admitting that finite beings exist only because God has made them, have talked about their natures as if he had not. While perfunctorily asserting that grace perfects nature, they have only too often looked upon the orders of nature and grace as virtually isolated from each other, rather like two flats on adjacent floors separated by a soundproof ceiling. Or, to change the metaphor, they have spoken as if the sole function of nature in relation to grace was to provide a kind of platform upon which grace can perform a supernatural dance. It is not surprising then that man's natural desire for the vision of God becomes a complete mystery and an embarrassment. If, however, we give full weight to the essential openness of nature to the divine activity, recognising that all finite beings are necessarily *incomplete*, so that they would collapse into utter non-existence but for the incessant conserving activity of God, we can surely see that nature is not just a platform upon which grace performs but the medium in which grace works. Only so can we do justice to St Thomas's twin assertions that grace both presupposes nature and perfects it.[1]

One of the consequences of this is that the Christian's attitude before God should be one that combines gratitude and contentment with expectancy and wonder; for whatever God has given us in the way of grace is more than we had any right to demand, and, whatever he has given us, it is always in his power to give more. There is in fact a double openness of nature for grace. At every stage there are a vast number of possibilities for further supernaturalisation, any (or none) of which God may choose to actualise; and whatever stage we have reached, there are an infinite number of further stages to any of which God may take us if he sees fit. It is in the light of such considerations as these

[1] *S. Th.*, I, i, 8 *ad* 2; I, ii, 2 *ad* 1.

that I should wish to interpret such a fine passage as this from M. Maritain:

> In supernatural operations, two activities are joined, but not juxtaposed: the activity of nature does not initiate what grace completes; from the beginning, nature acts as elevated by grace. If the roles of nature and grace in supernatural operation, in the vision of God in heaven and in the act of theological virtues here below, were *divided*, then there would be a mechanical addition. No! Precisely because our very essence and our natural powers of action are themselves docility and potentiality with regard to God, our supernatural acts emanate verily from our very depths, from the very roots of our soul and of our faculties. But they so emanate only *inasmuch as* the soul and its faculties are lifted up by grace and its energies, *inasmuch as* they are borne by these infused qualities to possibilities absolutely inaccessible to their nature alone.[1]

The writers whom I have mentioned are only some among the many Roman Catholic scholars who have in recent years explored afresh the theology of grace. Rahner himself, in his small book *Nature and Grace*, gives a formidable list of some others.[2] I shall conclude this discussion with a brief summary of the typical and conciliatory book by Fr Robert W. Gleason, S.J., published in 1962 under the simple title *Grace*. In contrast to the manuals, he stresses the importance of discussing sanctifying grace before actual grace, and not *vice versa*. Sanctifying grace, he insists, is not a thing but a participation in the life of God himself; therefore it must be investigated in terms of its own nature, rather than in terms of sin. Grace is an absolute quality which is a transcendent relation to God actuating us; de la Taille's phrase *actuation créée par acte incréé* is a translation into philosophical terms of the doctrine of the Greek fathers. The Incarnation sets up an ontological relation between Christ and all humanity, but this is only a fundamental or radical filiation, whose completion requires grace through the sanctifying action of Christ's humanity in the sacraments, especially baptism. Nevertheless, the grace of Christ operates hiddenly even in pagan man. It is often difficult, Gleason says, to know whether the Councils of Carthage and Orange are speaking of

---

[1] op. cit., pp. 256f.
[2] op. cit., pp. 32f.

sanctifying or of actual grace; not until the later works of St Thomas was the distinction satisfactorily drawn. Fr Gleason adds excellent appendices on Eastern Orthodoxy and Lutheranism; owing to his Occamism, we are told, Luther could neither unify his insights with the rest of Christian tradition nor even remain true to them.

In looking back on this discussion, it would be too much to claim that we have seen how to reconcile the fundamental differences between Protestantism and Catholicism, but we have perhaps been able to see more clearly what these differences really are. And the witness of Eastern Orthodoxy has shown pretty clearly that there are other points of view of which both Catholics and Protestants in the past have been totally ignorant. To have achieved this is not to have brought about reconciliation, but it is perhaps to have brought it nearer, and this in itself is something for which we ought to be grateful.

BODY, SOUL AND CREATION

THERE ARE A number of questions about the origin, nature and destiny of man, as an individual and as a species, in which both Christian theology and natural science have a special interest, and concerning which it is widely believed that these two disciplines are in some kind of deep-seated opposition. This impression is, I believe, mainly due to a misunderstanding about a fundamental Christian doctrine which underlies discussions in this realm, namely the doctrine of creation.

To many people the word 'creation' will simply suggest an act by which God is alleged to have brought the world or one of its constituents into existence at the beginning of its career, whenever that beginning may have been. The word is indeed sometimes used in this sense by theologians themselves, or at least by biblical scholars, as, for example, when the stories contained in the first two chapters of the book Genesis are described as 'creation-narratives'. In philosophical and dogmatic theology, however, 'creation' means much more than this, as is seen from the common assertion that it would still have application to finite beings even if they had always existed and therefore had no beginning at all. This can be illustrated very strikingly from the writings of St Thomas Aquinas, the greatest of the medieval theologians. St Thomas did in fact believe, in accordance with the interpretation of the Genesis stories which was current at his day, that the world had begun to exist at some particular date in the past and he was anxious to controvert the arguments of the Arab philosophers who claimed to prove by purely rational arguments, without any appeal to revelation, that the world had always existed and would always continue to exist. Nevertheless, he was convinced that reason itself could not settle the question; what was clear to him was that, whether the world had always existed or not, it must in either case be the creature of God.[1] 'That the world did not always exist', he writes, 'is held by faith alone and cannot be proved by demonstration.'[2] Everything except God is created, and to create is to make something out of nothing, but creation is no kind of change, for 'nothing' is not a being but the absence of any being.[3] The creation of a being is in fact identical with its conservation. 'As it depends on God's will that he brings things into being, so it depends on his will that he keeps them in being; for he keeps them in being only by always giving them being. Therefore if he withdrew his action from them they would return to non-existence.'[4] 'God causes this effect [sc. of being created] in things, not only when they first begin to be but as long as they are kept in being.'[5] For since God himself exists in eternity, creation is, from his standpoint, one timeless act by which the whole range of temporal existence is maintained in being; it is only from the temporal standpoint of the creature that creation is an act that begins when the creature begins. Nevertheless, *from the creature's standpoint* it is a continual and not a momentary act and it continues as long as the creature itself exists.[6] It is important that this should be kept in mind in the subsequent discussion, as otherwise quite unnecessary difficulties will arise. The view that God's creative activity is involved only when a creature begins its career is a hangover from the discredited seventeenth- and eighteenth-century doctrine known as deism;[7] it is certainly no part of traditional Christian teaching.

A more subtle but still important point is this; that creation is to be conceived as the imparting of being and not as the withholding of it. This assertion may sound cryptic and needs to be amplified. Some writers have thought it necessary, in order to protect the genuine freedom of the human will and to acquit God of direct responsibility for evil, to say that, within the

[1] *S.c.G.*, II, xxxi–xxxviii; *S. Th.*, I, xlvi.

[2] *S. Th.*, I, xlvi, 2c.

[3] *S.c.G.*, II, xv–xxi; *S. Th.*, I, xliv, xlv.

[4] *S. Th.*, I, ix, 2c.

[5] *S. Th.*, I, viii, 1c.

[6] For a fuller discussion cf. my *Existence and Analogy*, ch. vi.

[7] Cf. G. C. Joyce, *Encycl. of Religion and Ethics*, IV, pp. 533ff; R. S. Westfall, *Science and Religion in Seventeenth-century England*; R. H. Hurlbutt III, *Hume, Newton and the Design Argument*.

sphere of the creature's freedom, God withholds his own activity. Thus Captain D. H. Doig, in a very interesting article on the problem of evil,[1] has written as follows:

> The act of divine creation must have something paradoxical about it. It cannot confer any benefit on God to create something, because he has the fulness of perfection already. And the first need must be for the Creator to withdraw his universality and omnipotence from a certain sphere in which his creation can operate. ... Thus to express himself more fully he must surrender some freedom of action. His creation must be a positive act, but since it cannot add to what was already infinite, this must be balanced by a negative withdrawal.

Now it must of course always be remembered that words taken from human experience and applied to God must be understood analogically, and it would be unfair to press the suggestions of the notion of withdrawal beyond its proper limits. Nevertheless, the notion that God has to withdraw himself from a certain sphere in order that, on balance, the totality of being shall not be augmented by the act of creation does not seem to me to be a happy one. The classical tradition of Christian theism would maintain that, simply because the creature is finite and God is infinite, the creature's existence, real as it is, does not add anything to the existence of God; no 'withdrawal' is necessary because there is no augmentation to be counterbalanced. So far from the creature's freedom implying a withdrawal of God from its sphere, that freedom is itself a gift of God and so implies God's entry into it, though 'entry', no less than 'withdrawal', is a radically analogous term. Where free-will is involved it seems to me much more satisfactory to start from the traditional assertion that God moves all secondary causes according to their natures: physical causes according to the nature of physical causes, and voluntary causes according to the nature of voluntary causes. For, although this is a statement of the problem rather than its solution, it is at least a statement of the right problem and not of the wrong one. It takes account of two truths of Christian experience: first, that when a man acts in accordance with God's will, God is not excluded from the act but is in fact the primary agent in it; secondly that when a man tries to exclude God from the act and make himself the

[1] *Theology*, LXIX (1966), pp. 485ff.

primary agent, all that he manages to do is to introduce an element of sheer destruction and negation, an element which contravenes the man's own nature as fundamentally dependent upon God, an element which is not genuine activity but is rather deficiency in actuality, an element which goes against the creature's own inbuilt finality and is therefore self-frustrating and self-destructive. There is, I believe, deep truth and not mere slickness or paradox in the maxim that it is only in the order of negation and defect that the creature can be a primary cause. So long as he is acting in line with the authentic finality of the nature which God maintains in him he cannot keep God out, nor will he wish to do so. For the act by which the creature fulfils itself is simply the prolongation, in the finite realm of secondary causes, of the act by which God continually creates and conserves it. To try to exclude God from one's act is to repudiate one's ontological status as dependent upon God and so to frustrate oneself. In contrast, willingly to invite God as primary cause into one's act is not to abandon or diminish one's own freedom and spontaneity but to augment it. For in relations between persons, in contrast to relations between impersonal forces, provided the relations are authentically adjusted in accordance with the status and character of the parties, the influence of the one does not suppress but releases and enhances the freedom of the other; and this will be more and not less true when the former is the Creator himself. What I find unsatisfactory in Captain Doig's notion of 'withdrawal' is the suggestion that God withholds himself from the sphere in which he gives us freedom to act; rather I would wish to say that it is precisely by entering into it that he gives us freedom.

It should be unnecessary to add that the priority of God in this relationship is not a priority in time; it is not temporal but ontological. There is not an act of God, followed by an act of man; nor is there an act of man, followed by an act of God. There is one act, in which God is the primary cause and the creature is the secondary cause, and in which God exercises his primary cause by maintaining the creature's secondary causality and not by overriding or suppressing it. There are only two qualifications which I would wish to make to this assertion.

(1) I am excluding from consideration here acts of God

which are, in the strict sense, miraculous. Whether in these there is a real overriding of the secondary causality of creatures by divine intervention, and what the nature of such an over-riding would be, would need a separate discussion. My own tentative suggestion would be that even in these cases what is manifested is an abnormal mode of relation of the primary cause to the secondary causes rather than a suppression of the latter by the former. A miracle may be an unusually striking example of divine activity to minds such as ours in which familiarity tends to breed, if not contempt, at least insensitivity; but God is no more involved in it than he is in the ordinary course of nature. It is only to a deistic metaphysic that miracles will be seen as invasions by God into a normally godless universe. It is relevant to remark that the traditional arguments for the existence of God are based not upon occasional miracu-lous events but upon the existence and the normal functioning of the world, which, it is held, themselves depend upon the un-failing creative and conserving activity of God. For a fuller discussion I would refer the reader to the recent work by Fr Louis Monden, S.J., *Signs and Wonders: a study of the miraculous element in religion*.[1]

(2) It is an open question among scientists whether the basic events in the physical world are prescribed in all their aspects by strict causal laws or whether, on the other hand, all that can be specified by physical law, even in principle, is the statistical frequency with which events of a certain type occur and the probability of occurrence of any individual event. The second of these views is that of the 'Copenhagen' school; if it is correct (it certainly seems to be dominant) we shall have to say that in the individual events on the sub-atomic level, the primary causality of God is operative without the involvement of any secondary causes at all. This will, however, be true only of the individual events in their bare occurrence as contrasted with their place in the setting of their actual environment. Secondary causality is not abolished on the Copenhagen view, but its scope is limited to the determination of the frequency or the probability of events of a specified type and does not extend to the determi-nation of their individual occurrence. And, for theism, this

[1] New York: Desclée, 1966 (Original edition: *Le Miracle, Signe de Salut* (Bruges: Desclée de Brouwer, 1960)).

whole fabric of statistical secondary causality will itself be con-
served by the primary causality of God. To say this is not to
postulate a 'God of the gaps' in the proper and pejorative sense
of that term. What that term applies to is the view that God
does not operate in the realm that has at the present time been
brought within the scope of natural law, but only in that which
has not; and since the latter realm is constantly diminishing as
science advances, the view in question is rightly held to be un-
dignified and suicidal. I am saying something quite different:
not that God is in the gaps and nowhere else, but that God is
everywhere, including the gaps if there are any. Whether there
are any gaps is the business of the physical scientist and not of
the theologian. The structure of secondary causality is the subject of the positive sciences; the theologian is concerned with
the relation of secondary causality to the primary causality of
God. He will, of course, be suspicious of any doctrine of the
physical world which excludes from its account of secondary
causality any place for the effectiveness of volition; but so too
will the scientist if he is a human being. The detailed correla-
tion of physical law with human freedom is in any case the job
of the scientist and, perhaps, the philosopher, not of the theologian. The latter is concerned only to maintain that, however
secondary causes operate, they do so under the primary
causality of God, who is 'everywhere present and filleth all
things'.

If we now turn to consider the process of the evolution of the
physical and biological universe, we must envisage it all as
taking place against the background of the creative and conserving activity of God. Whether this process, in its physical
aspects, is capable of being understood simply in terms of the
laws of physics and chemistry or whether it needs the postula-
tion of some kind of immanent entelechy or 'drive', some *élan
vital*, in Bergson's phrase, is not, as I see it, a question in which
the theologian has any vested interest. Speaking as an outsider,
I find it very difficult to convince myself that the diversity, complexity and magnitude of evolution as it has actually occurred
is to be accounted for simply by natural selection acting upon
the material provided by the mutation and reshuffling of genes;
so do biologists such as Dr Robert Clark and, if I understand
him, Dr W. H. Thorpe, and such an amazingly well-informed

philosopher from the scientific angle as Dr Errol Harris.[1] However, the majority of biologists seem to be confident that nothing
beyond the laws of chemistry and physics is needed to explain
the evolutionary process; this is true even of Sir Alister Hardy,
who stresses the selective power of differences of habit as of not
less importance than pure natural selection.[2] The applied
mathematician will recall how the apparently teleological
variation-principles can be reduced to non-teleological differ-
ential equations.

The relevance of this emphasis upon creation as, from the
standpoint of the creature, a continuous and not a momentary
activity will be seen when we consider the question of the origin
of the human soul. Before doing this, however, I shall briefly
consider the relation between mentality and the physical organism throughout the evolutionary process, leaving the special
case of man for discussion later. As a matter of verbal clarification it should be noticed that, in ancient writers and in traditional Christian theologians, the word 'soul'—the Greek *psyche*,
the Latin *anima*—is used to denote the vital principle in any
living being, however lowly.

Turnips and wart-hogs, as well as men, possess souls, for they,
too, in their humble and different ways, are alive; when more
precision is needed, the soul of the turnip is described as 'vegeta-
tive', that of the wart-hog as 'sensitive' and that of the man as
'rational'; there is no implication that a soul necessarily survives the death of the body or that it is, in the modern sense of
the word, 'religious'. A vestige of this terminology persists in
our use of the word 'animal' to describe such beings as wart-
hogs, and of 'animate' and 'inanimate' to mean respectively
'alive' and 'dead'. (Incidentally, the word 'sensitive' has also
changed its meaning; today we should hardly describe the wart-
hog as having a 'sensitive soul', though we might so describe a
poet or an art-critic.) Without trying to decide the precise stage
of the evolutionary process at which the first glimmerings of
consciousness appear, I shall, in the present discussion, use the
word 'soul' to cover any kind of mental awareness or appetition,

[1] R. E. D. Clark, *The Universe: Plan or Accident?* (1961); W. H. Thorpe,
Science, Man and Morals (1965), ch. ii; E. E. Harris, *The Foundations of Metaphysics in Science* (1965), chh. xi–xiv.
[2] *The Living Stream* (1965), chh. v–vii.

and I shall now ask how we are to conceive the relation between soul and body.

There is a tendency among philosophers and scientists of what might be called the 'tough-minded' type to attempt to reduce mentality to the status of a mere function of the physical processes of the body. This is exemplified on the crudest level by the once fashionable assertion that 'the brain secretes thought as the liver secretes bile' and in a much more sophisticated and elusive way in Professor Gilbert Ryle's neobehaviourism, as set forth in his celebrated work *The Concept of Mind*. In spite of such disclaimers as 'Men are not machines, not even ghost-ridden machines. They are men—a tautology which is sometimes worth remembering',[1] he maintains 'To find that most people have minds (though idiots and infants in arms do not) is simply to find that they are able and prone to do certain sorts of things, and this we do by witnessing the sort of things they do.'[2] And it is clear from the whole context that 'the sort of things they do' refers simply to overt bodily behaviour. All the statements that are normally taken to be statements about mental acts and dispositions are thus interpreted as being purely about either actual bodily behaviour or the bodily behaviour that takes place or would take place under certain specifiable conditions. Ryle is thus led to the astounding assertion that, in the only sense in which he is willing to use the word 'mind', we do not experience our own minds in any way substantially different from the way in which we experience the minds of other people,[3] since we experience both simply by observing overt bodily behaviour. Against this neobehaviourist reductionism I shall assert, with common sense, that I have an immediate awareness of my own mind as a subject of consciousness, although this awareness is in important respects different from the awareness that I have of physical objects. I shall also assert that it is reasonable to believe that human bodies which are in their general structure and behaviour similar to mine have a subjective awareness associated with them in a way essentially similar to the way in which my subjective awareness is associated with mine. And, in spite of Descartes, I shall hold, with almost equal confidence, that

[1] op. cit., p. 81.
[2] ibid., p. 61.
[3] Cf. op. cit., p. 169.

non-human living physical bodies have types of awareness associated with them of a type that in each case is co-ordinated with the kind of physical body in question. It is, I admit, not easy to know just what it feels like to be an oyster or a mushroom; for the matter of that it is not easy for me to know exactly what it feels like to be Professor Ryle, or for him to know exactly what it feels like to be me. But it is not unreasonable to suppose that some kind and degree of mentality is to be found in the evolutionary scale well below the human level, and I am pretty sure that most biologists, like most human beings, assume this. Even the fox-hunter in the television programme, who denied his opponent's right to say that foxes did not like being hunted, on the ground that the opponent in question was not a fox, found himself obliged to defend his own assertion that the fox rather enjoyed the sport, by maintaining that, although he himself was not a fox either, he had lived among foxes all his life and knew what they felt like. It is, however, not essential to my next point that all living creatures have some kind of mental awareness, but only that some of them do, and in particular human beings. That point is the following: mentality cannot be reduced simply to physical quantities and processes, for the simple reason that the laws connecting physical quantities and describing physical processes make no reference whatever to mental states.

Put as baldly as this, the point may seem to be a platitude, but it is in fact so often ignored that it will be well to make it in more detail. The argument is simply this. You can only solve a mathematical equation for the variables that are in it. The variables that occur in the equations of physical science stand for purely non-mental quantities: masses, positions, electric charges, gravitational and electromagnetic fields, isotopic spins, strangenesses and whatever other concepts may be fashionable at the time. None of them stands for awareness, volition, surprise or pain. The equations enable one in principle (for their solution in practice may surpass the powers of man or computer) to derive from the values of these quantities at one moment their values at any later moment. (If the generally accepted view of quantum theory is correct, they do not enable one to do quite as much as this, but they certainly do not enable one to do more.) Thus, given the physical state of a living body at one moment, equations can in principle be constructed whose solution will specify its physical state at any subsequent moment. But the solution cannot specify the body's mental state, for none of the variables in the equation stands for anything mental. If there are laws which, when the physical state is given, specify the mental state, they are certainly not the laws of physics. *The equations that specify the physical process will be exactly the same whether the physical process is accompanied by mental process or not.* Therefore, if a physicist or biologist asserts that a certain type and degree of physical complexity in an organism is always accompanied by a certain type of mental awareness and appetition, he may conceivably be saying what is true, but its truth or falsehood in no way follows from the laws of physics. A similar point arises in connection with the question which is often discussed, whether any electronic computer that either exists now or may exist in the future can rightly be said to 'think'. Some of those who answer this question in the affirmative appear to hold that some kind of consciousness will necessarily appear in a computer which embodies a certain type of complexity; others, *à la* Ryle, appear to hold that thinking is not a matter of consciousness in any case, but only of overt physical behaviour. All of them are, I maintain, wrong. Whether such a machine is necessarily conscious, or potentially conscious, or never conscious is entirely undetermined by its physical structure and operation; this will be decided by something outside the realm of physics. A theist will, of course, say that, like the operation of physical law, it is decided in the last resort by the will of God: but he will add that God's conservation of the physical process is one thing and his decision about consciousness is another; there is no logical necessity connecting the two.

Thus for a theist it will be a matter for empirical investigation (unless a direct divine revelation has been vouchsafed on the question) whether consciousness has in fact been associated by God with organisms which have reached a certain level of physical complexity or with man-made machines of a certain type. Admittedly, such investigation may be very difficult to carry out, and in any given case the conclusion may be largely conjectural. We cannot, however, bypass the matter by simply asserting that such an association will always take place. A theist may think it is very probable that God will always bring it about or he may think that it is a rare privilege conferred by God on certain favoured organisms and machines, but there is no logical necessity one way or the other. The empirical investigation will indeed be difficult and may be inconclusive. It will clearly not be an empirical investigation of the type that is characteristic of the physical and biological sciences, for these, as we have already seen, are concerned simply with the physical aspects of their object. I have, however, argued elsewhere[1] that it is characteristic of the human mind that its perceptive activity does not terminate in the sense-datum which is the proper object of the physical sciences; it uses the sense-datum instrumentally as the *objectum quo*, through which it apprehends the intelligible object, the *objectum quod*, whether this latter be a lifeless or a living being. It is of course by entering into active relationship with them that we are able to acquire a knowledge of other beings that penetrates beneath the phenomenal level, and it is through this involvement and interchange that we convince ourselves that we are in relation with real beings and not just with groups of sense-data. We meet other human beings on the plane of our common humanity, dogs and cats on the plane of our common animality, and stocks and stones on the plane of our common materiality. There can be no *logical* guarantee that we are not mistaken in supposing that the people around us are subjects of consciousness like ourselves, but then there can never be a logical guarantee against an absolutely indetectible hallucination; it is indeed a truth of logic that what is indetectible cannot be detected. Nevertheless, from the fact that we are sometimes deceived it does not follow that deception is invariable or normal; and it is by acting on the principle that our senses do not normally deceive us that we learn to recognise the occasions when they do. How we are to decide whether there is genuine mental life in some extremely elaborate computer will indeed be a difficult problem, for the *objectum quo* with which it confronts us will be vastly different from those presented by the conscious beings with which we are normally familiar. Mr J. R. Lucas has forcefully argued[2] on logical

[1] *Words and Images*, pp. 70ff. Cf. pp. 98f *supra*.
[2] 'Minds, Machines and Gödel', in *Minds and Machines*, ed. A. R. Anderson. Briefly, the argument is that, while a calculating machine can handle data of any logical type inferior to its own, it is logically impossible for it to handle data of its own logical type. Minds, in self-reflection, do just this.

grounds that it is impossible for a calculating machine, however complex it may be, to simulate the mental activity of intelligent self-consciousness unless it is in fact intelligently self-conscious. If all machines of a certain kind are found to simulate this activity, it will show that they are something more than just machines. We shall then, as Mr Lucas remarks, have to recognise that there are two ways open to us of making intelligent beings: one that employs the old-fashioned method of sexual union and the other that uses the more up-to-date factory techniques. If he is right, we shall have a method by which, in principle, we may be able to recognise that a machine has an intelligent consciousness, for the manifestation of self-reflection will be a sufficient, though not perhaps a necessary, index. It must, however, be noted that this will be the index of a consciousness that is intelligent in the sense of being able to reflect upon its own activities; there can be no such index of a consciousness which is not in any way *self*-conscious, or which has only an un-formulated or 'unthematic' consciousness of itself as the subject, but not as the object, of its own activity. The fact in any case remains, that there can be no *a-priori* logical or physical necess-ity for any machine, or, for that matter, for any organism, to be conscious, since there are no variables in any physical equa-tion which stand for conscious activities or states, though it may be possible in some cases to recognise consciousness, by Lucas's criterion, *a posteriori*. The theist will, of course, assert that physi-cal and mental states alike are in the last resort due to the crea-tive activity of God; he will add that, even if the atheist were right in thinking that the physical states were self-explanatory, he would still be demonstrably wrong if he supposed that the mental states were necessary consequences of them.

Whatever may be the case about machines we have, I have suggested earlier on, solid grounds for supposing that, as a matter of fact though not of physical or logical necessity, certain complicated types of biological organism have associated with them subjects of consciousness which, following the traditional usage, I shall call 'souls'. (This will not exclude the application of the word 'soul' to the vital principle of a living organism which has not even a rudimentary consciousness; this we may guess to be the case with plants, though it would be difficult to prove it.) Nothing is implied about the nature of this conscious-

ness, but, since the consciousness and the physical organism—
the 'body'—are intimately related, it is reasonable to suppose
that the more elaborate and hierarchically structured types of
consciousness will be found in connection with the more elaborate types of body and especially those with a highly developed
central nervous system. The general view of neurophysiologists
that there is an association between the higher types of mental
life and a great development of the frontal lobes of the brain is
just the sort of thing we might expect. We must further recognise that, while the soul is intimately associated with the body,
it is not spatially extended through it in such a way that one
part of the soul is in one part of the body and another part in
another. There may, of course, be cases—perhaps sponges and
ant-hills provide examples—in which the total organism includes within itself lesser organisms, each of which has its own
vital principle, its own 'soul'; the fact will remain that the soul,
as the vital principle of the organism, is correlated with the
organism as such and hence it is inherently indivisible. If the
organism divides into two organisms, the soul will not be sub-
divided, though it may be replaced by two new souls; if the
organism decays and disintegrates, the soul may cease to exist.
But, because it is correlated to the organism as a whole, it is
essentially indivisible and unextended. If we are to speak of its
relations to the spatially distinct parts of the organism, we can
only say that it is *totum in toto et totum in aliqua parte*; it is related
as a whole, though in diverse ways, to the organism as a whole
and to every part of it. Whether in the case of a human being
the soul is something more than just the body's vital principle
is a question which we shall shortly consider; but even if it is
more it is certainly that. The point which I wish to stress at the
moment is this. Bodies can divide into fresh bodies, as when the
amoeba becomes two amoebae; they can eject parts of themselves and such parts can come together and unite into fresh
bodies, as happens in sexual reproduction. But souls can only
come into existence and cease to exist. There is nothing specially
mysterious or miraculous about this, and least of all to the theist.
For, as I have already emphasised, no special activity on the
part of God is involved in a being's *genesis* and *phthora*, its coming-
to-be and its passing-away; his creative activity is uniformly
involved in the whole course of its existence, however long or

short that may be. As long as beings exist God conserves them, and this is equally true whether they are bodies which are divisible, or souls which are indivisible, or living organisms composed of body and soul.

It has been the traditional belief of Christianity and of most, though perhaps not all, other religions that, in contrast with the souls of lower animals, the rational soul of a human being survives the death and decay of the body with which it is associated. Whether this immortality of the human soul is a necessary consequence of its rational nature has been disputed even within the tradition of scholasticism; not all the medieval philosophers agreed with St Thomas Aquinas on this point. It is, however, significant that, in contrast with the lower creation, man has a whole range of mental life which transcends the mere concern with the business of physical existence, and through which he is able, as it were, to stand outside and reflect upon his own embodied condition and, which is even more significant, to acquire a dim awareness of another realm, not of this world which is his real home and to which he ultimately belongs. There is nothing contrary to reason in the Christian doctrine according to which a human being is neither a pure animal nor a pure spirit, but a unity of both, this unity being dissolved at death and restored in the final resurrection, while in the intervening period the soul continues to exist although deprived of its material partner. Some of the questions that arise from this dual composition of man I have discussed elsewhere.[1] In particular it should be remarked that the nature of the time-process for a disembodied soul may be very different from that which it experiences in its normal embodied condition; for all we know, it may pass 'like a flash'. What I wish to stress at the moment is that, even if for a sub-human organism the consciousness is so narrowly limited in its concern with the operations of the body that its *raison d'être* ceases with the body's dissolution, there is no reason whatever why in the case of man this consciousness should not have a subject whose concern transcends, while including, the operations of the body and which therefore can still, so to speak, 'find something to do' when the body itself has died. From a different angle, we might say that, when

[1] Cf. *The Importance of Being Human*, ch. ii; *Christian Theology and Natural Science*, ch. vi.

bodily evolution (and especially its cerebral aspect) has reached the degree and type of development which we find in man, it can rightly and without maladjustment have a mental partner —a 'rational soul'—whose concern is not only with the material world and the body but also with a higher spiritual realm, and that just because the soul has this double concern, the body itself—or, it would be more accurate to say, the whole man, body and soul together—is given a point of entry into this other world in which the soul is rooted. The further point, that man has an openness towards the spiritual realm which makes it possible for him to be taken up by grace into the very life of God, is of the utmost importance but cannot be discussed here.[1] What I want to stress is that the traditional view that the soul of every human being is a fresh creation is much more reasonable than is sometimes recognised; for all that it really means is that the soul, not being extended in space as a material object is (though it is of course united with a material body), cannot be made out of pieces of other souls. This does not imply that the mental characteristics of a human being do not depend in any way upon the mental characteristics of his parents, that there is no inheritance of mental qualities. For a human being is not a loose conjunction of a totally unrelated soul and body; not, to speak colloquially, just any old soul and any old body thrown together anyhow. He is a real unity of two distinct but mutually adapted constituents, and, both at the first moment of his existence and throughout his subsequent life, the two fit together, develop together and influence each other. (The Aristotelian way of saying this is that the soul is the formal cause of the body's development and the body the material cause of the soul's, but the point can be made without bringing in either Aristotle or St Thomas.) There may thus very well be a registration of mental as well as physical peculiarities in the genetic material (the chromosomes, etc.) of the individual, and these may have been inherited from the parents according to the normal Mendelian laws. There will thus be an *indirect* transmission of mental characteristics from the souls of the parents to the soul of their child, since in parents and child alike these mental characteristics will be correlated with, and registered in, the genetic

[1] Cf. my *The Importance of Being Human*, ch. iv; *Grace and Glory, passim*; *Christ, the Christian and the Church, passim*; Appendix IV *supra*.

material in which, through the union of spermatozoon and ovum, the *direct* transmission from body to body takes place. And if we now cease to speak about the soul and the body separately and speak instead of the human being as the unified being who is constituted by their union, we can say quite simply that all the characteristics of a human being, both bodily and mental, are inherited from his parents. This does not, of course, deny the part that may be played in his subsequent development by his environment, his free decisions or the grace of God; it concerns simply his initial inherited endowment.

If the complaint is made that the account which I have given is very complicated, I can only reply that a human being is a very complicated kind of thing. It is much simpler to be either an angel or a machine, but this does not prove that either Descartes or Haeckel was right. We are not concerned with what is simple but with what is true.

BIBLIOGRAPHY

Where more than one edition of a work exists, reference has normally been made to the British edition if there is one.

ANDERSON, A. R., ed. *Minds and Machines*. Englewood Cliffs, N. J.: Prentice-Hall, 1964.

AULÉN, Gustaf. *The Faith of the Christian Church*. London: S.C.M. 2nd ed., 1961.

AYER, A. J. *Language, Truth and Logic*. London: Gollancz, 1936. 2nd ed., 1946.

BAILLIE, John. *The Sense of the Presence of God*. Oxford U.P., 1962.

BAKER, John Austin. *The Foolishness of God*. London: Darton, Longman and Todd, 1970.

BALTHASAR, Hans Urs von. *Cordula, oder der Ernstfall*. 1967.

BALTHASAR, Hans Urs von. *Essays in Theology, II: Word and Redemption*. New York: Herder, 1965.

BARRETT, C. K. *The New Testament Background: Selected Documents*. London: S.P.C.K., 1956.

BARTH, Karl. *The Knowledge of God and the Service of God according to the Teaching of the Reformation*. London: Hodder and Stoughton, 1938.

BASTABLE, Patrick K. *Desire for God*. London: Burns Oates and Washbourne, 1947.

BENARDETE, J. A. *Infinity: An Essay in Metaphysics*. Oxford: Clarendon Press, 1964.

BENT, Charles N. *Interpreting the Doctrine of God*. New York: Paulist Press, 1969.

BERGER, Peter L. *A Rumour of Angels: Modern Society and the Rediscovery of the Supernatural*. London: Allen Lane, 1970.

BETTENSON, H. *Documents of the Christian Church*. Oxford U.P., 1943.

BOCHEŃSKI, J. M. *The Methods of Contemporary Thought*. New York: Harper and Row, 1968.

BOUILLARD, Henri. *The Knowledge of God*. London: Burns and Oates, 1969.

BOUYER, Louis. *The Spirit and Forms of Protestantism*. London: Harvill Press, 1956.

BRAITHWAITE, R. B. *An Empiricist's View of the Nature of Religious Belief.* Cambridge U.P., 1955.

BROAD, C. D. *Examination of McTaggart's Philosophy.* Cambridge U.P., 1933, 1938.

BRUNNER, Heinrich Emil. *Man in Revolt: A Christian Anthropology.* London: Lutterworth Press, 1939.

CALLAHAN, Daniel, ed. *The Secular City Debate.* London: Collier-Macmillan, 1966.

CHAMBAT, Lucien. *Présence et Union: Les Missions des Personnes de la Sainte-Trinité.* Paris: Fontenelle, 1944.

CHAPMAN, H. John. *Spiritual Letters.* London: Sheed and Ward, 2nd ed., 1938.

CHARLESWORTH, M. J. *St Anselm's Proslogion.* Oxford: Clarendon Press, 1965.

CHOMSKY, Naom. *Language and Mind.* New York: Harcourt, Brace and World, 1968.

CHRISTIAN, William A. *An Interpretation of Whitehead's Metaphysics.* New Haven, Conn.: Yale U.P., 1959.

CLARK, R. E. D. *The Universe: Plan or Accident?* London: Paternoster Press, 1949.

COBB, J. B. *A Christian Natural Theology.* Philadelphia, Md.: Westminster Press, 1965.

CORETH, Emerich. *Metaphysics.* New York: Herder, 1968.

COX, Harvey. *The Secular City: Secularisation and Urbanisation in Theological Perspective.* London: S.C.M., 1965.

DENZINGER, H. *Enchiridion Symbolorum Definitionum et Declarationum de Rebus Fidei et Morum.* 33rd ed., A. Schönmetzer ed. Rome *et al*, 1965.

DEWART, Leslie. *The Foundations of Belief.* London: Burns and Oates, 1969.

DEWART, Leslie. *The Future of Belief: Theism in a World Come of Age.* London: Burns and Oates, 1967.

DUMÉRY, Henry. *Faith and Reflection.* Tenbury Wells: Fowler Wright, 1968.

DUMÉRY, Henry. *The Problem of God in Philosophy of Religion.* Evanston, Ill.: North-Western U.P., 1964.

EDWARDS, David L., ed. *The Honest to God Debate.* London: S.C.M., 1963.

EMMET, Dorothy M. *Whitehead's Philosophy of Organism.* London: Macmillan, 1932.

FARRER, Austin M. *Faith and Speculation: An Essay in Philosophical Theology.* London: A. and C. Black, 1967.

FARRER, Austin M. *Finite and Infinite*. London: Dacre Press, 1943. 2nd ed., 1959.

FARRER, Austin M. *The Freedom of the Will*. London: A. & C. Black, 1958.

FARRER, Austin M. *The Glass of Vision*. London: Dacre Press, 1948.

FERRÉ, Frederick. *Language, Logic and God*. London: Eyre and Spottiswoode, 1962.

FLEW, A. G. N. *God and Philosophy*. London: Hutchinson, 1966.

FLEW, A. G. N., and MacINTYRE, A., edd., *New Essays in Philosophical Theology*. London: S.C.M., 1955.

FINDLAY, J. N. *Language, Mind and Value*. London: Allen and Unwin, 1963.

FRANSEN, Peter. *The New Life of Grace*. Tournai: Desclée, 1969.

GARAUDY, Roger. *From Anathema to Dialogue: The Challenge of Marxist-Christian Cooperation*. With replies by Karl Rahner and J. B. Metz. London: Collins, 1967.

GARRIGOU-LAGRANGE, R. *Dieu, Son Existence et sa Nature*. Paris: Beauchesne, 1915. (E.T., *God, his Existence and Nature*. St Louis, Mo.: Herder, 1934.)

GEACH, Peter. *God and the Soul*. London: Routledge and Kegan Paul, 1969.

GIBSON, A. Boyce. *Theism and Empiricism*. London: S.C.M., 1970.

GILSON, Étienne. *Le Réalisme Méthodique*. Paris: Téqui, n.d.

GILSON, Étienne. *Réalisme Thomiste et Critique de la Connaissance*. Paris: Vrin, 1939.

GILSON, Étienne. *The Spirit of Medieval Philosophy*. London: Sheed and Ward, 1936.

GLEASON, Robert W. *Grace*. London: Sheed and Ward, 1962.

HAMILTON, Peter. *The Living God and the Modern World*. London: Hodder and Stoughton, 1967.

HARDY, Alister. *The Living Stream: A Restatement of Evolution Theory and its Relation to the Spirit of Man*. London: Collins, 1965.

HARRIS, Errol E. *The Foundations of Metaphysics in Science*. London: Allen and Unwin, 1965.

HARTSHORNE, Charles, *Anselm's Discovery: A Re-examination of the Ontological Proof of God's Existence*. La Salle, Ill.: Open Court Press, 1965.

HARTSHORNE, Charles. *The Logic of Perfection*. La Salle, Ill.: Open Court Press, 1962.

HARTSHORNE, Charles. *A Natural Theology for our Time*. La Salle, Ill.: Open Court Press, 1967.

HEALEY, F. G., ed. *Prospect for Theology*. London: Nisbet, 1966.

HEIMBECK, Raeburne S. *Theology and Meaning: A Critique of Metatheological Scepticism*. London: Allen and Unwin, 1969.

HEISENBERG, Werner. *Physics and Philosophy*. London: Allen and Unwin, 1958.

HICK, John and McGILL, Arthur C., edd. *The Many-Faced Argument: Recent Studies on the Ontological Argument for the Existence of God*. London: Macmillan, 1968.

HINTIKKA, Jaakko. *Models for Modalities*. New York: Humanities Press, 1969.

HODGSON, Leonard. *For Faith and Freedom*. Oxford U.P., 1956–7.

HURLBUTT III, Robert H. *Hume, Newton and the Design Argument*. Lincoln, Neb.: Univ. of Nebraska Press, 1965.

HUXLEY, Sir Julian. *Evolution in Action*. London: Penguin Books, 1963.

KENNY, Anthony. *The Five Ways: St Thomas Aquinas' Proofs of God's Existence*. London: Routledge and Kegan Paul, 1969.

KNOX, John. *The Humanity and Divinity of Christ: A Study of Pattern in Christology*. Cambridge U.P., 1967.

KÖRNER, Stephan. *The Philosophy of Mathematics: An Introductory Essay*. London: Hutchinson, 1960.

KÜNG, Hans. *The Council and Reunion*. London: Sheed and Ward, 1961.

LEWIS, H. D. *Freedom and History*. London: Allen and Unwin, 1962.

LEWIS, H. D., ed. *Clarity is not Enough: Essays in Criticism of Linguistic Philosophy*. London: Allen and Unwin, 1963.

LEWIS, H. D. *Our Experience of God*. London: Allen and Unwin, 1959.

LINDBECK, George A. *The Future of Roman Catholic Theology*. London: S.P.C.K., 1970.

LONERGAN, Bernard J. F. *Collection*. London: Darton, Longman and Todd, 1967.

LONERGAN, Bernard J. F. *Insight: A Study of Human Understanding*. London: Longmans Green, 1957.

LONERGAN, Bernard J. F. *Verbum: Word and Idea in Aquinas*. London: Darton, Longman and Todd, 1968.

LOSSKY, Vladimir. *The Mystical Theology of the Eastern Church*. London: James Clarke, 1957.

LUBAC, Henri de. *Augustinianism and Modern Theology*. London: Geoffrey Chapman, 1969.

LUBAC, Henri de. *The Mystery of the Supernatural*. London: Geoffrey Chapman, 1967.

LUBAC, Henri de. *Surnaturel: Études historiques*. Paris: Aubier, 1946.

LUCAS, J. R. *The Freedom of the Will*. Oxford U.P., 1970.

McLEAN, George F., ed. *Christian Philosophy and Religious Renewal*. Washington, D.C.; Catholic Univ. of America Press, 1967.

MACQUARRIE, John. *God-Talk: An Examination of the Language and Logic of Theology*. London: S.C.M., 1967.

MACQUARRIE, John. *Principles of Christian Theology*. London: S.C.M., 1966.

MALCOLM, N. *Ludwig Wittgenstein: A Memoir*. Oxford U.P., 1958.

MARÉCHAL, Joseph. *Le Point de Départ de la Métaphysique: Leçons sur le Développement historique et théorique du Problème de la Connaissance*. Louvain, 1922–49.

MARITAIN, Jacques. *The Degrees of Knowledge: Distinguish to Unite*. 2nd E.T. London: Geoffrey Bles, 1959.

MASCALL, E. L. *Christ, the Christian and the Church: A Study of the Incarnation and its Consequences*. London: Longmans Green, 1946.

MASCALL, E. L. *Christian Theology and Natural Science: Some Questions in their Relations*. London: Longmans Green, 1956.

MASCALL, E. L. *The Christian Universe*. London: Darton, Longman and Todd, 1966.

MASCALL, E. L. *Existence and Analogy*. London: Longmans Green, 1949.

MASCALL, E. L. *Grace and Glory*. London: Faith Press, 1961.

MASCALL, E. L. *He Who is: A Study in Traditional Theism*. London: Longmans Green, 1943. 2nd ed., enlarged, 1966.

MASCALL, E. L. *The Importance of Being Human: Some Aspects of the Christian Doctrine of Man*. New York: Columbia U.P., 1958.

MASCALL, E. L. *The Recovery of Unity: A Theological Approach*. London: Longmans Green, 1958.

MASCALL, E. L. *The Secularisation of Christianity: An Analysis and a Critique*. London: Darton, Longman and Todd, 1965.

MASCALL, E. L. *Theology and the Future*. London: Darton, Longman and Todd, 1968.

MASCALL, E. L. *Via Media: An Essay in Theological Synthesis*. London: Longmans Green, 1956.

MASCALL, E. L. *Words and Images*. London: Longmans Green, 1957.

MATSON, Wallace I. *The Existence of God*. Ithaca, N.Y.: Cornell U.P., 1965.

MATTHEWS, W. R. *God in Christian Thought and Experience*. London: Nisbet, 1930.

MATTHEWS, W. R. *The Purpose of God*. London: Nisbet, 1935.

MEYENDORFF, John. *St Grégoire Palamas et la Mystique Orthodoxe.* Paris, Ed. du Seuil, 1959.

MEYENDORFF, John. *A Study of Gregory Palamas.* London: Faith Press, 1964.

MOELLER, C., and PHILIPS, G. *The Theology of Grace and the Oecumenical Movement.* London: Mowbrays, 1961.

MONDEN, Louis. *Signs and Wonders: A Study of the Miraculous Element in Religion.* New York: Desclée, 1966.

MONTAGNES, Bernard. *La Doctrine de l'Être, d'après Saint Thomas d'Aquin.* Louvain: Publications Universitaires, 1963.

MUCK, Otto. *The Transcendental Method.* New York: Herder, 1968.

MUNITZ, Milton K. *The Mystery of Existence.* New York: Appleton-Century-Crofts, 1965.

NIEBUHR, Reinhold. *The Nature and Destiny of Man: A Christian Interpretation.* London: Nisbet, 1941, 1943.

O'MAHONEY, James. *The Desire of God in the Philosophy of St Thomas Aquinas.* London: Longmans Green, 1929.

OWEN, H. P. *The Christian Knowledge of God.* London: Athlone Press, 1969.

OWEN, H. P. *The Moral Argument for Christian Theism.* London: Allen and Unwin, 1965.

PIEPER, Josef, *The Silence of St Thomas.* London: Faber, 1957.

PIKE, Nelson. *God and Timelessness.* London: Routledge and Kegan Paul, 1970.

PITTENGER, W. Norman. *Christology Reconsidered.* London: S.C.M., 1970.

PITTENGER, W. Norman. *Process Thought and Christian Faith.* London: Nisbet, 1968.

PITTENGER, W. Norman. *The Word Incarnate: A Study of the Doctrine of the Person of Christ.* London: James Nisbet, 1959.

PLANTINGA, Alvin. *God and Other Minds: A Study of the Rational Justification of Belief in God.* Ithaca, N.Y.: Cornell U.P., 1967.

PLANTINGA, Alvin, ed. *The Ontological Argument from St Anselm to Contemporary Philosophers.* Garden City, N.Y.: Doubleday, 1965.

PONTIFEX, Mark. *The Existence of God; A Thomist Essay.* London: Longmans Green, 1947.

PRELLER, Victor. *Divine Science and the Science of God: A Reformulation of Thomas Aquinas.* Princeton, N.J.: Princeton U.P., 1967.

RAHNER, Karl, *Hearers of the Word.* Revised by J. B. Metz. London: Sheed and Ward, 1969.

RAHNER, Karl. *Nature and Grace and other essays.* London: Sheed and Ward, 1963.

RAHNER, Karl, *Spirit in the World*. London: Sheed and Ward, 1968.

RAHNER, Karl. *Theological Investigations*. London: Darton, Longman and Todd. Vol. I, 1961. Vol. II, 1963. Vol. IV, 1966.

RAHNER, Karl. *The Trinity*. London: Burns and Oates, 1970.

RAMSEY, Ian T., ed. *Prospect for Metaphysics: Essays of Metaphysical Exploration*. London: Allen and Unwin, 1961.

RICHMOND, James, *Theology and Metaphysics*. London: S.C.M., 1970.

ROBERTS, Louis. *The Achievement of Karl Rahner*. New York: Herder, 1966.

ROBINSON, J. A. T. *Honest to God*. London: S.C.M., 1963.

RUSSELL, Bertrand (Earl). *Human Knowledge: Its Scope and Limits*. London: Allen and Unwin, 1948.

RUSSELL, Bertrand (Earl). *An Outline of Philosophy*. London: Allen and Unwin, 1927.

SERTILLANGES, A. D. *L'Idée de Création et ses Retentissements en Philosophie*. Paris: Aubier, 1945.

SHERRARD, Philip. *The Greek East and the Latin West: A Study in the Christian Tradition*. Oxford U.P., 1959.

SONTAG, Frederick. *Divine Perfection: Possible Ideas of God*. London: S.C.M., 1962.

STEVENSON, J. *Creeds, Councils and Controversies: Documents illustrative of the History of the Church A.D. 337–461*. London: S.P.C.K., 1966.

STEVENSON, J. *A New Eusebius: Documents illustrative of the History of the Church to A.D. 337*. London: S.P.C.K., 1957.

TAVARD, George H. *Holy Writ or Holy Church: the Crisis of the Protestant Reformation*. London: Burns and Oates, 1959.

TAYLOR, A. E. *The Faith of a Moralist*. Vol. I: The Theological Implications of Morality. Vol. II: Natural Theology and the Positive Religions. London: Macmillan, 1930.

TEMPLE, William. *Nature, Man and God*. London: Macmillan, 1934.

TENNANT, F. R. *Philosophical Theology*. Cambridge U.P., 1928, 1930.

THILS, Gustave. *L'Infaillibilité Pontificale: Sources, Conditions, Limites*. Gembloux: Duculot, 1969.

THILS, Gustave. *Primauté Pontificale et Prérogatives Épiscopales: "Potestas ordinaria" au Concile du Vatican*. Louvain, 1961.

THORPE, W. H. *Science, Man and Morals*. London: Methuen, 1965.

TODD, John M., ed. *Problems of Authority: An Anglo-French Symposium*. London: Darton, Longman and Todd, 1962.

TORRANCE, Thomas F. *Space, Time and Incarnation*. Oxford U.P., 1969.

TRETHOWAN, Illtyd. *Absolute Value: A Study in Christian Theism*. London: Allen and Unwin, 1970.

TRETHOWAN, Illtyd. *The Basis of Belief*. London: Burns and Oates, 1961.

TRETHOWAN, Illtyd. *Certainty, Philosophical and Theological*. London: Dacre Press, 1948.

TRETHOWAN, Illtyd. *An Essay in Christian Philosophy*. London: Longmans Green, 1954.

URMSON, J. O. *Philosophical Analysis: its Development between the Two World Wars*. Oxford: Clarendon Press, 1956.

WARD, Maisie. *Return to Chesterton*. London: Sheed and Ward, 1952.

WESTFALL, Richard S. *Science and Religion in Seventeenth-Century England*. New Haven, Conn.: Yale U.P., 1958.

WHITE, Victor. *God the Unknown and other essays*. London: Harvill, 1956.

WHITEHEAD, A. N. *The Principle of Relativity with Applications to Physical Science*. Cambridge U.P., 1922.

WHITEHEAD, A. N. *Process and Reality: An Essay in Cosmology*. Cambridge U.P., 1929.

WHITEHEAD, A. N. *Science and the Modern World*. Cambridge U.P., 1926.

WHITEHEAD, A. N. and RUSSELL, B. *Principia Mathematica*. Cambridge U.P., 1910–13. (2nd ed., 1925).

WHITROW, G. J. *The Natural Philosophy of Time*. London: Nelson, 1961.

WILLIAMS, Bernard and MONTEFIORE, Alan, edd. *British Analytical Philosophy*. London: Routledge and Kegan Paul, 1966.

WITTGENSTEIN, Ludwig. *Tractatus Logico-Philosophicus*. London: Routledge and Kegan Paul, 1961.

WOODS, G. F. *A Defence of Theological Ethics*. Cambridge U.P., 1966.

WOODS, G. F. *Theological Explanation*. London: James Nisbet, 1958.

INDEX OF PROPER NAMES

The more important entries are printed in heavy type.